D1528337

Understanding Suicide: Why We Don't and How We Might

Understanding Suicide: Why We Don't and How We Might

James R. Rogers and David Lester

Library of Congress Cataloguing-in-Publication Data
is available via the Library of CongressMarc Database
under the LC Control Number 2009933128

Archives Canada Cataloguing in Publication
Rogers, James R.
    Understanding suicide : why we don't and how
we might / James R. Rogers and David Lester.
Includes bibliographical references.
ISBN 978-0-88937-359-4

    1. Suicide. 2. Suicide--Psychological aspects.
I. Lester, David, 1942-

RC569.R64 2009   362.28   C2009-904607-5

PUBLISHING OFFICES
USA: Hogrefe Publishing, 875 Massachusetts Avenue, 7th Floor, Cambridge, MA 02139
                  Phone (866) 823-4726, Fax (617) 354-6875, E-mail info@hogrefe.com
EUROPE: Hogrefe Publishing, Rohnsweg 25, 37085 Göttingen, Germany
                  Phone +49 551 49609-0, Fax +49 551 49609-88, E-mail publishing@hogrefe.com

SALES & DISTRIBUTION
USA: Hogrefe Publishing, Customer Services Department,
                  30 Amberwood Parkway, Ashland, OH 44805
                  Phone (800) 228-3749, Fax (419) 281-6883, E-mail custserv@hogrefe.com
EUROPE: Hogrefe Publishing, Rohnsweg 25, 37085 Göttingen, Germany
                  Phone +49 551 49609-0, Fax +49 551 49609-88, E-mail publishing@hogrefe.com

OTHER OFFICES
CANADA: Hogrefe Publishing, 1543 Bayview Avenue, Toronto, Ontario M4G 3B5
SWITZERLAND: Hogrefe Publishing, Länggass-Strasse 76, CH-3000 Bern 99

Hogrefe Publishing
Incorporated and registered in the Commonwealth of Massachusetts, USA, and in Göttingen, Lower
Saxony, Germany

Printed and bound in the USA
ISBN 978-0-88937-359-4

Table of Contents

Introduction

1

Introduction

Several years ago, Lester (2000) suggested that suicidology had come to an end. The thesis of that article was that very little of consequence had appeared in the last ten years that furthered our knowledge of suicide – no new theory and no ground-breaking research.

The end of the 20th Century produced an interesting trend in the scholarly world – a sense that everything was coming to an end. Francis Fukuyama (1992) declared that history had come to an end and that little of importance would happen in the future. David Lindley (1994) followed with a declaration that physics had discovered all that there was to be discovered, and John Horgan (1997a) declared that science in general had solved all of the puzzles. It seems clear that Fukuyama was wrong in asserting that nothing of importance would occur in world history in the future – the rise in global terrorism or climate change cannot be described as "of little importance" – but let us look at Horgan's views in more detail.

Horgan (1997a) argued that pure science had entered its twilight, that is, there are no more profound revelations that will occur. He noted that science as a whole was not ending but that *path-breaking* science was ending. He argued that scientists will continue to keep busy and make tiny advances, but that they will never achieve their most ambitious goals. He noted that scientists themselves, as well as the media, hype each new research finding, disregarding whether it is spurious or genuine, and this gives us the illusion that scientific research is making great progress. More recently, Horgan (1997b) has suggested that even applied science might be ending. After all, he noted, where are the nuclear fusion reactors that were predicted in the 1950s? Has the war on cancer declared by President Richard Nixon in 1971 been won yet?

The same seems to be true in the discipline of psychology, particularly with regard to theories of personality and systems of psychotherapy. The last major theory of personality was George Kelly's published in 1955, and the last major theories of psychotherapy were introduced by Albert Ellis and Fritz Perls in the 1960s and Arthur Janov in the 1970s. Since then, a degree in marketing would be more appropriate than a degree in psychology, for the so-called "new" theories proposed have been little more than re-packaging of the older theories, combined in a new mix and with new terms for old concepts – a "new improved product" that consumers should regard warily.

What of suicidology? Every ten years for the last thirty years Lester (1972, 1983, 1992, 2000) reviewed the suicidology literature as completely and extensively as he was able. The reviews cover the period 1897–1997. In the latest edition, Lester (2000) concluded that nothing of importance has been published in the 1990s! For each recent decade, Lester selected the major contributors to the field of suicidology: Edwin

Shneidman and Norman Farberow in the 1960s and Aaron Beck and David Phillips in the 1970s, for example. These people introduced new topics and research foci for suicidology and produced a large body of work on those topics. There was no one, in Lester's opinion, worthy to be chosen for the 1990s.

The topics for research in the 1990s were those which had been identified in earlier decades. Indeed, it was depressing to see the same kinds of research being conducted as has been published many, many times before. A large sample of subjects is administered depression, hopelessness, self-esteem and life stress scales to predict suicidal behavior using a multiple regression model. A sample of suicidal subjects is examined for its psychiatric characteristics. (How many more times must we read about comorbidity as an indicator for suicidality?) A set of social indicators is entered into (again) a multiple regression analysis to predict suicide rates over time or over regions. A few brains are examined for a dozen or so biochemicals in up to 30 or so brain areas, with inconsistent findings. In this last case, it is obvious that the reports on suicide are often side issues – the goal of the study was to explore biochemical causes of depression or schizophrenia but the investigators saw that they could produce an additional paper or two by studying the suicides in the sample.

In addition, some topics in suicidology have been removed from our purview, topics such as sex differences in suicidal behavior or the variation of suicidality over the menstrual cycle. It is not that we solved the problems or adequately tested theories of these phenomena. It seems rather that we simply lost interest. For example, with regard to sex differences in suicidal behavior, despite the many papers and books published on the topic, there have been almost no empirical tests of relevant theories in the last twenty years. Rather we read simple discussions of the topic. This has been particularly true recently of the female suicide rate in China which appears to be higher than the male suicide rate. Dozens of papers have noted this difference (almost all using the same WHO data), and most have speculated on the causes. However, no paper has attempted to test a theory for this difference!

In the 1990s, a number of suicidologists argued that we needed a meaningful and generally agreed-upon terminology for suicidology, and several papers appeared on this topic (e.g., O'Carroll et al., 1996). A meaningful terminology that was generally agreed upon would be useful (although getting general agreement might be difficult) and there continues to be work in this area (e.g., Silverman, Berman, Sanddal, O'Carroll, & Joiner, 2007) but what we really need are good theories and, in particular, good competing and incompatible theories, combined with methodologically sound empirical tests of hypotheses generated from these competing theories.

Let us give two examples. Henry and Short's (1954) theory of suicide and homicide, regardless of how well it predicts and explains suicidal phenomena, is a complex theory. It has many assumptions, proposes many hypotheses, and cleverly interweaves psychological and sociological concepts. In contrast, psychological models of suicidal behavior imply (by using multiple regression techniques) that suicidal behavior is simply a weighted sum of various psychological states and traits – a little bit of hopelessness plus a little bit of stress, etc. There are rarely any interaction terms, and certainly no tests of theories of the form $S = (A + B^2)/(\sqrt{C} - \log D)$, where S, A, B, C and D are psychological or behavioral variables, theoretical forms that are common in the natural sciences.

Consider Durkheim's (1897) classic sociological theory of suicide. There are four types of suicide based on two dimensions (social integration and social regulation). Two dimensions provide a zonal analysis with four types such as high social integration plus low social regulation, etc. These four types do not match Durkheim's four types. Rootman (1973) noted this and reported a preliminary study, but his study has been largely ignored. Instead, sociologists simply examine correlations of variables such as divorce and birth rates with suicide rates. They never empirically demonstrate that variables such as divorce or birth rates are measures of social integration or social regulation. Are divorced people less socially integrated or socially regulated than married people? An empirical justification of this assumption is never presented in a sociological paper on suicide. Even the dominance of Durkheim's theory has been criticized by Gibbs (1994) who wrote on "Durkheim's heavy hand in the sociological study of suicide."

So is this the end of suicidology? Perhaps, but we think not. In order that it may not be the end, in this book we critique respectfully the field of suicidology while making *constructive* suggestions for what needs to be done in the future. We hope that these suggestions will provide the groundwork for a new beginning for suicidology. Our aim in this book is not review the whole field. There are books that provide a broad and thorough introduction to suicidology such as the *Comprehensive Textbook of Suicidology* by Ronald Maris, Alan Berman and Morton Silverman (2000) and summaries of research and theory up to 1997 by Lester (2000).

In Chapter 2 we will first review the general methodological issues that are major problems for research into suicidal behavior. Some of these issues are present in all research, but others are specific to research into suicidal behavior.

In the next four chapters (Chapters 3 through 6), we critique the four major disciplines that contribute to our understanding of suicide. To be sure, we acknowledge that there are disciplines (major and minor) that also contribute (criminal justice, economics, political science and public health, to name just a few), but we feel that our criticisms and recommendations for the disciplines we have selected also apply to the others.

In the next section, we critique and make recommendations for a number of research topics in the field of suicidology. In this section, again, we are not attempting to review the whole field, but rather we have chosen representative examples of different areas of research. For example, the critique and recommendations in Chapter 8 on studies of sexual abuse and suicidality are relevant to many topics of study, including substance abuse and suicidality, eating disorders and suicidality, borderline personality disorder and suicidality, and so on. The chapter on sex differences has been chosen to illustrate the issue of "fads" in suicidology, topics that arouse great interest for a period of time and are then abandoned without any of the major questions fully answered. However, some of the chapters in this section do address seminal issues in the field, assessing suicidal risk and the formulation of typologies of suicidal individuals.

Finally, we draw together our thoughts after this endeavor and we present a summary of our recommendations for the field of suicidology. We hope that you will be stimulated and even provoked by our thoughts and recommendations, and that you will be motivated to prove that we have not reached "the end of suicidology."

References

Durkheim, E. (1897). *Le suicide*. Paris: Felix Alcan.

Fukuyama, F. (1992). *The end of history and the last man*. New York: Free Press.

Gibbs, J. P. (1994). Durkheim's heavy hand in the sociological study of suicide. In D. Lester (Ed.), *Emile Durkheim: Le Suicide 100 years later* (pp. 30–74). Philadephia: Charles Press.

Henry, A. F., & Short, J. F. (1954). *Suicide and homicide*. New York: Free Press.

Horgan, J. (1997a). *The end of science*. New York: Broadway Books.

Horgan, J. (1997b). Facing up to the decline of science. *Chronicle of Higher Education*, 43(40), A52.

Lester, D. (1972, 1983, 1992, 2000). *Why people kill themselves*. Springfield, IL: Charles Thomas.

Lester, D. (2000). The end of suicidology. *Crisis*, 21, 158–159.

Lindley, D. (1994). *The end of physics*. New York: Basic Books.

Maris, R. W., Berman, A. L., & Silverman, M. M. (2000). *Comprehensive textbook of suicidology*. New York: Guilford.

O'Carroll, P. W., Berman, A. L., Maris, R. W., Moscicki, E., Tanney, B. L., & Silverman, M. (1996). Beyond the Tower of Babel. *Suicide & Life-Threatening Behavior*, 26, 237–252.

Rootman, I. (1973). A cross-cultural note on Durkheim's theory of suicide. *Life-Threatening Behavior*, 3, 83–94.

Silverman, M. M., Berman, A. L., Sanddal, N. D., O'Carroll, P. W., & Joiner, T. E. (2007). Rebuilding the tower of Babel: A revised nomenclature for the study of suicide and suicidal behaviors. *Suicide and Life-Threatening Behavior, 37,* 264–277.

2

General Methodological Issues

The goal of the present book, as we have discussed in the Introduction, is to critique the field of suicidology and make constructive suggestions for future research and theory. In Part 1, the contributions of several disciplines to our understanding of suicide (such as psychology and sociology) are reviewed and proposals made for future studies in those fields. In Part 2, several topics in suicidology (such as twin studies and studies of the association between sexual abuse and subsequent suicidality) are reviewed and, again, proposals made for future studies on those topics.

There are however, some general problems and issues in the field of suicidology, and the purpose in the present chapter is to review and discuss these general issues. This chapter is organized around the following areas: the accuracy of suicidal classifications, the method of substitute subjects, subject bias, control groups, sample size, the validity of measures, ecological and time series research, statistical versus clinical significance, and problems with literature searches.

Accuracy of Suicidal Classifications

Completed Suicide

The problems of making reliable and valid psychiatric diagnoses of psychiatric patients are large and have received a great deal of discussion and debate. Indeed, one of the major reasons that the American Psychiatric Association is now preparing the 6th revision of their Diagnostic and Statistical Manual is to improve the reliability and validity of psychiatric diagnoses.

One would think, at first glance, that the field of suicidology would not have this problem. Surely a death from suicide or an attempt to kill oneself is easily certified. Certainly, the classification of suicidal acts is less problematic than the classification of psychiatric disorders. However, a closer examination of the classification issue in suicidology suggests that, even here, problems exist.

First, for completed suicide, many central statistical offices rely on the certification of death made by coroners and medical examiners. These individuals have a variety of backgrounds, including law and medicine. In some regions of the world, juries of lay men and woman, under the guidance of a judge, make this decision.

In rare cases, the decision is not simple. Some men hang themselves for auto-erotic sexual activity. Hanging produces an erection and so can accompany masturbation.

Occasionally, the man fails to remove his head from the noose and dies (Shankel & Carr, 1956) making a determination of suicide likely in the absence of disconfirming evidence. In other cases, it is difficult to distinguish between suicide and murder. There are several famous "suicides" for whom murder rather than suicide is suspected, including the film star Marilyn Monroe, the United Nations diplomat Povl Bang-Jensen, and the President of Chile, Salvador Allende (Lester, 1996a).

Douglas (1967) attacked the validity of official suicide rates based on the proposition that the social characteristics of the society affected the decisions of coroners and medical examiners. For example, if the religion of a society condemned suicide harshly, then more suicides would be "covered up" and classified as from another cause as compared to a society which did not condemn suicide as harshly. Douglas asserted that this phenomenon could account for differences in suicide rates by religion, sex, age, and other variables. His argument became well-known and widely accepted, despite the fact that he, himself, produced no supporting empirical evidence.

When coroners and medical examiners are uncertain about the cause of death, they can label the death as "undetermined" or, in England, as an "open verdict." Barraclough (1970, 1974) found that a change in coroner affected the proportion of open verdicts in English jurisdictions and could account for regional differences in suicide rates (such as England versus Scotland). Several studies have presented cases to coroners from different nations and found differences in how they would classify the deaths (Atkinson, Kessel & Dalgaard, 1975; Brooke, 1974). A number of researchers have investigated this phenomenon in order to identify factors that may account for these differences.

For example, Farberow, MacKinnon and Nelson (1977) studied 202 counties in western states in the United States and found that suicide rates were higher if the coroner was a pathologist and lower if the coroner was a lawyer. Similarly, Ajiki et al. (1991) found that the suicide rate in a Japanese prefecture was dependent on whether a medical examiner or medical practitioner certified the deaths. Jarvis et al. (1991) found that the certification of deaths in a sample of Canadian medical examiners was affected by their religion, the size of the town in which they worked and their experience. Thus, there are a number of professional, social and individual differences that may impact the official classification of deaths related to suicide.

Typically, when researchers themselves study all of the deaths in a community, as opposed to relying on "official" data, they find that the actual suicide rate is grossly underestimated. For example, Clarke-Finnegan and Fahy (1983) found a suicide rate in Galway County of 13.8 per 100,000 per year as compared to the official rate of 5.8.

Suicide rates are also different when calculated from police records rather than the records of medical examiners, with rates based on police records generally lower (William et al., 1987). The suicide rate is also typically higher if more post-mortems are ordered in a region (Asencio et al., 1988). In addition, the characteristics of the decedent also affect the certification of death. For example, in England, Salib (1996) found that an open verdict was more likely than a judgment of suicide if there were problems with alcohol, use of an overdose for the method of suicide, no evidence of intent, and no prior psychiatric history.

On the other hand, Jennings and Barraclough (1980) found no effect on the number of suicide verdicts versus open or accidental verdicts after changes in the law about certification of death in England. While these results may suggest greater consistency in certification despite changes in law and legal procedures, alternatively, they could suggest that changes in the law and legal procedures may not be able to overcome the impact of professional, social, and individual differences as they relate to these three classifications or verdicts.

Recommendation 2.1: It is important for sound epidemiological research and socio-logical studies of suicide that rates of completed suicide are accurate. Public health agencies should work with coroners and medical examiners to ensure that death records supplied to central government agencies are free from bias introduced by differing professional, legal, religious and economic perspectives. For example, coroners in Pennsylvania have for many years prepared two death certificates, one for the government and a special one for funeral directors to ensure that insurance companies do not withhold payment of the death benefit.

Calculating Suicide Rates

(1) The Population Base
Almost all nations of the world calculate their suicide rates based on "per 100,000 of the population per year." However, the number of suicides by children and young adolescents has been very small. Indeed, in some jurisdictions, deaths of people under a certain age are rarely classified as suicides, presumably because we cannot be sure that children have a mature (and accurate) conception of what death is. Therefore, including children and young adolescents in the population base makes little sense and results in a downwardly biased estimate of the suicide rate. Interestingly, Israel is the only nation that uses the population aged 15 and over as the base for suicide rates.

Recommendation 2.2: Since suicide in very young people is rarely, if ever, classi-fied as such, rates should be calculated on a population base that does not include young children so as to provide a more accurate statistical picture of suicide. It would be appropriate if an organization like the World Health Organization con-vened a meeting to suggest an appropriate age range to use for this population base.

(2) Age-Adjusted Suicide Rates
Occasional sociological studies of aggregate suicide rates use age-adjusted suicide rates which control for differences between regions (or years) in the age distribution in the population. Using age-adjusted suicide rates might change the results of research. For example, Lester (1992a) found that the divorce rate predicted the crude suicide rate in the United States over time, but not the age-adjusted suicide rate. Age-adjusted suicide rates make better sense for research since they control for differences in age in the populations. However, suicide rates could be standardized for other variables also, such as the sex distribution, religious affiliations, etc. Broadening the somewhat exclu-

sive focus on age-adjusted suicide rates to include other important variables may lead to a more comprehensive understanding of the relation between suicide and other sociological factors.

Recommendation 2.3: More use should be made of age-adjusted suicide rates in research, as well as suicide rates that are adjusted for other demographic variables such as sex and religious affiliation when those characteristics are relevant to the research question.

(3) Opportunity-Based Suicide Rates

Suicide rates could be based on the availability of means for suicide. For example, suicide rates using car exhaust could be calculated as suicides per 100,000 cars per year, suicides by firearms as suicides per 100,000 guns per year, etcetera (Lester, 1992b). Analyses based on method opportunity or accessibility might provide an alternative perspective on suicide as a function of method that may have important implications for social policy in general and suicide prevention in particular. This idea is common in criminology where, for example, bank robbery rates can be calculated as robberies per 100,000 of the population per year or as robberies per 1,000 banks, per year.

(4) Other Measures

Thorson (1993) suggested that studying the percentages of deaths due to suicide might be of interest. In support of this suggestion, Lester (1994) found different ecological correlates across the states of America using this measure as compared to those using the suicide rate.

Recommendation 2.4: Rather than being tied to the typical 'rate per 100,000 per year' measure, researchers should explore the effect of using suicide rates calculated in logical, alternative ways on the results of their studies. Inclusion of alternative approaches may lead to a more fine-grained understanding of suicide and impact the refinement and development of theories of suicide.

The Time of Death

Rich et al. (1985) compared the date of the suicidal act and the date of death on the death certificate and found them to be the same in only 46% of the suicides. In addition to representing a discrepancy of great importance for studies of the distribution of suicides over the days of the week, these results bring into question the accuracy of documentation related to other information collected through official agencies.

The Source of the Information

Fishman and Weimann (1997) found that the classification of motives for suicides in Israel were quite different if official records were used rather than press reports. For example, 16.1% of suicides reported in the press involved romantic or love motives versus only 1.2% from official records. Mental problems were more common in the official records (58.9%) than in press reports (27.6%). When differences such as these are seen in empirical data, it is difficult to determine objectively which source leads to the more appropriate classification.

Missing Nations

The sample of nations reporting suicide rates to the World Health Organization is quite small. For 1980, Lester (1996b) was able to obtain a sample of only 64 nations with consistent data over a period of years. In fact, out of the current 192 member nations in the United Nations, the WHO report for December 2005 lists rates for only 95 nations (www.who.int/mental_health/prevention/suicide_rates/en/). Most African nations and many South American nations do not collect and report suicide rates for the whole nation.

Furthermore, given that culture plays a large role in affecting suicide rates, it is surprising that nations do not report suicide rates by ethnicity. For example, Belgium has both Fleming and Walloon cultural groups, but does not report their individual suicide rates. Similarly, the suicide rate of the Basques in France and Spain is unknown.

In Africa, the situation is worse. Most of the nations created by the colonial powers have several ethnic groups combined. When the suicide rate of an African nation is reported, for example, Zimbabwe (Lester & Wilson, 1988), no effort is made to distinguish between the ethnic groups (in the case of Zimbabwe, the major groups are the Ndebele and the Shona).

Recommendation 2.5: Efforts must be made, perhaps by the WHO, to get more nations to report suicide rates and to encourage nations to collect data by ethnicity.

Attempted Suicide

Diekstra (1997) commented on the apparent confusion over terminology and definitions in suicidology, especially with regard to nonfatal suicidal behavior. For those engaging in non-lethal suicidal actions, a variety of terms have been used – attempted suicide, parasuicide, deliberate self-harm or self-injury, intentional self-injury and nonfatal or nonlethal self-destructive behavior – and the milder forms of these actions begin to resemble self-mutilation. In fact, Silverman (2006) listed 36 different terms used for suicidal attempts! The problem with the term "attempted suicide" is that it implies that the individuals were trying to kill themselves. Since many who have attempted suicide deny suicidal intent, this term seems to be inappropriate.[1]

The choice of term may also affect responses in surveys. Respondents may be asked whether they have attempted suicide, inflicted harm on themselves or particular

---

[1] Diekstra noted that, in addition to research issues involved in this labeling, there may be effects on the attempted suicides themselves and on the members of their social networks which may be stigmatic and influence the prognosis for the individuals. For example, if the term attempted suicide is use in a vignette of a patient, all other features being the same, lay people tend to perceive more psychopathology in the patient.

methods may be specified (e.g., Have you ever tried to hang yourself, etc.). While each of these terms may be interpreted by the researchers as indicating a "suicide attempt," respondents may not be assigning the same meaning to the terms. Schwarz (1999) has provided empirical support for this concern using more general data highlighting the impact of survey wording on responses. His analysis demonstrated how alternative ways of asking the same question can drastically impact the results.[2] Similarly, Safer (1997) found that anonymous surveys resulted in a higher incidence of suicidality in the respondents than identifiable surveys. Clearly, prevalence rates may depend critically upon the exact wording used and the perception of anonymity of the respondents.

The critical issues in classifying behaviors as attempted suicide concern motivation and the lethality of the injury. In terms of motivation, if an individual admits to having an intent to die and if the injury is sufficiently severe, then the term "attempted suicide" may make good sense. However, if neither of these conditions is met, then self-injury as a classification seems more appropriate. A complication with regard to motivational determination, of course, is that the reported intent following the behavior may be different than the intent preceding the behavior (Andriessen, 2006). There may be a variety of reasons why an individual would reinterpret his or her motivations following the behavior, including the potential for secondary gain (Shea, 1999). For example, true intent prior to the behavior could be reported as no intent after the act in order to avoid hospitalization, protect loved ones from emotional distress, or as a function of self-denial. Similarly, no intent to die prior to the behavior could be reported as suicidal intent afterwards in order to help gain access to health care resources or enlist support from significant others.

Another consideration in this regard has to be the length of time between the behavior and the assessment of intent. Clearly, an empirical question that needs to be addressed is whether self-report of intent changes as a function of the length of time between the act and the self-report. It seems reasonable to consider that post-event cognitive processing may influence the self-report of intent to die. Thus, there may be a variety of individual and contextual-based reasons that a report to die after the act is reinterpreted by the individual. The potential discrepancy between pre-act and post-act reports of behavioral motivation and possible reinterpretations as a function of time with regard to intent to die could substantially impact the accuracy of classification.

The lethality of the behavior is another critical issue. Engaging in a highly lethal behavior may lead to a clearer classification of a suicide attempt. However, at lower levels of lethality, the distinction between an attempt, a "gesture" and self-mutilation becomes more difficult to make. An added complication in classifying suicide attempts as a function of lethality is that the medical-based judgment of the level of lethality (i.e., the medical likelihood that the behavior will result in death) may be very different from the subjective understanding by the suicidal individual. For example, a person may mistakenly believe that taking a certain combination of medications will

---

[2] For example, when asked if they are in favor of the death penalty for murder, the majority of American respondents say yes; but if asked to choose between the death penalty and life imprisonment without parole, the majority choose the life sentence (Lester, 1998).

result in death when, in fact, the combination is not lethal. Alternatively, a person may believe that overdosing on a medication or combination of medications will not be lethal when, in fact, it is, and it is only through rapid intervention that the person survived. Here it seems that reported intent to die combined with perceptions of lethality versus medically-based judgments of lethality can lead to very different classifications.

Differentiating suicide attempts from behaviors such as self-mutilation and other self-injurious behaviors is a function of identifying both motivation and lethality. Rather than being simplistic, however, this is a complex determination if we are to accurately classify such behaviors as suicide attempts. While identifying intent may be complicated by considering the potential that pre-act and post-act intent could be different, the use of an objective measure of suicidal intent such as the scale devised by Beck and his associates (Beck et al., 1974) may be helpful. It may also be possible to modify this scale so as to assess pre-act intent as well as post-act intent. Similarly, the use of a measure of the medical level of seriousness of the self-injury in combination with a subjective rating of the expected lethality may advance classification efforts related to suicide attempts.

Recommendation 2.6: Although it is important to agree upon a set of terms for deliberate self-harm, it is more critical that researchers use both objective and subjective approaches to assessing the suicidal intent and medical lethality involved in the acts of their research subjects. Only if this is done can researchers evaluate the comparability of the samples used in the different published reports of research.

The Method of Substitute Subjects

Neuringer (1962) noted that the subject of greatest interest to suicidologists is completed suicide. However, it is obvious that the subjects of our investigation are no longer available for psychological research – they are dead. Consequently, we are left with two less satisfactory methods for studying individuals who have died by suicide: the method of residuals and the method of substitute subjects.

In the *method of residuals*, we study materials left behind by the suicides – suicide notes, diaries, the results of psychological tests if the person had ever been a patient, and the memories of friends and relatives. The validity of such data is rarely determined, observational distortion occurs, and control groups are difficult to establish (Pouliot & De Leo, 2006).[3]

For example, in psychological autopsy studies in which an investigator interviews friends and relatives about the events in the suicide's recent life and their psychological state, often with the aim of establishing a psychiatric diagnosis, not only is the accuracy of the reports of friends and relatives not studied, but the investigators typically do not employ a control group of people dying from causes other than suicide and they

---

[3] We will discuss the problem of control (or comparison) groups in our discussion of research into suicide notes in Chapter 12.

are not "blind" as to the cause of death of the suicide.[4] The aim of establishing a psychiatric diagnosis is likely to solicit a confirmatory bias with researchers expecting to find a diagnosis and, therefore, focusing more on supportive than disconfirming data. As an example of having a priori knowledge regarding the cause of death, Robins, Murphy, Wilkerson, Gassner and Keyes (1959) reported that 126 of the 134 (84%) completed suicides in their sample were psychiatrically disturbed. However, they arrived at this result fully cognizant that they were asking about individuals who had died by suicide.

Thus, all that this "scientific" report tells us is that the authors believed that all suicides were psychiatrically disturbed. It is not a scientific fact.

Recommendation 2.7: In judgments made based on an analysis of "residuals" of suicides, consideration must be given to the issue of the reliability of those data including the potential for recall and confirmatory bias in methods such as the psychological autopsy. In addition, appropriate control groups must be incorporated in these approaches, and those making judgments must be "blind" as to who is a suicide and who is a control subject.

The second method is the *method of substitute subjects* in which the researchers study attempted suicides who are alive and often a captive subject pool in the hospital or clinic. This approach has been criticized on the grounds that attempted suicides as a group do not resemble completed suicides as a group. The groups differ in many easily observable ways – the proportion of men is greater among the completed suicides than among the attempted suicides, for example – and so may differ in psychological characteristics and psychodynamics. Farberow and Shneidman (1955) compared those who threatened suicide, attempted suicide and completed suicide and found no differences between the groups in demographic or sociological variables or early family experiences. However, the groups did differ in psychiatric diagnosis, methods used for the suicidal acts, and previous suicidal history. Maris (1971) also reported different patterns of symptoms and experiences between attempted and completed suicides. Thus, the study of individuals who have made suicide attempts as proxies for individuals who have died by suicide represents a major problem in suicidology.

There seems to be no unique solution to this problem. However, Lester, Beck and Trexler (1975) classified a sample of attempted suicides into three groups based on their suicidal intent. They used an objective measure of suicidal intent based upon the circumstances of the suicidal act (involving such items as whether the attempters took care to isolate themselves from others) and upon the self-report of the attempters (who could respond to the question of whether they intended to die with yes, no or I don't know).

Using either method of classification, Lester and his colleagues found that the average score of the three groups on measures of depression and hopelessness increased monotonically from the group with the lowest suicidal intent to the group with the higher intent. Thus, they argued that it would be possible to extrapolate to the group with the highest suicidal intent, those who died by suicide, who could not be adminis-

---

[4] The problem of the biases of the investigator is called "experimenter bias" (Rosenthal, 1966).

tered the measures of depression and hopelessness, to conclude that they would have had even higher levels of depression and hopelessness. In a follow-up study of these same attempters, Lester, Beck and Mitchell (1979) found that those who subsequently died by suicide had as a group the highest scores for depression and hopelessness when they were tested after their earlier nonlethal suicide attempt.

This methodology has rarely been used subsequently. Investigators occasionally include suicidal intent as a correlate in their research, but this is not sufficient. Correlations between variables address only linear trends in data, and an overall linear trend may mask nonlinearity or curvilinear trends within those same data. For example, the scores of subjects with the highest level of suicidal intent could be lower than those with moderate suicidal intent. But, if scores for both of these groups are much higher than those of the group with the lowest suicidal intent, the correlation coefficient might still be moderate to strong and statistically significant even though the trend was no longer monotonic. Based on this scenario, an interpretation of a positive correlation between intent and say, hopelessness, as indicating that an increase in intent is related to an increase in hopelessness across the range of intent, would be inaccurate and misleading as would an extrapolation of that conclusion to suicides. Therefore, *only monotonic trends in data collected on substitute subjects can be used for extrapolation to suicides.*

Recommendation 2.8: Researchers studying attempted suicides with the hope of generalizing the results to those who have died by suicide must classify the attempted suicides into at least three groups based on their suicidal intent.

Subject Bias

The problems mentioned above raise another methodological issue in suicide research, namely subject bias. Subject bias refers to biases introduced into research as a result of the selection of subjects for the research (Lester, 1969). Subjects who are not chosen or who do participate in research may differ, not simply in sociodemographic characteristics, but more importantly in psychological characteristics, from those who do participate.

Diekstra (1977) discussed the implications of the fact that many individuals who engage in nonfatal suicidal behavior do not come to the attention of medical and mental health institutions – the so-called "tip of the iceberg" phenomenon. By far the larger proportion of suicidal people eludes study by researchers. How do these "invisible" attempted suicides differ from those who are "visible" to researchers? Do they differ in demographic, behavioral and psychological characteristics? Do the circumstances of their suicidal actions differ, and are there different risk factors for the two groups?

Diekstra noted that those who take a nonlethal overdose may be more likely to become the subject of study (because of the likelihood that a significant other may take them to an emergency room) than someone who tries to die by suicide by jumping but is prevented from doing so by the intervention of others. The fact that the majority of attempted suicides are females may be a result of the different methods chosen by women and men, with a greater likelihood of being taken to a health service after using the methods preferred by women. The visible and invisible attempters may also differ in social class and ethnicity (since, for example, African Americans and other ethnic minorities may be less likely than Whites to use mental health services).

Diekstra further noted that visible attempters may have become visible because of their greater level of psychiatric disturbance. This may lead researchers to conclude that all attempters are more disturbed than the group as a whole really is. Additionally, attempts at suicide made early in life may be more likely to remain invisible than attempts made later in life, and so we may misread the developmental trajectories of suicidal careers.

Recommendation 2.9: Researchers studying attempted suicides should include attempters who do not come to the attention of medical services.

Examples of subject-related bias in suicidological research include biased recall, effects of hospitalization, recruitment settings, and missing subjects. These areas are discussed below.

Recall Bias

Most of the research on attempted suicides is conducted with individuals *after* their suicide attempt. They are, at this point in time, typically in a medical or psychiatric facility. This introduces many confounding effects, including the cathartic effect of the suicide attempt, the influence of therapeutic intervention, including the effects of any medications prescribed, the effects of the reactions of significant others, tissue and brain damage as a result of the attempt, psychological effects from disfigurement, and a tendency for individuals to act "normal" and contrite in order to facilitate release from the hospital. Any of these potential confounding influences or their combinations may impact the ability of individuals to provide accurate data related to their suicidal behaviors.

Effect of Hospitalization

Hospitalized suicidal individuals are often treated differently from other patients, especially if they are evaluated to be at high risk for suicide (Simon, 2006). As a result they may be guarded closely and put on "suicide watch," effectively limiting their autonomy and freedom of movement. In addition, they may be met with hostility from the staff because of the added strain that the increased level of surveillance places on ward resources. Consequently, the suicidal patient may experience a variety of emotions, including guilt, frustration, anger, shame, and feeling despised by the staff. The strength of these potential emotional reactions is likely to be exacerbated in the case of involuntary hospitalizations and impact motivation and attitude toward interviewers and researchers alike.

Recruitment Settings

The source of suicidal subjects for research will have a great impact on the research. Siewers and Davidoff (1943), for example, compared two groups of attempted suicides, one admitted to a general hospital and one admitted to a psychiatric hospital and found that the two groups differed greatly. The attempters from the general hospital were younger and less psychiatrically disturbed than those from the psychiatric hospital. They differed in occupation, religious affiliation, method of suicide and the presence of organic diseases. These results underscore the potential limitations in understanding that can result from limited sampling strategies.

To take an example from another field, fifty years ago, research on homosexuals recruited subjects who were in psychotherapy or clients of psychiatric clinics. As a result, the research showed that homosexuals were much more psychiatrically disturbed than heterosexuals. As homosexuality became more acceptable, it was possible to recruit homosexual participants for research from the community, and the research then showed that homosexuals were similar in psychological health to heterosexuals.

Missing Subjects

As we mentioned above, many suicidal individuals remain "undetected" by researchers, and these invisible suicidal individuals may differ in important ways from those who are visible. Even among the visible suicidal individuals, however, not all may be available for study. For example, Shneidman and Farberow (1961) identified 5,906 attempted suicides in Los Angeles County in 1957, but they could obtain data on only 2,652 of these people. The 2,652 for whom data were available might have differed considerably from the 3,254 for whom data were not available. Shneidman and Farberow, in the same study, found that only 36 percent of those who died by suicide in Los Angeles County that year left suicide notes. Individuals leaving suicide notes may differ, and not be representative, of all those who died by suicide in the county that year.

Furthermore, the problem noted earlier, that not all completed suicides in a community are officially recorded as suicide, means that many suicides are omitted from studies. This problem may influence data on suicidal behavior, especially with groups such as Native Americans. For example, Marshall and Soule (1988) found 33 Native American suicides in a region of southwest Alaska in 1979 to 1984 that were not recorded as such officially. Including these suicide deaths raised the official suicide rate from 7.3 to 36.9 per 100,000 per year. Additionally, Andress (1977) noted that, in California, many Native Americans have Mexican surnames and so, when dead, are classified as Hispanics rather than as Native Americans. These "missed" and mislabelled suicides may affect the outcome of research studies in unpredictable ways.

Recommendation 2.10: Researchers should consider potential sources of subject bias in creating research designs, and they develop strategies to control for this critical research confound. In the absence of control, researchers should identify potential uncontrolled sources and interpret their results accordingly.

Control Groups

An important feature of good research is the choice of a control or comparison group. This choice has a critical effect on the results obtained. The choice of a control group for studies of suicidal individuals depends upon the way in which suicidal behavior is conceptualized. Most commonly, suicidal behavior is seen as an extreme reaction to depression, and so depressed nonsuicidal individuals are often chosen as the control group. Since suicidal individuals tend to have high levels of depression, *all research should control for the level of depression in studies of suicidal behavior*. This is often not done. Another common conceptualization is to view suicidal individuals as psychiatrically disturbed, and so nonsuicidal psychiatric patients are often used as the control group. Therefore, the level of psychiatric disturbance is another critical characteristic that needs to be controlled for in research.

Recommendation 2.11: Studies of suicidal individuals should always control for the level of depression and the type and severity of psychiatric disturbance among other potentially confounding factors.

However, alternative conceptualizations of suicidal behavior do exist. Suicide may be viewed as aggression directed inwardly onto the self as opposed to outwardly onto others (Menninger, 1938). In this case assaultive and murderous individuals would constitute an appropriate control group. For example, Pokorny (1965) compared completed and attempted suicides with assaulters and murderers, primarily for differences in place of occurrence of the act, place of residence, the timing of the act, and demographic characteristics of the individuals. He found that the murderers and completed suicides were different in all the variables except sex, and he concluded that suicide and murder were committed by different types of people. Attempted suicides resembled the completed suicides in some respects (such as race and place of residence) but the murderers in other respects (such as timing and age). The assaulters were similar in all respects to the murders. What would be interesting, of course, would be psychological comparisons of these four groups.

Suicidal behavior may also be viewed as an impulsive act, and suicidal individuals may lack control. Indeed, recent physiological studies of suicidal individuals have shown some similarities between them and arsonists, eating disorder patients and obsessive-compulsive disorder patients. Appropriate control groups based on this conceptualization would include other types of impulsive patients as well as non-impulsive groups.

The way in which suicidal individuals are characterized, therefore, will affect critically the choice of an appropriate control group. At this stage of suicidology research, there is little value in comparing suicidal individuals with "normal" people in order to understand the psychological and social factors leading to suicide.[5]

---

[5] The only reason to compare suicidal individuals with "normal" individuals would be to devise psychological tests to predict which individuals in the general population are potentially suicidal.

Recommendation 2.12: Alternative comparison groups should be utilized in studies of suicidal individuals, such as assaultive people and those with other acting-out behaviors.

Finally, suicidal and nonsuicidal individuals differ in a variety of characteristics. When studying the important features of suicidal individuals, it is important to control for extraneous variables by matching the subjects in the suicidal and control groups – for variables such as sex, age and psychiatric disorder if these are deemed to be confounding variables, that is, variables which are not the focus of study.

Sample Size

It might seem an obvious comment or criticism to focus on sample size. Obtaining an adequate sample size is clearly important for research in all fields. However, completed suicide is rare in that only between ten and twelve individuals per 100,000 kill themselves in the United States each year. Obtaining adequate sample sizes is not easy.

Most of the psychological research into suicidal behavior involves reasonable sample sizes. However, occasional papers appear with small samples, such as a brief note by one of the authors of this book on funeral costs. This research included only six suicides (Lester & Ferguson, 1992)!

One area in which the issue of sample size is a significant problem is that of brain studies. There have been many studies of the brain tissue of suicides versus controls subjects, and many of those studies have used inadequate sample sizes. The concentrations of neurotransmitters and binding sites in the brain can be affected by many factors, including characteristics of the subjects (age, sex, diagnosis, prior medications, etc.) and features of the analysis (time since postmortem, chemical agents used, etc.). The only way to control for these factors in the analysis of the data is to have large samples and to use multivariate statistical techniques. The samples sizes used are often woefully inadequate to do this properly. For example, Allard and Norlein (1997) in their study of the density of dopamine uptake sites in the caudate nucleus studied the brains of only thirteen depressed suicides (and nineteen controls).

Recommendation 2.13: It is important to obtain adequate sample sizes for research into suicide, especially for physiological studies.

Validity of Measures

The issue of validity is critical to research using measurement instruments and, in fact, it is technically a misnomer to claim that measures are or are not valid. Validity is a characteristic of interpretation of measures, not of the measures themselves (Hoyt, Warbasse & Chu, 2006). For example, suggesting that the Beck Depression Inventory (BDI) is a valid measure is not accurate from a psychometric perspective. However, the interpretation of scores on the BDI as indicating levels of depression may or may not be valid. In the case of the BDI, of course, the interpretation of scores as indicative of depression is generally accepted based upon numerous validity investigations.

The foundation required for valid interpretations is measurement reliability. That is, for valid interpretation of scores, those scores must first demonstrate an acceptable level of reliability (e.g., consistent or stable scores and internal consistency for the scale items). Thus, reliability is a characteristic of measurement scores, while validity is associated with interpretations of those scores. Although adequate levels of measurement reliability can be obtained across samples, settings and time, it is equally likely that reliability fluctuates across these factors. Since reliability cannot be assumed, it is incumbent on researchers to investigate and report sample-specific reliability estimates for the measures they use in research whenever possible. In the absence of reliability data or in cases of questionable reliability, interpretations of results are highly suspect.

While measurement reliability provides the foundation for valid interpretations, it does not ensure validity. For example, scores on a measure may be relatively consistent over time and scale items may be internally consistent, but the scores may not be measuring what a researcher assumes they are measuring. This may be especially relevant when measures are used in new or diverse sample. In cases of new or diverse samples, despite prior evidence that interpretations of measures are valid, researchers should create designs that allow them to address the question of validity in some way.

Of particular importance here is the issue of cultural validity. There has been considerable debate as to whether interpretations of scores on psychological scales developed in one culture have validity in other cultures. Most inventories have been developed using undergraduates, mainly White undergraduates. Are these inventories useful for African-Americans, non-students, and those in different countries, such as those from Muslim nations? It is incumbent on researchers to demonstrate the reliability of their measures and the validity of their interpretations in their data rather than uncritically assuming reliability and validity.

Recommendation 2.14: Researchers must provide sample-specific evidence for the reliability and validity of the measuring instruments used in their research, especially when using measures devised in one type of setting or population but applied by the researchers in a new type of setting or population.

Ecological and Time-Series Research

There are several methodological problems with correlational studies of aggregate suicide rates. (1) With regard to ecological studies, such as those conducted across the states in America, it has been argued that researchers should control for spatial autocorrelation, that is, the fact that social variables in neighboring regions are similar because of the geographic proximity (Odland, 1988). Regression analysis assumes independent data points, and the existence of spatial autocorrelation means that the data points are not independent. Only one ecological study on suicide that we could find examined the impact of spatial autocorrelation in the analysis of the data (Wasserman & Stack, 1995).

(2) As with studies of individuals, there may be biases in the choice of samples in ecological studies. For example, Lester and Stack (1989) explored the effect of the method for choosing nations in cross-sectional ecological studies. Their samples included: (i) all nations with available data, (ii) European nations, (iii) industrialized nations, and (iv) a random sample of nations from each region of the world where each region provided the appropriate proportion of nations given the number of nations in each region. The results for the four samples were not identical.

Similarly, Cutchin and Cutchin (1999) compared the results of ecological correlates of suicide rates over the American states, counties in New England and townships in Vermont. The bivariate correlations between predictor variables (such as unemployment and proportion of minorities) showed little consistency across the samples, factor analyses indicated very different factor structures, and the results of the multiple regressions were quite different. Interestingly, Cutchin and Cutchin noted that the explanatory power of the predictor variables decreased as the size of the regions decreased.

(3) The results of time-series studies often differ from those obtain from ecological studies (over regions). Recently, panel data research designs have become more popular, in which the data sets combine ecological and time-series data in one large data set, a research design which may confound variations over time and region.

Recommendation 2.15: Researchers should make an effort to determine whether their results apply to variations in suicide rates over time, over place or both.

Recommendation 2.16: Researchers should investigate the impact of their choice of their sample of regions on the results of their ecological studies.

Statistical Significance

Suicidologists have had great difficulty in identifying meaningful correlates and predictors of suicidal behavior. Because of this Neuringer and Kolstoe (1966) suggested adopting less stringent criteria for statistical significance in suicide research, perhaps allowing rejection of the null hypothesis at the 10% level instead of the 5% level. This is an intriguing idea which has never been followed up, but it would result in the appearance of a larger proportion of "significant" results that were never replicated.

The use of "data-mining" (examining data sets using multiple statistical tests) in order to identify a publishable "finding" is also problematic from a statistical perspective. Data-mining often results in researchers reporting spurious associations that appear meaningful (Austin, Mamdani, Juurlink & Hux, 2006). Although there are statistical techniques for correcting for multiple statistical tests on the same data set, often researchers do not report how many analyses they undertook before "discovering" one to report.

Related to this is the possibility that many published research findings are false. Io-annidis (2005) identified many reasons for this, including (i) there are only a small number of studies on the topic, (ii) effect sizes are smaller, (iii) there is a greater number and less preselection of tested relationships in each report, (iv) there is greater flexibility in designs, definitions, outcomes and analytic modes, and (v) there are financial and other interests and greater prejudice involved. To this, we might add the failure of researchers and journals to be willing to publish negative results. In a different field (that of sex differences for genetic effects), Patsopoulos, Tatsioni and Ioannidis (2007) examined 432 claims of sex differences in 77 articles. Appropriate documentation was found for only 12.7% of these 432 claims. Of 60 claims with the best internal validity, only one was consistently replicated in at least two other studies.

Statistical versus Clinical or Practical Significance

The issue of statistical versus clinical or practical significance is a concern across quantitative research in suicidology. At issue here is the interpretation of statistical significance as *ipso facto* suggesting that a difference is important in any meaningful context. For example, Rogers, Lewis and Subich (2002) found that scores on the Suicide Assessment Checklist (SAC: Rogers, 1990) differentiated, at a statistically significant level, psychiatric emergency patients as a function of their reason for referral. However, with their sample size of 1969 protocols, even the mean difference of only 0.79 on the SAC between individuals who were referred following an attempted suicide and those who were referred for suicidal thoughts or feelings was statistically significant. It would be difficult to argue that a .79 mean difference on a measure where scores can range from 11 to 108 would have any clinical or practical meaning. While this is an extreme example, it demonstrates the impact of sample size on statistical significance and the potential for over-interpretation if researchers rely solely on statistical significance in their work (Tracey, 2000). Even with larger mean differences, researchers must provide support for an interpretation of clinical relevance beyond relying on statistical significance alone. Reporting effect sizes and confidence intervals around sample estimates, in addition to reporting the results of statistical tests of significance, can begin to address this important issue. Nonetheless, substantive arguments must also be proposed to support claims for the clinical or practical usefulness of results.

Recommendation 2.17: Researchers must continue to move beyond a sole reliance on statistical significance in interpreting quantitative research in suicidology to address issues of the clinical and practical usefulness of their results.

Problems with Literature Searches

A frequent complaint in recent years has been over the proliferation of the literature. More and more journals appear, at higher and higher prices, making it harder for libraries to subscribe to a comprehensive set of journals in any field. This, of course, has happened also in suicidology. Whereas there were roughly 1,000 articles on suicide in the 1960s, this rose to about 2,000 in the 1970s, 3,000 in the 1980s, and some 5,000 in the 1990s. Becoming aware of all of these papers is time-consuming.

In addition, the switch to CD-ROM and online access to this literature has had two effects. The first is that searching by the word "suicide" has increased the number of "useless" hits. For example, the word "suicide" is sometimes used in an article when the research has nothing to do with suicide. Similarly, suicide is sometimes mentioned in passing in an Introduction or Discussion section of an article, and sometimes the word is used metaphorically.

More important is that the CD-ROM data bases go back only a few years. Thus, it is easy for scholars to locate recent sources to cite in their article, but they sometimes remain ignorant about earlier research on their topic. Consequently, they tend to repeat research which has already been conducted and published without being aware of this or not having an understanding as to how the more current literature builds on or perhaps differs from earlier work in the area. It is critical that suicidology remembers what is past and builds on this past rather than repeating it.

A similar phenomenon results when using online data bases. Often hundreds or thousands of relevant articles are identified, typically sorted by date. Researchers tend to scan the first dozen or so articles (that is, the most recent) and rarely check all of the abstracts.

Recommendation 2.18: Researchers should remain cognizant of the limitations of online and CD-ROM access to the literature and take care to acquaint themselves with research on and theory about suicide prior to the last few years.

Conclusions

Overall, the field of suicidology is susceptible to methodological issues inherent in any area of research in the social and behavioural sciences. In addition, unique issues related specifically to the study of suicide and other suicide-related behaviors create difficult challenges for researchers in this area. Nonetheless, good science dictates the need for researchers to be aware of the strengths and limitations of methodological approaches to suicide research and to apply their critical and creative energies to overcome those limitations.

References

Ajiki, W., Fukunaga, T., Saijoh, K., & Sumino, K. (1991). Recent status of the medical examiner system in Japan. *Forensic Science International*, 51, 35–50.

Allard, P., & Norlein, M. (1977). Unchanged density of caudate nucleus dopamine uptake sites in depressed suicide victims. *Journal of Neural Transmission*, 104, 1353–1360.

Andress, V. R. (1977). Ethnic/racial misidentification in death. *Forensic Science*, 9, 179–183.

Andriessen, K. (2006). On "intention" in the definition of suicide. *Suicide & Life-Threatening Behavior*, 36, 533–538.

Asencio, A. P., Gomez-Beneyton, M., & Llopis, V. (1988). Epidemiology of suicide in Valencia. *Social Psychiatry & Psychiatric Epidemiology*, 23, 57–59.

Atkinson, M., Kessel, N., & Dalgaard, J. (1975). The comparability of suicide rates. *British Journal of Psychiatry*, 127, 247–256.

Barraclough, B. M. (1970). The effect that coroners have on the suicide rate and the open verdict rate. In E. Hare & J. Wing (Eds.), *Psychiatric epidemiology*, pp. 361–365. London, UK: Oxford University Press.

Barraclough, B. M. (1974). Classifying poisoning deaths by motivation. *Acta Psychiatrica Scandinavica*, 50, 625–635.

Beck, A. T., Schuyler, D., & Herman, I. (1974) Development of suicidal intent scales. In A. T. Beck, H. Resnick, & D. Lettieri (Eds.), *The prediction of suicide*, pp. 45–56. Philadelphia: Charles Press.

Brooke, E. (1974). Suicide and attempted suicide. *WHO Public Health Papers*, #58.

Burgess, A. W., & Hazelwood, R. R. (1983). Autoerotic asphyxial deaths and social network response. *American Journal of Orthopsychiatry*, 53, 166–170.

Clarke-Finnegan, M., & Fahy, T. (1983). Suicide rates in Ireland. *Psychological Medicine*, 13, 385–391.

Cutchin, M. P., & Cutchin, R. R. (1999). Scale, context, and causes of suicide in the United States. *Social Science Quarterly*, 80, 97–114.

Diekstra, R. F. W. Parasuicide: (1997). Is it a distinct phenomenon? In A. J. Botsis, C. R. Soldatos, & C. N. Stefanis (Eds.), *Suicide: Biosocial approaches*, pp. 177–185. New York: Elsevier.

Douglas, J. D. (1967). *The social meanings of suicide*. Princeton, NJ: Princeton University Press.

Farberow, N. L., MacKinnon, D., & Nelson, F. (1977). Suicide. *Public Health Reports*, 92, 223–232.

Farberow, N. L., & Shneidman, E. S. (1955). Attempted, threatened, and completed suicide. *Journal of Abnormal & Social Psychology*, 50, 230.

Fishman, G., & Weimann, G. (1997). Motives to commit suicide. *Archives of Suicide Research*, 3, 199–212.

Hastings, D. W. (1965). The psychiatry of Presidential assassinations. *Lancet*, 85, 294–302.

Hoyt, W. T., Warbasse, R. E., & Chu, E. Y. (2006). Construct validation in counselling psychology research. *The Counseling Psychologist*, 34, 768–805.

Ioannidis, J. P. A. (2005). Why most published research findings are false. *PloS Medicine*, 2, #8.

Jarvis, G. K., Boldt, M., & Butt, J. (1991). Medical examiners and the manner of death. *Suicide & Life-Threatening Behavior*, 21, 115–133.

Jennings, C., & Barraclough, B. M. (1980). Legal administrative influences on the English suicide rate since 1900. *Psychological Medicine*, 10, 407–418.

Lester, D. (1969). The subject as a source of bias in psychological research. *Journal of General Psychology*, 81, 237–248.

Lester, D. (1992a). Effect of using age-adjusted suicide rates on time-series studies of the American suicide rate. *Perceptual & Motor Skills*, 75, 778.

Lester, D. (1992b). Social correlates of opportunity-based suicide rates. *Psychological Reports*, 71, 154.

Lester, D. (1994). An alternative measure of the frequency of suicide and homicide and its social correlates. *Perceptual & Motor Skills*, 79, 606.

Lester, D. (1996a). *An encyclopedia of famous suicides*. Commack, NY: Nova Science.

Lester, D. (1996b). *Patterns of suicide and homicide in the world*. Commack, NY: Nova Science.

Lester, D. (1998). *The death penalty*. 2nd edition. Springfield, IL: Charles Thomas.

Lester, D., Beck, A. T., & Trexler, L. (1975). Extrapolation from attempted suicide to completed suicide. *Journal of Abnormal Psychology*, 84, 563–566.

Lester, D., Beck, A. T., & Mitchell, B. (1979). Extrapolation from attempted suicide to completed suicide. *Journal of Abnormal Psychology*, 88, 78–80.

Lester, D., & Ferguson, M. (1992). An exploratory study of funeral costs for suicides. *Psychological Reports*, 70, 938.

Lester, D., & Stack, S. (1989). Bias resulting from the choice of sample and results of cross-national analyses of suicide rates. *Quality & Quantity*, 23, 221–223.

Lester, D., & Wilson, C. (1988). Suicide in Zimbabwe. *Central African Journal of Medicine*, 34, 147–149.

Maris, R. (1971). Deviance as therapy. *Journal of Health & Social Behavior*, 12, 113–124.

Marshall, D. L., & Soule, S. (1988). Accidental deaths and suicides in southwest Alaska. *Alaska Medicine*, 30(2), 45–52.

Neuringer, C. (1962). Methodological problems in suicide research. *Journal of Consulting Psychology*, 26, 273–278.

Neuringer, C., & Kolstoe, R. H. (1966). Suicide research and the nonrejection of the null hypothesis. *Perceptual & Motor Skills*, 22, 115–118.

Odland, J. (1988). *Spatial autocorrelation*. Beverly Hills, CA: Sage.

Patsopoulos, N. A., Tatsioni, A., & Ioannidis, J. P. (2007). Claims of sex differences. *Journal of the American Medical Association*, 298, 880–893.

Pokorny, A. D. (1965). Human violence. *Journal of Criminal Law, Criminology & Police Science*, 56, 488–497.

Pouliot, L., & De Leo, D. (2006). Critical issues in psychological autopsy studies. *Suicide & Life-Threatening Behavior*, 36, 491–510.

Rich, C., Young, D., Fowler, R., & Rosenfeld, S. (1985). The difference between date of suicidal act and recorded death certificate date in 204 consecutive suicides. *American Journal of Public Health*, 75, 778–779.

Robins, E., Murphy, G. E., Wilkinson, R. H., Gassner, S., & Keyes, J. (1959). Some clinical considerations in the prevention of suicide based on a study of 134 successful suicides. *American Journal of Public Health*, 49, 888–899.

Rogers, J. R., Lewis, M. M., & Subich, L. M. (2002). Validity of the Suicide Assessment Checklist in an emergency crisis center. *Journal of Counseling & Development*, 80, 493–502.

Rosenthal, R. (1966). *Experimenter bias in behavioral research*. New York: Appleton-Century-Crofts.

Safer, D. J. (1997). Self-reported suicide attempts by adolescents. *Annals of Clinical Psychiatry*, 9, 263–269.

Salib, E. (1996). Predictors of coroners' verdicts. *Medicine, Science & the Law*, 36, 237–241.

Schwarz, N. (1999). Self-reports: How the question shapes the answer. *American Psychologist*, 54, 93–105.

Shankel, L. W., & Carr, A. C. (1956). Transvestism and hanging in a male adolescent. *Psychiatric Quarterly*, 30, 478–493.

Shea, S. C. (1999). *The practical art of suicide assessment*. New York: Wiley.

Shneidman, E. S., & Farberow, N. L. (1961). Statistical comparisons between committed and attempted suicides. In N. L. Farberow & E. S. Shneidman (Eds.), *The cry for help*, pp. 19–47. New York: McGraw-Hill.

Siewers, A. B., & Davidoff, E. (1943). Attempted suicide. *Psychiatric Quarterly*, 17, 520–534.

Silverman, M. M. (2006). The language of suicidology. *Suicide & Life-Threatening Behavior*, 36, 519–532.

Simon, R. I. (2006). Patient safety versus freedom of movement. In R. I. Simon & R. E. Hales (Eds.), *Textbook of suicide assessment and management*, pp. 423–439. Washington, DC: American Psychiatric Punlishing.

Temoche, A., Pugh, T. F., & MacMahon, B. (1964). Suicide rates among current and former mental institution patients. *Journal of Nervous & Mental Disease*, 138, 124–130.

Thorson, J. A. (1993). To die with your boots on. *Psychological Reports*, 72, 843–854.

Tracey, T. J. G. (2000). Issues in the analysis and interpretation of quantitative data: Deinstitutionalization of the null hypothesis test. In S. D. Brown & R. W. Lent (Eds.), *Handbook of counselling psychology (3rd edition)*, pp. 177–198. New York: Wiley.

Wasserman, I., M., & Stack, S. (1995). Geographic spatial autocorrelation and United States suicide patterns. *Archives of Suicide Research*, 1, 121–129.

Williams, P., De Salva, D., & Tansella, M. (1987). Suicide and the Italian psychiatric reform. *European Archives of Psychiatry*, 236, 237–240.

Part 1: The Disciplines

3

Psychological Research Into Suicide[6]

Currently in the Western world, suicide is a conscious act of self-induced annihilation, best understood as a multidimensional malaise in a needful individual who defines an issue for which suicide is perceived as the best solution (Shneidman, 1987; p. 157).

Due to the nature of psychology, it is often difficult to distinguish between research that is "psychological" and research that is not "psychological." As suggested in the quote by Shneidman, this difficulty is heightened in the field of suicidology as a function of its multidimensional and, consequently, multidisciplinary nature. If we define psychology broadly as the study of mind and behavior, it is difficult to construct inclusion and exclusion criteria for deciding which research in suicidal behavior can be appropriately identified as psychological. According to Patton (1990), the fundamental disciplinary questions that differentiate psychology from other social science disciplines are "Why do individuals behave as they do?" and "How do human beings behave, think, feel, and know?" (p. 153). Although applying these questions to help differentiate between psychological, sociological, and anthropological research can be helpful, they are not particularly useful in distinguishing psychological research from research in the related human science disciplines of counseling, medicine, nursing, and psychiatry.

The distinction between the "psychological" and the "non-psychological" in suicidology is especially problematic when one considers the historical roots of psychological thought, that is, psychology's early grounding in philosophy. For example, how does one draw a clear line between the philosophical writings of individuals such as Hume (1783/1929), Kierkegaard (1954), Nietzsche (1886/1966), Heidegger (1962), Sartre (1957), and Camus (1955) related to suicide and "pure" psychological research perspectives? Similarly, in considering psychological research, how would one rationalize the exclusion of a consideration of the major theoretical writings as they relate to the study of suicide in light of an expectation that theory and research are or ought to be linked in a reciprocal relationship (Pedhazur & Schmelkin, 1991)?

Given the areas of overlap between psychological research in suicidology and research based in other disciplines and narrow versus broad definitions of research in general, reasonable individuals could differ in their categorizations of psychological research in this area. Rather than focus on the specific outcomes of psychological research into suicide, which would require the establishment of somewhat artificial boundaries around what is and is not psychological research, this chapter will attempt to overview the past, present, and future of psychological research in suicidology in

---

[6] An earlier version of this chapter appeared as Rogers (2001a).

the Western world in terms of general methodological focus. The first section of the chapter presents a brief overview of the major philosophical and theoretical traditions related to the understanding of suicide. The second section provides a brief analysis of the pragmatic focus of research in suicidology in the United States prompted by the 1966 creation of the Center for the Studies of Suicide Prevention by the National Institute of Mental Health (Resnik & Hathorne, 1972). Finally, section three presents a discussion of trends and directions for future psychological research in the area of suicidology with a specific focus on macro and complexity theories.

As a final caveat, while certainly not intended as a comprehensive review of the psychological study of suicide and suicidal behavior, reference will be made to some of the extant literature in the field in support of the methodological overview. Consequently, omissions in terms of referenced work are reflective of this focus as opposed to any commentary on the quality, importance, or impact of specific works in the field.

Psychological Study Of Suicide In The Past: The Philosophical And Theoretical Traditions

This section briefly outlines the major philosophical and theoretical perspectives related to suicide. This philosophical overview provides a backdrop for the subsequent presentation of four of the major theoretical models in psychology. The importance of theory in advancing understanding and guiding research has been argued in both the general philosophy of science literature (e.g., Lynd, 1939; Lykken, 1991) and in the psychological literature as it relates to suicidology (e.g., Lester, 1988; Rogers, 2003). Thus, this section is intended to provide a basis for the interpretation of the current status of psychological research in suicidology as it relates to philosophical and psychological theory.

Philosophical Perspectives

According to Stillion and McDowell (1996), suicides or self-murders in some form or another have probably occurred almost as long as human beings have been in existence. Early suicide in the form of self-sacrifice has evolved over the millennia to encompass many other dimensions including self-punishment (e.g., the death of Judas Iscariot in 33 A.D.) and rational control over death (e.g., the death of Socrates in 399 B.C.). In the early Christian tradition, suicide was additionally viewed as a means of self-martyrdom and it was not until around 400 A.D. that suicide began to be defined as a crime against God and the state (Stillion & McDowell, 1996). This process of redefinition culminated in 1256–1272 A.D. with Thomas Aquinas's conceptualization of suicide as a clear sin against God.

With the publication of *Biathanatos* (Donne, 1644/1982) and continuing with Hume's (1783/1929) *Essay on Suicide*, the strict definition of suicide as a sin began to be challenged from a philosophical perspective. During the time period of these two publications, the development of secular laws prohibiting suicide and attempts to define it as an illness (Esquirol, 1838; Merian, 1763) were under way. According to Stillion and McDowell (1996), the writings of Freud (1917/1961) established the foundation for the interpretation of suicide as a sign of mental illness. In contrast to defining suicide as a crime, sin, or illness, the existential writings of Hume (1783/1929), Kierkegaard (1954), Nietzsche (1886/1966), Heidegger (1962), Sartre (1957), and Camus (1955) argued that suicide can be an expression of freedom and responsibility and, as such, may represent an existential choice (see also, Rogers, 2001b). In fact, much of the contemporary discussion related to rational suicide (e.g., Rogers & Britton, 1994; Rogers, Gueulette, Abbey-Hines, Carney & Werth, 2001; Werth, 1992/1996) and physician assisted suicide (e.g., Battin,1998; Hendin, 1998; Werth & Rogers, 2005) is linked to existential thought in this area.

Psychological Perspectives

In his review of the issue of suicide from the perspective of classical psychological theories, Lester (1988) suggested that, in contrast to the attention given the subject of suicide in the sociological literature, none of the major contributing theorists in psychology have focused specifically on suicide. Despite this lack of specific attention to the topic, however, Lester (1988) and Leenaars (1990) have discussed a number of psychological theories and highlighted their interface with the field of suicidology.

For example, according to Leenaars (1990), the psychological study of suicide can be traced to the early theoretical work of Sigmund Freud. As indicated previously, Freud's (1917/1961) writings have been used to benchmark the interpretation of suicide as a sign of mental illness. Although Freud's conceptualization of suicide from the psychodynamic perspective was not extensively articulated, his recognition of many of the associated clinical features such as guilt, loss, revenge, humiliation, depression and the view of suicidal behavior as a form of communication clearly predated and influenced the directions of subsequent empirical research (Lester, 1988). Additionally, Freud's early conceptualization of the dynamics of eros and thanatos as the life and death instincts has, in many ways, presaged the current literature in suicidology investigating the genetic and neurobiological correlates of suicide (e.g., Mann & Arango, 1998).

Social learning theory (Bandura, 1977) has also been suggested as a useful theoretical model for the study of suicidal behavior (Leenaars, 1990; Lester, 1988). In fact, Lester concluded that the research evidence for a learning component in suicidal behavior was "overwhelming" (p. 61). Imbedded in the stimulus/response/reinforcement paradigm of general learning theory, social learning theory includes attention to the transmission of suicidal attitudes and behaviors through social and family-based learning experiences. Bandura's (1977) extension of the basic learning model to include observational learning has found particular attention in suicidology as an heuristic for understanding the occurrence of suicidal behavior in families (e.g., Platt, 1993; Rogers & Carney, 1994), suicide clusters, pacts, and mass suicides (Lester, 1988).

Similarly, the cognitive behavioral perspective on suicide with its general focus on depression, hopelessness, and the role of cognition has been identified by Leenaars (1990) as having important implications for the study of suicide. According to

Leenaars, the link between the cognitive perspectives and suicide is most clearly articulated in the writings of Beck and his colleagues (e.g., Beck, Shaw, Rush, & Emery, 1979). Within this model, negative and often unrealistic views and expectations of one's self, the future, and the world lead to feelings of helplessness and hopelessness. These feelings can become overwhelming and lead one to suicide as a means of escaping the associated negative affect. Intervention in the cognitive model focuses on identifying the automatic and involuntary cognitions and testing those for empirical validity (e.g., Ellis & Newman, 1996).

While the above psychological theories address the issue of suicide in limited ways and as extensions of their larger theoretical perspectives, Shneidman (1987) developed a theory specific to suicide based on Murray's (1938) conceptualization of personality and consists of the three characteristics of press, perturbation, and pain. According to the model, press refers to "events done to the individual to which he or she reacts" (p. 174). While press can be both positive and negative, threatening presses are those most relevant to suicide. Perturbation refers to the state of being upset and pain is interpreted as psychological pain related to unrealized or blocked need fulfilment. Individuals experiencing high levels of press, pain, and perturbation and who are motivated to escape that pain are those who commit suicide.

Although these four theories have been identified by Lester (1988) and Leenaars (1990) as having much to offer the area of suicidology in terms of theoretical understanding and guidance for empirical research, this promise has not been realized (Lester, 1988). What has occurred, instead, is a piecemeal investigation of empirically identified variables associated with suicidal behavior with little or no translation into broader theoretical perspectives.

Recommendation 3.1: The major classical theories of personality and human behavior, plus more recent proposals, should be explored further for their implications for explaining suicidal behavior. Testable hypotheses should be proposed, and research to test these predictions carried out.

Psychological Research into Suicide in the Present: Pragmatics in Action

The contemporary study of suicidal behavior in the United States can be traced back to the work of Shneidman, Farberow and Litman in the late 1950s and the subsequent creation of the Center for the Studies of Suicide Prevention by the National Institute of Mental Health (NIMH) in 1966 (Resnik & Hathorne, 1972). In combination, the investigations of Shneidman and his colleagues and the national initiative were instrumental in prompting the scientific community to begin to systematically investigate suicidal behavior as an important area of inquiry. The major methodological result of NIMH policy and funding initiative was that research in suicide took on a predominantly pragmatic character. That is, the predominant focus in contemporary suicidology in the United States became the identification of risk and protective factors that influence suicidal behavior as opposed to understanding and theory development. This pragmatic focus resulted in the identification of a variety of biological, psychological, and sociological correlates of suicide and suicidal behavior (e.g., Blumenthal & Kupfer, 1990). Although the ultimate goal of this approach was to provide a basis for predicting and preventing suicide (e.g., Blumenthal & Kupfer, 1990; Maris, Berman, Maltsberger & Yufit, 1992; Rogers, Alexander & Subich, 1994), there is little evidence to suggest that it has resulted in any reduction in the overall suicide rate (Kachur, Potter, James, & Powell, 1995; Lester, 1998) or increased the ability to predict suicide (Maris, Berman, Maltsberger & Yufit, 1992).

As a secondary effect, the pragmatic approach to the problem of suicide prompted by NIMH has contributed to the general lack of attention to theoretical grounding in the extant research. That is, much of the current psychological literature in suicidology is written from an atheoretical or micro-theoretical perspective as opposed to proceeding from well articulated theoretical positions and retrospectively informing those theories. Additionally, much of the existing theory-linked research is a result of post hoc theorizing (Pedhazur & Schmelkin, 1991). This lack of prospective and broad theoretical grounding has had at least two effects on the knowledge base in suicidology. First, rather than the development of a coherent body of knowledge, the atheoretical, micro-theoretical, and post hoc approaches have resulted in the identification of a wide array of correlates to suicidal behavior with little understanding regarding how they are interrelated and may coalesce at the individual level to lead one to a decision to commit suicide. Second, as indicated earlier, without clearly identified theoretical specifications, it is difficult to unambiguously differentiate between psychological research and research emanating from other closely related fields.

As an example of atheoretical research in the psychological study of suicide, Mireault and De Man (1996) investigated predictors of suicidal ideation among elderly individuals. Although these authors identified their research as being based on a multifactor theory of suicide, it was not grounded in any clear psychological theory and was, in fact, atheoretical in nature. In their design, the authors identified a set of correlates of suicidal behavior from prior empirical investigations and cast them in a regression model to identify significant predictors of elder suicide. The authors made no attempt to place their findings within a theoretical framework.

Rogers (1992) is an example of theorizing at the micro level. Here, he suggested that the well-documented relationship between alcohol consumption and suicidal behavior could be understood based on the work of Steele and Josephs (1990). He suggested that the link might best be conceptualized as a function of the construct of "alcohol induced myopia" introduced by Steele and Josephs as part of their cognitive-social model for understanding alcohol's cognitive and behavioral effects. Rogers highlighted the overlap between the concept of alcohol induced myopia and the concept of tunnel vision or cognitive constriction which has often been identified as being associated with suicide (e.g., Shneidman, 1987). While making this link to cognitive-social theory may result in some degree of practical and heuristic value, it occurs in isolation from other empirically observed relationships to suicidal behavior and does not necessarily advance the field toward better understanding at a macro theoretical level.

In a similar fashion, Platt (1992) provides an example of the post hoc approach. In this research, Platt was interested in investigating the relationship of previous suicide attempts and exposure to suicidal behavior with current suicidal behavior. Although his research questions were not originally derived from social learning theory (Bandura, 1977), he interpreted his results as a test of the observational learning model. Based on his analyses, he concluded that there was little evidence to support an observational learning component for suicidal behavior. Critiquing Platt (1992), Rogers and Carney (1994) highlighted the post hoc nature of both his analyses and theoretical conclusions. These authors suggested that, in order to appropriately test the observational learning paradigm, one would need to specify the theory a priori, derive testable hypotheses from the theory, and develop a methodology that would allow interpretation back to the theory. As suggested by Pedhazur and Schmelkin (1991), "Post hoc theorizing should not be confused with the meaningful and necessary process of theory refinement, revision, reformulation, or whatever the case may be, in light of research findings" (p. 185). These authors make their case regarding the importance of theory further by stating:

> Meaningful hypotheses cannot emerge in a theoretical vacuum. Admittedly, the theory from which a given hypothesis was derived is frequently implicit. The researcher may not even be aware of the theoretical orientation that has led him or her to advance and test a given hypothesis. Yet it is the theory that renders the hypothesis and the variables that it refers to, relevant to attempts to explain a given phenomenon. Moreover, it is theory that gives coherence and integration to a set of hypotheses designed to explain a given phenomenon. (p. 185)

Finally, psychological research in suicidology has generally adhered to the deficit model embedded in the mental illness tradition. Based in this model, researchers have focused on discovering the deficiencies of suicidal as compared with non-suicidal individuals. These deficiencies have then been interpreted as risk factors and, very often, their absence has been interpreted as protective factors. Two notable exceptions to this deficit model have been in the areas of "reasons for living" and "rational" suicide.

In the first exception to the deficit model, Linehan, Goodstein, Nielson, and Chiles (1983) constructed the Reasons for Living Inventory in an attempt to assess the "adaptive, life-maintaining characteristics of non-suicidal people" (p. 276). This effort at exploring the issue of suicide from a non-deficit perspective was mirrored by Westefeld and his colleagues with the construction and psychometric development of the College Student Reasons for Living Inventory (Westefeld, Cardin, & Deaton 1992). While this approach can potentially be useful in understanding suicidal individuals through the study of non-suicidal people, it continues to be overshadowed by research from the deficit perspective.

Rational suicide represents the other major area of departure in the contemporary psychological literature from the deficit model of suicide. Prompted in part by the emergence of the AIDS pandemic and the issue of physician assisted suicide, but with clear historical ties into the philosophical work of Hume (1783/1929), Kierkegaard (1954), Nietzsche (1886/1966), Heidegger (1962), Sartre (1957), and Camus (1955), rational suicide has become a recent focus in the psychological literature (e.g., Werth, 1996). In contrast to the reasons for living research, the rational suicide issue has gained momentum through its connection with other right to die policy issues (e.g., Rogers, 1996) and can be expected to continue to impact the psychological study of suicide into the next century.

In summation, the current pragmatic approach to the psychological study of suicidal behavior has resulted in the development of a clearer picture of relevant correlates of suicide. This approach has clearly been important in the developmental process of the relatively young field of suicidology. These efforts, however, have not resulted in the expected reduction in suicidal behaviors nor have they increased predictive efficacy. In general, the psychological research in the area of suicidal behavior evidences a clear lack of theoretical cohesiveness. Psychological research in suicidology in the future should focus on the development of macro theories in order to provide organizing structures for what is currently known about suicide and human behavior in general. Future efforts directed at organization and cohesiveness have the potential to move the field well beyond the current stage of risk and protective factor identification that has been the hallmark of contemporary psychological investigations into suicide and may provide a reasonable link to the re-emerging issue of rational suicide. This process should lead to a greater understanding of suicidal people and, perhaps, to the development of more effective strategies and interventions for working with suicidal individuals.

Based on the conclusion that research in suicidology has been largely atheoretical, at the micro-level, post hoc and deficit-oriented, the following recommendations are offered.

Recommendation 3.2: Research should be based on hypotheses derived from psychological theory rather than conducted at a purely empirical level and then related back to any theory that seems relevant.

Recommendation 3.3: Efforts should be made to summarize the findings from the existing atheoretical research, using meta-analyses where appropriate to identify reliable findings and their range of applicability.

Recommendation 3.4: Previously proposed micro-level and post hoc theories should be identified and reviewed, and testable (and competing) hypotheses derived and tested.

Recommendation 3.5: More theories derived from the study of other behaviors should be explored for their applicability as explanations for suicidal behavior.

Recommendation 3.6: Alternatives to the deficit-oriented models of suicidal behavior should be proposed (for example, models based on "positive psychology" and resilience), and theories proposed to explain suicidal behavior carried out for growth-oriented (as conceived by humanistic psychologists) motives.

The Future of Psychological Research in Suicidology: Macro Theories, Chaos, and Complexity

There have been efforts to search for and propose new theories of suicidal behavior. For example, Lester (1990) reviewed the major theories of criminality and proposed parallel theories of suicide (classical, positivist individualistic, social structure, learning, social control, social reaction and social conflict).

Joiner and Rudd (2000), agreeing that suicide science needs "new life" and that a theoretical vacuum exists in the field of suicidology, invited leading psychological theorists, many of whom had not considered suicidal behavior hitherto, to apply their theories and research programs to the topic. Their book had the title "Suicide Science" and was subtitled "Expanding the Boundaries." Among the perspectives represented were self-regulation models, the role of shame and guilt, and a looming vulnerability model.

This final section provides some examples of areas for future psychological research in suicidology for the millennium. The first example is an outline of the early stages of development of a macro theory that may serve to organize the current body of knowledge in suicidology and link it with a broader theory of human behavior based in existential (e.g., Yalom, 1980) and constructivist (e.g., Mahoney, 1991) theories. This will be followed by a brief presentation of chaos and complexity theoretical perspectives that have been applied in the realm of the physical sciences and seem to have promising applications in psychology (e.g., Masterpasqua & Perna, 1997).

An Existential-Constructivist Model

Following his review of the issue of suicide from the perspective of psychological theories, Lester (1988) suggested that advancements in the psychological study of suicidology might accrue through attempts to integrate the current body of knowledge with "classic psychological theories of human behavior" (p. 122). The existential-constructivist model for understanding suicide (Rogers, 2001b) represents such an attempt at integration. This conceptualization attempts to combine classical existential theory derived from the work of Yalom (1980) and rooted in the philosophical literature (e.g., Kierkegaard, 1954; Nietzsche, 1886/1966) with critical constructivism as discussed by Mahoney (1991) and Neimeyer and Mahoney (1995).

This model posits that the existential issues of death, meaninglessness, isolation, freedom, and responsibility provide the underlying motivational dynamics for the development of individual and shared constructions of meaning. These constructions, according to Neimeyer (1995), are the result of the "basic human quest to seek relatedness, connection, and mutuality of meaning in spite of our uniqueness, using the common grounding provided by our language and our embodiment to form an inter-subjective bridge between our phenomenal worlds" (p. 2) and include our world views and perceptions of reality, as well as our interpretations of ourselves, others, and relationships.

With its focus on the adaptive viability of constructions (Mahoney, 1991) and attention to human cognitive processes, this model can reasonably incorporate and explain many of the correlates of suicide and suicidal behavior identified through pragmatic research endeavors. Furthermore, the existential-constructivist model potentially allows for an integrative consideration of the various risk and protective factors in a human motivational context, thereby, enhancing our overall understanding of suicide. Additionally, with its grounding in existentialism, the existential-constructivist framework may provide a reasonable basis for conceptualizing the emerging issue of rational suicide and help guide research around this important topic in the future.

The existential-constructivist theory was presented here as just one example of a number of possibilities for developing macro theories of suicide that may serve to link the current empirical knowledge base with classical psychological theories of human behavior. As suggested by Lester (1988) and supported by Pedhazur and Schmelkin's (1991) general philosophy of science discussion, what is needed in future psychological research in suicidology is the development of multiple macro theories of this type that can be empirically tested and validated. Efforts in this process should result in advances in the psychological understanding of suicide well beyond the current level.

Chaos and Complexity Theories

Given the lack of the current pragmatic focus of psychological research in suicidology to result in increased predictive efficacy and a reduction in the suicide rates (Lester, 1994, 1998), a number of authors have suggested that psychology in general, and the psychological study of suicidology specifically, may benefit from a consideration of the various non-linear dynamic systems perspectives including chaos and complexity theories (e.g. Lester, 1994; Mishara, 1996; Masterpasqua & Perna, 1997; Rogers, 1995, 1997). According to Eidelson (1997), chaos and complexity theories have evolved from investigations into the behavior of complex, dynamic, and interactive systems and have revealed that determinism and randomness often coexist, the whole is often more than the sum of its parts, instability is common, and behavioral change is frequently abrupt and discontinuous. Related to human behavior, Perna and Masterpasqua (1997) suggested that:

> We can no longer rely on models based on insulated, linear, and closed systems to explain a self in context and in continuous construction. We see the sciences of chaos and complexity as offering these new models and metaphors. They offer a basis from the physical and natural sciences from which to understand a postmodern self in ôcontinuous construction and reconstruction. (p. 7)

Chaos and complexity theories have already begun to appear in the psychological literature as models and metaphors for advancing the understanding of such psychological issues as dissociative disorder (Derrickson-Kossman & Drinkard, 1997), psychological trauma (Lasser & Bethory, 1997), and the psychotherapeutic process (Mahoney & Moes, 1997). Thus, investigating their application to the study of suicide seems an appropriate direction for psychological research in the next millennium.

Non-linear dynamic systems perspectives include chaos theory (e.g., Gleick, 1987) and the complexity theories of self-organized criticality (Bak & Chen, 1991) and catastrophe modeling (Stewart & Peregoy, 1983). These three general models and their possible impact on the psychological study of suicidology will be briefly described below.

Chaos Theory

In his discussion of the difficulties inherent in the prediction of suicide, Lester (1994) suggested that the non-linear theory of chaos may have significant implications for suicidologists. Based on the work of Lorenz (1979) and Gleick (1987), Lester introduced the concept of *sensitive dependence on initial conditions* into the psychological literature in suicidology. According to Lester (1994), "In suicidology, we expect and therefore search for major events which might lead to suicide subsequently, whereas perhaps the causes of suicide are more subtle" (p. 187). Similarly, Rogers (1995) suggested that this concept may have far-reaching implications for the field of suicidology in that "events in peoples' lives that have been viewed as having little or minor significance in terms of a causal relationship to suicidal behavior, may actually play a substantially greater role" (p. 139).

At the basis of chaos is the paradox that unpredictable behavior (i.e, suicide) can and does occur within predictable systems. According to Perna and Masterpasqua (1997), "Another way to understand this apparent paradox is that systems in chaos are determined, but not by linear methods. Chaos represents nonlinear deterministic behavior" (pp. 9–10). Translated into the psychological study of suicidology, chaos theory may provide a useful metaphor for understanding the inability of research to result in useful predictive models at the individual level. By giving up the unobtainable goal of individual prediction and incorporating the concepts of sensitive dependence on initial conditions and nonlinear modeling, the application of chaos theory to suicidology has the potential to move the field to a greater level of understanding of suicide and suicidal individuals.

Self-Organized Criticality

Self-organized criticality is a theory developed by Bak and Chen (1991) in order to explain how large interactive systems can evolve or self-organize toward a critical state in which a minor incident can lead to a catastrophic event. This state of precarious equilibrium has been referred to by Eidelson (1997) as the edge of chaos and a critical state between order and disorder. According to Eidelson, the classical example of self-organized criticality is the behavior of a pile of sand:

> As sand is slowly added from above, the pile's height increases until the slope reaches a critical state. At that point, any additional grains of sand will cause an avalanche of unpredictable magnitude. In fact, the distribution of landslides is best described by a power law, with a small slide far more likely than a large one. But perhaps most intriguing is the premise that the same conditions can produce different outcomes on dif-

ferent occasions. What remains relatively constant, however, is the critical state that the pile must return to before the next avalanche will occur. (p. 54–55)

Rogers and McGuirk (1997) have suggested that the use of self-organized criticality as a metaphor for suicidal phenomena may have heuristic value. According to these authors, when applied to suicidal behavior, the self-organized criticality model may aid psychologists "in understanding the relative unpredictability of suicidal behavior and help explain why seemingly minor events can lead to suicidal and non-suicidal behaviors within the same individual at different points in time" (p. 139).

In their discussion of psychological systems and the self-organizing process, Rogers and McGuirk (1997) suggested that, at a basic level, one could consider the human cognitive, affective, and symbolic systems as three of the possible psychological components of the complex system for modeling purposes. Each of these systems have their own self-organizing processes that interpret and assimilate new relevant information. Additionally, these systems interact in reciprocal ways and self-organize at a meta-system level. The meta-system, or individual, constantly self-organizes to what appears to be a state of equilibrium representing stability and some degree of behavioral predictability. This state of equilibrium, however, is only one of many possible equilibrium states and is actually the result of many "self-organized, far from equilibrium dynamical systems" (Eidelson, 1997, p. 43). Consequently, the equilibrium state represents a stable picture of the system or individual constantly at the edge of chaos.

In terms of suicide, Rogers and McGuirk (1997) suggested that self-organized criticality and the concept of multiple possible equilibrium states might be useful in explaining some current observations regarding suicidal behavior. For example, they suggested that the concept of multiple possible equilibrium states could be applied to the understanding of both resilience to negative life events and to suicidal crises, that is, a threatened equilibrium state may lead to a shift or re-organization to a different equilibrium state or, alternatively, to a catastrophic event such as suicide.

The application of self-organized criticality to the psychological study of suicide seems to have promise when considering the implications of the theory at the superficial level as presented here. Certainly, the theory appears to provide an appropriate metaphor for thinking about suicide and suicidal behavior and for organizing some of the empirical literature in suicidology. The challenge for the psychological study of suicidology in the future will be, as suggested by Eidelson (1997), to move from metaphor to modeling if complexity theories in general are going to advance the knowledge base in the behavioral sciences.

Catastrophe Modeling

Catastrophe theory provides a method for conceptualizing how smooth changes in the independent variable can lead to sudden changes in the dependent variable (Stewart & Peregory, 1983). Thus, related to human behavior, it attempts to explain "sudden changes or discontinuities in behavior that occur even though the underlying causative factors are continuous" (p. 140; Rogers, 1995).

Of a variety of catastrophe models, Rogers (1995) suggested that the cusp catastrophe model may be most appropriate for considering suicidal phenomena. Accordingly, in his brief discussion of catastrophe modeling, Rogers suggested that:

> The cusp catastrophe model, one of a number of general catastrophe models, seems particularly suited to a consideration of suicidal behavior. In general, the cusp catastrophe model suggests that smooth changes in independent variables (e.g., press and perturbation) are sometimes associated with sudden discontinuous or abrupt changes in the independent [dependent] variable (e.g., non-suicidal coping responses lead to suicide). Additionally, in some circumstances the same event history of the independent variables (e.g., identical levels of press and perturbation) can result in very different final values on the dependent variable (e.g., nonsuicidal coping responses at one time and a suicidal response at another time). This characteristic of divergence may have explanatory implications for suicidal behavior in the absence of an objectively identified triggering event. (p. 140)

As with chaos and self-organized criticality, catastrophe theory and specifically the cusp catastrophe model appear to provide useful metaphors for the psychological study of suicide for the next millennium. The translation of the non-linear dynamic systems models into the behavioral sciences is at a very early stage. However, based on the use of these models in other areas of psychology and the brief discussion of their possible impact on the psychological study of suicide, efforts directed at interpreting these models in suicidology seem warranted.

Recommendation 3.7: Efforts should be made to develop new macro-theories of suicidal behavior based on previously applied micro-theories of suicidal behavior or by drawing upon theoretical developments in other fields and disciplines.

Recommendation 3.8: Testable hypotheses should be derived from these macro-theories of suicidal behavior so that the relevance and applicability of the theories can be tested.[7]

Conclusion

Despite its connection to the philosophical writings of the 18th Century and the more recent translations of classical psychological theory to address suicide and suicidal behavior, psychological research in suicidology barely goes back 40 years. Psychological research since the 1950s in this area has been focused on the pragmatic issues of prediction and intervention but has yet resulted in any reduction in the suicide rate or improved the ability to predict suicide at the individual level.

---

[7] It is noteworthy that, for example, theories of suicide based on chaos and complexity theories have not, so far, generated testable hypotheses or any research.

As suggested in this chapter, psychological research in suicidology in the next millennium may benefit from a focus on the development of macro theories that integrate the extant knowledge of suicide correlates with classical psychological theories of human behavior. Additionally, the field may benefit from efforts aimed at developing theoretical models based on the non-linear dynamic systems perspectives of chaos, self-organized criticality, and catastrophe modeling, as well as other complexity theories, for understanding suicide and suicidal individuals.

Finally, perhaps it is time for suicidologists to let go of the hope of prediction that has driven much of the psychological research to date and increase the focus of gaining a clearer understanding of suicide at the individual level. As suggested by Lykken (1991):

> A natural scientist is not embarrassed because he cannot look at a tree and predict which leaves will fall first in the autumn or the exact path of the fall or where the leaf will land. Maybe individual lives are a lot like leaves; perhaps there is a very limited amount one can say about the individual case, based on a knowledge of leaves in general or people in general, without detailed, idiographic study of that particular case and even then it is hard to know how the winds will blow from one day to the next. (pp. 18–19)

References

Aquinas, T. (1975). *Summa theologica (Vol. 38)*. London: Blackfriars. (Original work written 1265–1272)

Battin, M. P. (1998). Ethical issues in physician assisted suicide. In M. Uhlmann (Ed.), *Last rights? Assisted suicide and euthanasia debate*, pp. 111–145. Grand Rapids, MI: Eerdmans.

Bek, P., & Chen, K. (1991). Self-organized criticality. *Scientific American*, 264(January), 46–53.

Camus, A. (1955). *The myth of Sisyphus, and other essays*. (J. O'Brien, Trans.). New York: Knopf.

Derrickson-Kossmann, D., & Drinkard, L. (1997). Dissociative disorders in chaos and complexity. In F. Masterpasqua & P. A. Perna (Eds.), *The psychological meaning of chaos: Translating theory into practice*, pp. 117–145. Washington, DC: American Psychological Association.

Donne, J. (1982). *Biathanatos.* (M. Rudick & M. P. Battin, Trans.). New York: Garland. (Original work published 1644).

Eidelson, R. J. (1997). Complex adaptive systems in the behavioral and social sciences. *Review of General Psychology*, 1, 42–71.

Ellis, T. E., & Newman, C. F. (1996). *Choosing to live: How to defeat suicide through cognitive therapy*. Oakland, CA: New Harbinger Publications.

Freud, S. (1961). Mourning and melancholia. In J. Strachey (Ed. And Trans.), *The standard edition of the complete psychological works of Sigmund Freud (Vol. 14)*, pp. 243–258. London: Hograth Press. (Original work published 1917)

Gleick, J. (1987). *Chaos: Making a new science*. New York: Viking.

Heidegger, M. (1962). *Being and time*. (J. Macquarrie & E. Robinson, Trans.). New York: Harper & Row.

Hume, D. (1929). *An essay on suicide*. Yellow Springs, OH: Kahoe. (Original work published 1783.)

Joiner, T., & Rudd, M. D. (Eds.). (2000). *Suicide science: Expanding the boundaries*. Boston: Kluwer Academic.

Kierkegaard, S. (1954). *Fear and trembling/The sickness unto death*. (W. Lowrie, Trans.). Garden City, NY: Doubleday.

Lasser, C. J., & Bathory, D. S. (1997). Reciprocal causality and childhood trauma: An application of chaos theory. In F. Masterpasqua. & P. A. Perna (Eds.), *The psychological meaning of chaos: Translating theory into practice*, pp. 147–176. Washington, DC: American Psychological Association.

Leenaars, A. A. (1990). Psychological perspectives on suicide. In D. Lester (Ed.), *Current concepts of suicide*, pp. 159–167. Philadelphia: Charles Press.

Lester, D. (1988). *Suicide from a psychological perspective*. Springfield, IL: Charles C. Thomas.

Lester, D. (1990). *Understanding and preventing suicide: New perspectives*. Springfield, IL: Charles C. Thomas.

Lester, D. (1994). Reflections on the statistical rarity of suicide. Crisis, 15, 187–188.

Lester, D. (1998). Preventing suicide by restricting access to methods for suicide. *Archives of Suicide Research*, 4, 7–24.

Linehan, M. M., Goodstein, J. L., Nielson, S. L., & Chiles, J. A. (1983). Reasons for staying alive when you are thinking of killing yourself: The Reasons for Living Inventory. *Journal of Consulting and Clinical Psychology*, 51, 276–286.

Lorenz, E. (1979). *Predictability: Does the flap of a butterfly's wings in Brazil set off a tornado in Texas?* Paper presented at the American Association for the Advancement of Science, Washington, DC.

Lykken, D. T. (1991). What's wrong with psychology anyway? In D. Cicchetti & W. M. Grove (Eds.), *Thinking Clearly about Psychology. Volume 1: Matters of Public Interest*, pp. 3–39. Minneapolis, MN: University of Minnesota Press.

Lynd, R. S. (1939). *Knowledge for what?: The place of social science in American culture.* Princeton, NJ: Princeton University Press.

Mahoney, M. J. (1991). *Human change processes: The scientific foundations of psychotherapy.* New York: Basic Books.

Mahoney, M. J., & Moes, A. J. (1997). Complexity and psychotherapy: Promising dialogues and practical issues. In F. Masterpasqua & P. A. Perna (Eds.), *The psychological meaning of chaos: Translating theory into practice*, pp. 199–224. Washington, DC: American Psychological Association.

Masterpasqua, F., & Perna, P. A. (1997). *The psychological meaning of chaos: Translating theory into practice.* Washington, DC: American Psychological Association.

Mireault, M., & DeMan, A. F. (1996). Suicidal ideation among the elderly: Personal variables, stress and social support. *Social Behavior and Personality*, 24, 385–392.

Mishara, B. L. (1996). A dynamic developmental model of suicide. *Human Development*, 39, 181–194.

Murray, H. A. (1938). *Explorations in personality.* New York: Oxford University Press.

Neimeyer, R. A. (1995). An invitation to constructivist psychotherapies. In R. A. Neimeyer & M. J. Mahoney (Eds.), *Constructivism in psychotherapy*, pp. 1–8. Washington, DC: American Psychological Association.

Neimeyer, R. A., & Mahoney, M. J. (Eds.). (1995). *Constructivism in psychotherapy.* Washington, DC: American Psychological Association.

Nietzsche, F. (1966). *Beyond good and evil.* (W. Kaufmann, Trans.). New York: Vintage. (Original work published 1886.)

Patton, M. Q. (1990). *Qualitative evaluation and research methods (2nd edition).* Newbury Park, CA: Sage.

Pedhazur, E. J., & Schmelkin, L. P. (1991). *Measurement, design, and analysis: An integrated approach.* Hillsdale, NJ: Lawrence Erlbaum Associates.

Rogers, J. R. (1990). Female suicide: The trend toward increased lethality in method of choice and its implications. *Journal of Counseling and Development,* 69, 37–38.

Rogers, J. R. (1992). Suicide and alcohol: Conceptualizing the relationship from a cognitive-social paradigm. *Journal of Counseling and Development*, 70, 540–543.

Rogers, J. R. (1995). Chaos and suicide: The myth of linear causality. In D. Lester (Ed.), *Suicide '95: Proceedings of the 28th Annual Conference of the American Association of Suicidology*, pp. 139–140. Washington, DC: American Association of Suicidology.

Rogers, J. R. (1996). Assessing right to die attitudes: A conceptually guided measurement model. *Journal of Social Issues, 52*, 63–84.

Rogers, J. R. (2001a). Psychological research into suicide. In D. Lester (Ed.), *Suicide prevention: Resource for the Millennium*, pp. 31–44. Philadelphia: Brunner-Routledge.

Rogers, J. R. (2001b) Theoretical grounding: The "missing link" in suicide research. *Journal of Counseling and Development*, 79, 16–25.

Rogers, J. R. (2003) The anatomy of suicidology: A psychological science perspective on the status of suicide research. *Suicide and Life-Threatening Behavior*, 31, 9–20.

Rogers, J. R., & Britton, P. J. (1994). AIDS and rational suicide: A counseling psychology perspective or a slide on the slippery slope. *The Counseling Psychologist*, 22, 171–178.

Rogers, J. R., Alexander, R. A., & Subich, L. M. (1994). Development and psychometric analysis of the suicide assessment checklist. *Journal of Mental Health Counseling*, 16, 352–368.

Rogers, J. R., & Carney, J. V. (1994). Theoretical and methodological considerations in assessing the "modeling effect" in parasuicidal behavior: A Comment on Platt (1993). *Crisis*, 15, 83–89.

Rogers, J. R., Gueulette, C. M., Abbey-Hines, J., Carney, J. V., & Werth, J. L., Jr. (2001). Rational suicide: An empirical investigation of counsellor attitudes. *Journal of Counseling and Development*, 79, 365–372.

Rogers, J. R., & McGuirk, H. A. (1998). Self-organized criticality and suicidal behavior. In J. McIntosh (Ed.), *Suicide '97: Proceedings of the 30th Annual Conference of the American Association of Suicidology*, pp 139–140. Washington, DC: American Association of Suicidology.

Sartre, J. P. (1957). *Existentialism and human emotions*. (B. Frechtman, Trans.). New York: Philosophical Library.

Shneidman, E. S. (1987). A psychological approach to suicide. In G. R. VandenBos & B. K. Bryant (Eds.), *Cataclysms, crises, and catastrophes: Psychology in action*, pp. 151–183. Washington, DC: American Psychological Association.

Stewart, I. N., & Peregoy, P. L. (1983). Catastrophe theory modeling in psychology. *Psychological Bulletin*, 94, 336–362.

Werth, J. L., Jr. (1992). Rational suicide and AIDS. *The Counseling Psychologist*, 20, 645–659.

Werth, J. L., Jr. (1996). *Rational suicide?: Implications for mental health professionals.* Washington, DC: Taylor & Francis.

Werth, J. L., Jr., & Rogers, J. R. (2005). Assessing for impaired judgment as a means of meeting the "duty to protect" when a client is a potential harm-to-self: Implications for clients making end-of-life decisions. *Mortality*, 10, 7–21.

Yalom, I. D. (1980). *Existential psychotherapy*. New York: Basic Books.

4

Psychiatric Research

This chapter will review some of the research into suicidal behavior conducted by those in the field of psychiatry. The goal here is not to provide a complete review of the field, but rather to take three illustrative topics, present some of the research on those three topics, and then make recommendations for future psychiatric research on suicidal behavior. The three topics will come from genetics (twin studies of suicidal behavior), physiological research (brain studies of the μ opioid receptors), and diagnosis-based studies (PTSD).

However, before getting to these three illustrative topics, we must discuss two major problems in psychiatric research, namely, the diagnostic system and the difficulties in general of conducting research on psychiatric patients.

Problems with the Psychiatric Diagnostic System

The diagnosis of psychiatric disorders is governed by the American Psychiatric Association which produces a Diagnostic and Statistical Manual (DSM). DSM-I in 1952 and DSM-II in 1968 were etiological based, that is, incorporated ideas about physiological, psychological and social causal factors of psychiatric disorders (Castillo, 1997). DSM-III in 1980 switched to a disease-centered paradigm and from causes to description. Each disorder was now considered a separate brain disease. The motivation for this switch was to improve the reliability and validity of diagnosing patients since available evidence indicated that mental health professionals had very low rates of agreement about diagnoses, as low as 54% (Beck et al., 1962). There have been many serious critiques of the psychiatric diagnostic approach, some of which argue that we should abandon it (e.g., Kutchins & Kirk,1991; Albee, 1998). Some have argued that researchers should study psychological phenomena (behaviors such as hallucinations or delusions) rather than psychiatric diagnoses (e.g., Persons, 1986).

DSM-IV-TR based diagnoses have greater reliability than the earlier DSMs, but it still has many problems (Beutler & Malik, 2002). Many of the categories ("diseases") do not predict future symptoms, events or course, and there are still sexual and racial biases in the system (Faravelli et al., 2005). The DSM also assumes that psychiatric disorders are qualitatively different from normal behaviors, whereas the reality seems to be that they often differ only quantitatively. If this is the case, then an all-or-nothing approach to diagnosis (this patient has a major depressive disorder whereas this patient does not) is faulty. The DSM also assumes that each of the 400 diseases is a discrete entity in contrast to the view of some psychologists and psychiatrists that some of the categories reflect a single basic dimension. For example, a dimension labeled "negative emotionality" could include at one extreme anxiety and depression rather than separating these two emotions into two different types of disorder (anxiety disorders and mood disorders) (Comer, 2008). On the positive side, DSM-IV-TR incorporated a slight shift in that it recognized explicitly that no physiological cause has been identified for most psychiatric disorders, but it still maintained a descriptive paradigm rather than an etiological paradigm.

There have also been serious criticisms of the whole conception of personality disorders which are now on a separate "axis" of the diagnostic system. The classification of the personality disorders is based on a categorical model (a patient either has a particular personality disorder or does not). Some psychologists have argued that a dimensional system would make better sense, that is, patients would receive a score on the extent to which they have each "dimension" (Costa & McRae, 1992). However, there has been disagreement as to what the basic dimensions should be, but the consensus seems to be that, eventually, the DSM will switch to a dimensional model (Derlega, Winsted & Jones, 2005), thereby rendering all prior research into personality disorders irrelevant to current research and theory!

It can be argued that a psychiatric diagnostic system that does not take into account the causes of a disorder will impede progress. Would medicine have been as successful in curing sick individuals if there was an illness, for example, called "fever"? People who had this illness might all be given aspirin or acetominophen regardless of whether the fever was caused by malaria, influenza, or colitis.

Let us consider the affective disorders and, in particular, depressive reactions. The older physiological theories of depression focused on the role of serotonin, and the popular anti-depressants are SSRIs – selective serotonin reuptake inhibitors – which, as their name implies, increase the levels of serotonin in the brain. Psychoanalytic theories of depression focus on the suppression and repression of anger felt toward others, resulting in the anger being turned inward on to the self. Learning theories of depression focus on learned helplessness and on the lack of positive reinforcers for the depressed individual, either because significant others do not reward the individual appropriately or because the individual lacks the interpersonal and work-oriented skills that would elicit rewards from others. The labeling theory of depression would argue that many people who are experiencing simple sadness or grief over loss are now labeled as depressed and encouraged to take medications (Horwitz & Wakefield, 2007).

In a study of suicidal behavior in depressed individuals, to group together these five types of depressed individuals with no regard to the cause of their depression makes little sense. Progress in psychiatric research into any disorder or symptom, including suicide, will not make progress until an etiologically-based diagnostic system is developed.

Recommendation 4.1: Psychiatric research into suicide requires the development of a better diagnostic system, one that takes into account causes rather than relying on the phenomenology of symptoms.

Difficulties In Conducting Research on Psychiatric Patients

There are many difficulties in conducting psychiatric research aside from problems with the diagnostic system. Let us review some of these.

(1) Subject analogs:

It is not always possible to study the types of people we are interested in. For example, to explore the theory that the dopamine pathways in the brain are responsible for schizophrenia, much of the research exploring the effects of phenothiazines and amphetamines on neurotransmitters was done on the brains of rats. Many studies of individuals with phobias are conducted on undergraduates who have a dislike or an aversion to touching some particular object, but who are not necessarily phobic about the object. In the study of suicide, often those who attempt suicide are used as subject analogs for completed suicides and there is no clear evidence that this approach is appropriate.

(2) Stimulus analogs:

Psychiatric research often uses a different stimulus from those in real life. For example, Schachter (1971), in his study of whether psychopathic individuals might have responded differently to the parental punishment that they received as children, explored the impact of electric shock on adult psychopaths.

(3) Response analogs:

Psychiatric research sometimes uses a different response from those emitted in real life. To take Schachter's study again, he was interested in whether psychopaths could learn appropriate behavior in real life, but in his research he explored how fast they could learn a maze. Analogs of all three kinds limit the generalizability of the results of the research to real world situations.

(4) Sampling errors:

Psychiatric research often introduces bias because of sampling errors. It is much more common to study chronic cases with a disorder rather than acute cases, patients who are intact and less deteriorated, and patients in treatment rather than those in the community. In suicidology, for example, studies of attempted suicides typically focus on those that come to the attention of medical or psychiatric units and less often focus on those in the community who recover (medically and psychiatrically) without seeking treatment.

(5) Medication:

Typically, psychiatric research studies patients who are on medication. It would be un-ethical to withhold treatment from patients so that the research could rule out the impact of medication on the results of the dependent variable. Thus, there is no straightforward way to assess the effectiveness of medication in random controlled trials.

Recommendation 4.2: Psychiatric research into suicidal behavior must take into account the treatment history (especially medications), current medications and adherence to treatment regimen of the subjects.

(6) Single testing:

Typically, a researcher tests each patient only once. Petrie (1967) tested schizophrenic patients on a measure of augmenting (over-estimating the intensity of stimuli) versus re-ducing (under-estimating the intensity of stimuli). When she tested a group of schizo-phrenics, she found that the majority were reducers. She did not, however, conclude that schizophrenics were reducers. She went back several weeks later and then again a third time. Each time, the majority of the patients were reducers, but she noticed that different patients were reducers on each occasion. She concluded that schizophrenics were aug-menters and that reducing was a defense against an overwhelmingly intense perception of stimuli. Occasionally the defense breaks down, and the true nature of their augment-ing breaks through.

Symptoms can be infrequent events. Single session testing will miss observing the impact of these symptoms.

(7) Specific versus general deficits:

Often psychiatric researchers have a hypothesis that a particular type of patient will per-form worse on a particular task. They give this task to a group of these patients and a control group and find that, indeed, the target group performed worse on the task. The problem is that these patients may perform worse on all tasks and not just on this specific one. Thus, there may be a general deficit and not a specific deficit. This may be true, for example, of depressed patients. Their depression may result in poor performance on all tasks rather than the ones that are the focus of study.

(8) Control groups:

It is often very unclear which control groups to use in psychiatric research. This problem is discussed in Chapter 12 where the problem of the control group for suicide notes is discussed. If suicide is construed as a depressive symptom, then non-suicidal depressed patients may be an appropriate control group. However, if suicide is construed as an ag-gressive act (with the aggression turned inward on to the self), then murderers may be a more appropriate control group.

Recommendation 4.3: Research into suicide should experiment with the use of other control groups beyond depressed non-suicidal patients. Aggressive and impulsive subjects might provide interesting and useful insights.

(9) Correlational studies:

Much psychiatric research is correlational in design, and the experimenter does not manipulate an independent variable to see its impact on the dependent variable. Therefore, cause-and-effect conclusions cannot be drawn. If variable A is correlated with variable B, then A can cause B, B can cause A, or some third variable can cause both A and B which, as a result, are associated. All too often, correlational studies are the basis for cause-and-effect conclusions which are, therefore, not warranted.

In the next three sections, we are going to take three typical areas of research on suicidal behavior and explore the problems in the research and make suggestions for improvements.

Twin Studies Of Suicidal Behavior[8]

One of the few methodologically sound approaches for studying whether a behavior or trait is inherited is to use twins. A sound design must compare monozygotic (identical or MZ) twins and dizygotic (fraternal or DZ) twins. However, there are still methodological problems associated with this approach.

(1) Since there is evidence that MZ twins are treated more similarly by their parents than DZ twins (Wilson, 1931), it is essential that a group of MZ twins raised apart be studied. If the members of MZ twins reared apart are found to resemble each other, then the resemblance cannot be attributed to similar rearing, but must result from genetic resemblance. Many published studies of the genetics of behaviors, especially in earlier times, did not study MZ twins reared apart. For example, in Kallman's (1952) study of homosexuality in MZ and DZ twins, the MZ twins were all reared together. In a review of research on schizophrenia, Slater (1968) reported a concordance rate of 60 percent for MZ twins reared together, 13 percent for same-sex DZ twins reared together, and 5 percent for opposite-sex DZ twins reared together. In the whole history of schizophrenia research up to that time, only 15 MZ twin pairs separated earlier in life, and only one who had schizophrenia, had been identified. The concordance rate was 60 percent. This shows the difficulty in obtaining a large sample of MZ twins separated early in life one of whom has the target behavior.[9]

---

[8] Studies of the genetics of suicidal behavior can utilize family studies, adoption studies and molecular genetics, in addition to twin studies ((Baldessarini & Hennen, 2004). For a recent review of twin studies, see Voracek and Loibl (2007).

[9] In research on the genetics of a personality trait, every MZ twin pair separated early life can be studied because all the twins can be given a personality test. But for rare behaviors such as schizophrenia and suicide, most such pairs have to be discarded since neither member has the target behavior.

(2) In many studies, no effort is made to find DZ twins reared apart. If MZ twins reared apart are more similar than DZ twins reared together, it has been assumed that a genetic contribution has been demonstrated. However, for the MZ twins to be reared apart, they must have undergone a trauma in infancy – the death or separation of their parent(s). Thus, current studies prefer that the samples of both the MZ twins and the DZ twins be reared apart (e.g., Bouchard & Hur, 1998) so that both groups are equivalent in experienced trauma.

(3) A further methodological problem in twin studies is the accuracy of establishing zygosity. Before the advent of DNA testing, zygosity was determined by methods such as physical resemblance, blood type, fingerprints, and height. The conclusions from these different measures are not always in agreement. The use of physical resemblance is especially poor. In a study by Scarr-Salapatek, Carter-Saltzman, Katz and Barker (1979) of 342 twin pairs in one community, they found that 28 percent of the families could not agree on whether the twins were identical or not based on their physical appearance. In a study by Jablon, Neel, Gershowitz and Atkinson (1967), a small sample of twins was given blood testing, fingerprinting and asked their opinion: 122 were DZ on the basis of their blood; 7 were identical on the basis of their blood but differed in height, weight and eye/hair color and so were probably DZ; 103 were identical on the basis of blood and appearance; and 25 were unassigned. The twins' personal opinion agreed well with the assignment on the basis of their blood (only 5.4 percent disagreed), but fingerprinting was less satisfactory (22.6 percent disagreed).

(4) Several reports have appeared of a single twin pair, concordant or discordant for suicidal behavior. These reports should not be included in tallies of MZ and DZ twin pairs. First, there may be a bias in whether concordant or discordant pairs are deemed interesting enough to be reported in the scholarly literature. Second, it may be difficult to locate all of the published reports on single twin pairs. For example, Roy (1992) included a report by Zaw (1981) of a MZ twin pair concordant for completed suicide, and Juel-Nielsen and Videbech (1970) listed "scattered reports" of MZ twin pairs discordant for suicidal behavior from eleven scholarly reports, none of which were considered by Roy. Thus, the results are likely to be more valid if twin pairs only from large samples are considered.

(5) One simple problem often overlooked, is that DZ twins can be of opposite sex. For example, in their study of suicidal behavior in twins, Roy and Segal (2001) included opposite-sex twin pairs in their DZ sample. It is important to compare MZ twins with *same-sex* DZ twins. Kringlen (1986) found that opposite sex DZ twins had lower concordance rates for schizophrenia than same-sex DZ twins. Thus, sex may be an important confounding factor in research of this type.

(6) Related to this is that fact that the concordance rates sometimes vary by sex, and so the sex of the twins should be taken into account. Kringlen (1986) found that MZ female twins had higher concordance rates for suicide than MZ male twins.

(7) One useful technique when studying MZ twins is to find MZ twins *discordant* for the target behavior, for then, since the twins are identical genetically, any differences between them must result from experiential factors. For example, in a study of MZ twins discordant for schizophrenia, Pollin and Stabenau (1986) found that the twin diagnosed with schizophrenia was more likely to have a central nervous system disease as a child,

birth complications and somatic illnesses and to be smaller when born.

(8) Many other problems and biases are present in twin studies (see Kendler, 1993). For example, it has been noted that there may be a recruitment bias in seeking twins to participate in research – Lykken, McGue and Tellegen (1987) found that male twin pairs and DZ twin pairs are less likely to volunteer for research studies than females and MZ twins.

Recommendation 4.4: Research on suicidal behavior in twins must employ more rigorous methodologies to address these and other potentially confounding issues.

Recommendation 4.5: MZ twins reared apart MUST be studied if interpretations are going to be drawn regarding genetic versus environmental influences.

Recommendation 4.6: Twin studies of suicide must control for depression in order to decide whether it is suicidal behavior *per se* that is inherited or merely depression.

Completed Suicide

The results of the following studies are summarized in Table 4.1.

Kallman's (1953) report of a twin study of suicide is especially poor. He reports that one and possible three more MZ twin pairs out of 18 pairs were concordant for completed suicide as compared to zero out of 21 DZ twin pairs.[10] In this report he does not define what he means by "possibly concordant," he does not described the source of the twins, and he does not report the sex of the twin pairs (other than stating that the definitely concordant twin pair was male). It may be assumed that the MZ and DZ twins were all raised together. In reviewing this study, Haberlandt (1967) noted that "possibly concordant" means that one twin completed suicide while the other twin showed non-lethal suicidal behavior (a suicide attempt or suicidal ideation). Clearly, this definition of concordance can be criticized from a number of perspectives.

In earlier reports by Kallman (Kallman et al., 1946, 1947, 1949) results from this sample were also reported. In the 1946 and 1947 reports, the sex of the twin pairs was noted, but none of the 3 MZ twin pairs or the 8 DZ twin pairs were concordant. These 11 cases were part of Kallman's series of some 2,500 twin pairs obtained from mental institutions, tuberculosis hospitals, old age homes and "certain other sections" in the state of New York. In the 1949 report, the sample had grown to 24 twin pairs. None of the 8 MZ twin pairs or the 16 DZ twin pairs were concordant, but the sex of the DZ twin pairs was not stated. In these reports, Kallman also referd to six or seven historical cases. It is by no means clear whether his 1953 report includes these historical cases or not.

---

[10] Lester (1968) noted that many authors (e.g., Fuller and Thompson, (1960) cite Kallman's (1953) study as showing that there are no genetic factors in suicide. In fact, counting the three possibly concordant MZ pairs in his sample as concordant, a Fisher exact test shows p = 0.04 in favor of MZ twins being more concordant than DZ twins, which is statistically significant (Lester, 1968).

Juel-Nielsen and Videbech (1970) reported on twins from a Danish registry, comprising all twins born in Denmark 1870–1920. This twin sample is of same-sex twin pairs. In 19,484 cases, one or both twins died before the age of six, leaving 11,828 twin pairs alive for at least six years. Of these 6,723 were traced and 4,565 untraced. In the sample involving suicides studied by Juel-Nielsen and Videbech, 19 pairs were MZ (14 males and 5 females) and 58 were DZ (42 males and 16 females). Four (3 male and one female) of the 19 MZ twin pairs were concordant for completed suicide versus none of the 58 DZ twin pairs. These same data appear to have been reported by Hauge, Harvald, Fischer, Gotlieb-Jensen, Juel-Nielsen, Raebild, Shapiro and Videbech (1968), but these authors did not disaggregate the data by sex.

Juel-Nielsen (1979) later reported on 10 of the MZ twin pairs (of whom one was only "probably" MZ) from the Danish Twin Study concordant for affective disorder. Of these ten pairs, only three pairs were concordant for completed suicide. Harvald and Hauge (1965) also reported data from this sample of twins and reported that 4 of the 21 MZ twin pairs were concordant for suicide (19%), and none of the same-sex DZ twin pairs or the 37 DZ opposite-sex twin pairs.

Roy, Segal, Centerwall and Robinette (1991) reported data from the NAS-NRC Twin Registry formed from a search of all birth certificates for white, male, multiple births for 1917–1927 in 39 American states. 15,924 twin pairs were located where both twins had served in the armed forces. The zygosity of the twins was established with an algorithm using blood type, responses to a questionnaire, fingerprints, eye and hair color, height and weight. The typing has been found in other studies to be 90 percent accurate. One hundred sixty-five twin pairs contained at least one completed suicide. Five of the 53 MZ twin pairs were concordant for completed suicide versus two of the 112 DZ twin pairs. These percentages (9.8% versus 1.8%) were found by Roy et al. to be statistically significant at the .035 level.

Roy et al. also collected a sample of 11 twin pairs with at least one completed suicide from responses to a letter requesting such pairs and from two "other sources of referral." Two of the 9 MZ twin pairs were concordant for completed suicide versus neither of the 2 DZ twin pairs. The two concordant MZ pairs were both male, the seven non-concordant twin pairs comprised three male pairs and four female pairs. The two non-concordant twin pairs were female-female and female-male (see point [5] above in the introduction to this section on twin studies).

Nonfatal Suicidal Behavior

The results of the following studies are summarized in Table 4.1.

Roy, Segal and Sarchiapone (1995) studied 32 twin pairs from a study of twins, together with three extra cases found by the investigators, one member of which had completed suicide. Of the 26 MZ twin pairs (13 male pairs and 13 female pairs), 10 co-twins had attempted suicide (2 men and 8 women); of the 9 DZ twin pairs (one male pair, 4 female pairs and 4 opposite-sex pairs), none of the co-twins had attempted suicide. Roy et al. noted that ten of the 35 pairs were concordant for psychiatric diagnosis (9 of the MZ twin pairs and one DZ twin pair).

Roy and Segal (2001) reported on 13 MZ and 15 DZ twin pairs, one of whom completed suicide. Four of the MZ twin pairs and none of the DZ twin pairs were concordant for suicide. (For the MZ twin pairs, three pairs had one completed and one attempted suicide; the fourth pair had two completed suicides.). Roy and Segal did not report these results by sex.

Statham et al. (1998) studied a twin sample of 2,716 pairs collected by the Australian National Health and Medical Research Council. The zygosity was based on self-report, but a comparison of self-report and DNA testing for 190 pairs from the sample revealed 100 percent agreement. The concordance rates were higher for suicidal thoughts in the MZ twins than in the same-sex DZ twins (44% versus 26% for females and 41% versus 31% for males) and for serious suicide attempts (29% versus 0% for females and 12% versus 0% for males).

Cho et al. (2006) studied 724 adolescent twin pairs, female-female (141 MZ pairs and 114 DZ pairs), male-male (141MZ pairs and 131 DZ pairs), and mixed sex (197 DZ pairs). The means age of the adolescents was 15.6 years. The concordance rates for suicidal ideation were 23.3% for the MZ twins and 8.5% for the same sex DZ twins. The percentages for attempted suicide were 37.5% and 25.0%, respectively.

Fu et al. (2002) did not present their data in a manner that would fit into Table 4.1. In a study of 4774 twin pairs, both of whom served in the American military during the Vietnam era, they found that having a twin who had experienced lifetime suicidal ideation increased the risk of having suicidal ideation in the co-twin above and beyond the role of psychiatric disorder. They also found that having a twin who had attempted suicide increased the risk of attempting suicide in the co-twin above and beyond the role of psychiatric disorder. For both of these effects, the effect was stronger for MZ twins than for DZ twins.

Discussion

Lester (1968) noted that the size of the samples typically used in these twin studies is woefully small. Assuming a suicide rate of 10 per 100,000 per year, the chance of finding concordant pairs in Kallman's (1953) sample of 39 twin pairs is 39×10^{-4} or one two-hundred and fiftieth of a pair.

In many of the more recent reports, one of the twin pair is still alive and so may become suicidal and even complete suicide later. As a result, the true concordance rate may be higher than calculated. For example, the discordant DZ twins reported by Holland and Gosden (1990) were only 20 years old, and Cho et al. (2006) studied adolescent twins. In addition, the surviving twin may receive some psychological or psychiatric treatment (formal or informal) that may reduce the likelihood of suicide, thereby reducing the concordance rate.

There are many confounding factors to be taken into account in twin studies on suicide. Segal and Bouchard (1993) found that the grief reaction after the loss of a twin is more intense in MZ twins than in DZ twins (see also, Pompili et al., 2006). This more intense grief reaction may be a confounding factor in the higher concordance rate for suicide in MZ twins.

Statham et al. (1998) found that the MZ twins in their sample had much more frequent social contact than the DZ twins, raising the possibility of contagion effect. However, their sample consisted of 2,716 twin pairs, with high concordance rates for serious attempted suicide in the MZ twins (319 MZ twin pairs were concordant for serious suicide attempts) and zero concordance in the DZ twins. Yet they reported data on ages at attempting suicide in only nine pairs! In three of these pairs, the ages of the twin at the time of the attempts were almost the same – 2 MZ twin pairs and 1 DZ twin pair – a surprise since the concordance rate for DZ twin pairs was reported as zero percent. In only one of these three twin pairs was the twin ignorant about the suicide attempt of the co-twin, thus ruling out contagion. The numbers reported by Statham et al. in this section of their report appear to be erroneous.

It has been suggested that an inherited psychiatric disorder is behind the higher concordance rate for suicide in MZ twins. Statham et al. (1998) tried to control for this variable by calculating a multiple regression to predict suicidal behavior in MZ and DZ twins. For the MZ twins, controlling for psychiatric history and psychosocial variables did not eliminate the significance of attempting suicide in the twins as a predictor of attempting suicide in the co-twin. For the DZ twin pairs, however, attempting suicide in one twin did not predict attempting suicide in the co-twin after controls for psychiatric diagnosis and other variables.

The etiology of suicide is obviously not exclusively genetic and certainly not the result of a dominant gene, since this would result in a 100 percent concordance rate in the MZ twin pairs. Psychosocial factors and stressors must play a role. In addition, there is obviously a high concordance in these twin pairs for psychiatric illness, particularly affective disorders. Thus, it is hard to know whether the low but significantly higher concordance rate for suicide in MZ twins is a result of that increased concordance for psychiatric illness. For example, Juel-Nielsen (1979) noted that two of the three MZ twin pairs concordant for completed suicide in his sample were also concordant for manic-depressive disorder and the third pair was concordant for manic-depressive disorder/affective personality disorder.

There is good evidence, based on much rigorous research designs than that used in the studies of suicide reviewed above, that many psychiatric disorders (including schizophrenia and the mood disorders) have a genetic component in their etiology (McGuffin, Marusic & Farmer 2001). It may be that the twin studies reviewed here of suicide in MZ and DZ twin pairs raised together are simply confirming this.

Suggestions for Future Research

Two suggestions can be made for future research. First, the rarity of completed suicide makes it unlikely that researchers will identify enough MZ and DZ twin pairs raised to apart to satisfy the demands of a sound twin study of completed suicide. Thus, it would seem imperative to switch to nonfatal suicidal behavior as the target behavior to be studied.

Recommendation 4.7: Research into suicidal behavior in twins should focus on non-fatal suicidal behavior.

Second, since obtaining MZ and DZ twin pairs raised apart is critical, it would be useful for suicidologists to collaborate with Bouchard's twin study ongoing at the University of Minnesota in which twin pairs separated early in life and raised apart are being studied longitudinally.

Brain Studies

The purpose of this section is not to provide a review of brain research on suicidal behavior, but rather to take one small topic and illustrate the problems in the research. There are four papers on μ opioid receptors in the brains of suicides. Gross-Isseroff, Dillon, Israeli and Biegnon (1990) noted that the opioid system appeared to be related to depression and so they decided to study the opioid system in suicides. They obtained the brains of 14 suicides and matched them for age, sex and postmortem delay with 14 control subjects who died from other causes. They studied μ opioid receptor density in 17 areas of the cortex and thalamus. They found that there was a correlation between μ opioid receptor density and age, and so they divided the subjects by age (above and below the median age of 41) and conducted ANOVAs on the data. The group sizes were, therefore 6, 5, 6 and 7. They found significant differences in μ opioid receptor density only in the younger subjects and only in four of the 17 brain areas studied.

Let us look at this study in detail. First, the sample size was very small, with only 14 subjects in each group. After splitting the groups by age, the largest sample size was 7 and the smallest 5. With sample sizes this small, reliable significant differences are hard to identify.

Second, the suicides and controls were matched for age. Therefore, it does not seem necessary to bring age into the analysis as a second independent variable. Third, related to this, the design is two dependent samples, for which there is an appropriate t-test. After splitting the groups by age, the young subjects consisted of 6 suicides and 5 controls; the older subjects 6 suicides and 7 controls. Therefore, their statistical analysis did not use the matched design. Having matched the subjects, the authors then analyzed the data as if there were independent samples.

Fourth, the authors found four significant differences at the 5% level out of 34 analyses conducted. After correcting for multiple tests, these 4 differences cannot be considered to be valid.

Fifth, and finally, without matching the suicides with the controls for psychiatric disorder, it is impossible to know whether the differences identified are relevant to depression or to suicide or some other important variable not included in the matching criteria. The study, as designed, throws no light on suicide.

The next study was conducted by Gabilondo, Meana and Garcia-Sevilla (1995) who compared 15 brains from suicides with 15 brains from controls, matched for age and postmortem delay (but not sex). They studied three areas – the frontal cortex, the head of caudate and the thalamus. They found a significant difference only in the frontal cortex in the number of binding sites, with the brains of the suicides having a higher density. Whereas Gross-Isseroff studied small regions in the frontal cortex, Gabilondo et al.

studied the frontal cortex on a more global level. This study has most of the defects of the study by Gross-Isseroff et al, in particular, the presence of psychiatric disorder as a confounding factor.

Gonzalez-Maeso et al. (2002) studied μ opioid receptors as a side-issue in a larger study of neurotransmitters. Their sample sizes were 28 (although only 27 of the target group were suicides), and all of the target group were chosen on purpose as having mood disorders. The groups were matched for age, sex and postmortem delay. The two groups did not differ in μ opioid activity in the frontal cortical membranes. Again, psychiatric disorder (in this case, the mood disorders) was a confounding variable in the study.

Escriba, Ozaita and Garcia-Sevilla (2004) studied mRNA expression of the μ opioid receptors in the frontal cortex of suicides and controls since, they argued, the results of radioligand binding studies do not necessarily indicate alterations in molecular events. They compared 500 milligrams of frontal cortex from each of 12 suicides and 11 controls, matched for age, sex and postmortem delay. The authors noted that the controls had no family history of psychiatric disturbance. They found that the mRNA expression of the μ opioid receptors was augmented in the brains of the suicides. As before, these two groups differed in psychiatric disturbance, thereby confounding the results, and the sample sizes were small. In addition, 12 suicides cannot be matched with only 11 controls and, whereas Gross-Isseroff, Dillon, Israeli and Biegnon (1990) studied 17 different brain areas (with different results for each area), Escriba et al. apparently studied only one area.

There are several conclusions from the review of this small area of research.

(1) Researchers into brain function in suicides should expand their approaches to research design and statistical analysis to strengthen their ability to draw appropriate inferences.

(2) Researchers into brain function in suicide do not seem to be primarily interested in suicidal behavior *per se*. They are most likely interested in psychiatric disorders, primarily, mood disorders, and they study suicides since they assume that most suicides are depressed. Indeed, Gonzalez-Maeso et al. (2002) purposely chose only depressed suicides for their study. This approach may account for their failure to match the suicides and control subjects for psychiatric disturbance.

The conclusion we draw is that this research sheds little, if any, light on the etiology of suicide. Consequently, based on this review, for brain research to be useful in understanding suicide, we make the following recommendations:

Recommendation 4.8: Studies of the brain of suicides must utilize large sample sizes.

Recommendation 4.9: Suicides and controls must be matched, not only for sex, age, ethnicity and post-mortem delay, but also confounding factors such as depression.

Recommendation 4.10: Researchers should study more than one brain area. Indeed, it might be useful for researchers into brains to come to some consensus about which brain areas should be sampled in research so that research from different research teams can be more easily compared.

Recommendation 4.11: Research on the brains of suicides would be improved if the research was designed to study suicidal behavior and not merely a peripheral analysis of data collected for a project on some other behavior (such as schizophrenia or depressive disorders).

Suicide And Post-Traumatic Stress Disorder

The aim of this section is to take one area of psychiatric research into suicide and explore what recommendations can be made for the future. Again, the aim is not to survey the whole field, nor even to provide a comprehensive review of this one topic.

Research on suicide and post-traumatic stress disorder (PTSD) dates primarily from 1990 on, and so it is a relatively new area of investigation. The first noteworthy fact about the research is that the samples chosen vary widely. The initial focus was on those who fought in wars, especially the Vietnam War in the 1960s and 1970s. Retuning veterans showed a high incidence of a variety of psychiatric problems, including drug abuse and suicidal behavior, and the incidence of PTSD soon became the focus of the research (e.g., Hendin & Haas, 1991).

Researchers interested in domestic violence (or interpersonal violence) then explored this association (e.g., Thompson et al., 1999), as did those interested in criminal victimization such as rape (Ullman & Brecklin, 2002). Researchers also studied samples of psychiatric patients in general (Floen & Elklit, 2007) and with specific problems such as anxiety disorders (Khan et al., 2002), and samples of the general population (Kessler et al., 1999) and students (Mazza, 2000).

This diversity of subjects makes identifying consistent trends more difficult, but it is important for ascertaining the generality of the findings.

Recommendation 4.12: Psychiatric research should be carried on a variety of clinical and non-clinical subjects in order that the generality of the associations between PTSD and suicidal behavior can be ascertained.

The next issue concerns the operational definitions of the behaviors. The operational definition of suicidal behavior (and the particular behavior chosen for study) is an issue throughout the field of suicidology. Is the target behavior ideation, attempted suicide or completed suicide or, instead, a score on an inventory designed to assess suicidal risk. The same issue arises for PTSD. Some researchers use a simple psychiatric diagnosis using DSM criteria (Hendin & Haas, 1991), others use exceeding a cut-off score on a standardized inventory (Freeman et al., 2000), others study full and sub-threshold PTSD (Marshall et al., 2001), others look at particular areas of PTSD symptomatology (Murphy et al., 2003), and some explore both current PTSD and lifetime PTSD (Oquendo et al., 2003). These different approaches to defining both suicidal behavior and PTSD limit the ability to synthesize the literature in this area and draw conclusions about the relation between them.

Recommendation 4.13: Since there typically exists a variety of operational measures for each target behavior, researchers should consider using two or more operational measures and comparing the results obtained with each measure.

There are three methodologies possible in studies of suicide and PTSD: (1) looking for the existence of PTSD in samples of suicidal individuals (Rudd et al. 1993), (2) looking for the existence of suicidal behavior in samples of PTSD individuals (Hendin & Haas, 1991), and examining the association in a sample of individuals (Mazza, 2000).

Recommendation 4.14: The strengths and limitations of these three different methodologies should be identified, and the associations examined for each methodology separately. Attempts to synthesize the results from these approaches should be grounded in a theoretical framework that can advance understanding of the relations.

Research into suicide and PTSD rarely takes into account sequencing, a problem made worse when there are other comorbid problems, such as anxiety disorders and drug abuse and environmental trauma such as assault or combat. Studies of PTSD and attempted suicide need to take into account the timing of the appearance of suicidal behavior, the appearance of PTSD and the traumata. In order words, what was the premorbid psychological state of the individual? Only s small portion of individuals who experience a trauma develop PTSD, and this link between PTSD and suicidality must be affected by what individuals bring to the situation, both past experiences and their psychological and psychiatric state.

In studies of PTSD and completed suicide, obviously the PTSD preceded the suicidal death. However, suicides often have a history of suicidal behavior, and so the individual completing suicide may have made suicide attempts earlier in life or had an affective disorder or other suicide-related characteristic. Did the suicide attempt or the depressive disorder precede the trauma and the appearance of PTSD? This point is critical in studies which target "lifetime" suicidal behavior.

Recommendation 4.15: Psychiatric research must take into account the timing and sequencing of experiential events, the appearance of symptoms and behaviors, and the development of the target behavior.

Discussion

The aim in this chapter has been to take three small areas of psychiatric research into suicide, examine the problems that characterize the research, and make recommendations for the future. We realize, of course, that some of the studies cited here were designed as preliminary studies, and the investigators intended to carry out later, more rigorous research. We realize also that there are many sound studies published which increase our understanding of suicide. This is especially true of the studies on PTSD and suicide, only some of which were mentioned above.

However, as we have shown, there are often methodological weaknesses in the research which impede progress in understanding suicide. Furthermore, the pressures on researchers from the agencies that fund the research and from the home institutions that employ the researchers (and award tenure and promotion) encourage the publication of scholarly papers regardless of their merit. "Publish or perish" may be trite advice, but it is nonetheless valid, and it often results in publications that do not advance our understanding of the target behavior.

References

Albee, G. W. (1998). Is the Bible the only source of truth? *Contemporary Psychology*, 43, 571–572.

Baldessarini, R. J., & Hennen, J. (2004). Genetics of suicide. *Harvard Review of Psychiatry*, 12, 1–13.

Beck, A. T., Ward, C. H., Mendelson, M., Mock, J. E., & Erbaugh, J. (1962). Reliability of psychiatric diagnoses. *American Journal of Psychiatry*, 119, 210–216.

Beutler, L. E., & Malik, M. L. (Eds.). (2002). *Rethinking the DSM*. Washington DC: American Psychological Association.

Bouchard, T. J., & Hur, Y. M. (1998). Genetic and environmental influences on the continuous scales of the Myers-Briggs Type Indicator. *Journal of Personality*, 66, 135–149.

Castillo, R. J. (1997). *Culture and mental illness*. Pacific Grove, CA: Brooks/Cole.

Cho, H., Guo, G., Iritani, B. J., & Hallfors, D. D. (2006). Genetic contribution to suicidal behaviors and associated risk factors among adolescents in the U.S. *Preventive Science*, 7, 303–311.

Comer, R. J. (2008). *Fundamentals of abnormal psychology*. New York: Worth.

Costa, P. T., & McRae, R. R. (1992). The five-factor model of personality and its relevance to personality disorders. *Journal of Personality Disorders*, 6, 343–359.

Derlega, V. J., Winstead, B. A., & Jones, W. H. (2005). *Personality*. Belmont, CA: Thomson Wadsworth.

Escriba, P. V., Ozaita, A., & Garcia-Sevilla, J. A. (2004). Increased mRNA expression of α_{2A}-adrenoceptors, serotonin receptors and μ opioid receptors in the brains of suicide victims. *Neuropsychopharmacology*, 29, 1512–1521.

Faravelli, C., Ravaldi, C., & Truglia, E. (2005). Unipolar depression. In C. Faravelli, D. J. Nutt, J. Zohar, & E. J. L. Griez (Eds.), *Mood disorders*, pp. 79–101. New York; Wiley.

Floen, S. K., & Elklit, A. (2007). Psychiatric diagnoses, trauma, and suicidality. *Annals of General Psychiatry*, 6(12), 1–8.

Freeman, T., Roca, V., & Moore, W. M. (2000). A comparison of chronic combat-related posttraumatic stress disorder (PTSD) patients with and without a history of suicide attempt. *Journal of Nervous & Mental Disease*, 188, 460–463.

Fu, Q., Heath, A. C., Bucholz, K. K., Nelson, E. C., Glowinski, A. L., Goldberg, J., Lynos, M. J., Tsuang, M. T., Jacob, T., True, M. R., & Eisen, S. A. (2002). A twin study of genetic and environmental influences on suicidality in men. *Psychological Medicine*, 32, 11–24.

Fuller, J. L., & Thompson, W. R. (1960). *Behavior genetics*. New York: Wiley.

Gabilondo, A. M., Meane, J. J., & Garcia-Sevilla, J. A. (1995). Increased density of μ opioid receptors in the postmortem brain of suicide victims. *Brain Research*, 682, 245–250.

Gonzalez-Maeso, J., Rodriguez-Puertas, R., Meane, J. J., Garcia-Sevilla, J. A., & Guimon, J.

60   Psychiatric Research

(2002). Neurotransmitter receptor-mediated activation of G-proteins in brains of suicide victims with mood disorders. *Molecular Psychiatry*, 7, 755–767.

Gross-Isseroff, R., Dillon, K. A., Israeli, M., & Biegon, A. (1990). Regionally selective increases in μ opioid receptor density in the brains of suicide victims. *Brain Research*, 530, 312–316.

Haberlandt, L W. F. (1967). Aportación a la genética del suicidio. *Folia Clinica Internacional*, 17, 319–322.

Harvald, B., & Hauge, M. (1965). Hereditary factors elucidated by twin studies. In J. V. Neel, M. W. Shaw & W. J. Schull (Eds.), *Genetics and the epidemiology of chronic disease*, pp. 61–76. Washington, DC: USGPO.

Hauge, M., Harvald, B., Fischer, M., Gotlieb-Jense, K., Juel-Nielsen, N., Raebild, I., Shapiro, N., & Videbech T. (1968). The Danish twin register. *Acta Geneticae Medicae et Gemellologiae*, 17, 315–331.

Hendin, H., & Haas, A. P. (1991). Suicide and guilt as manifestations of PTSD in Vietnam combat veterans. *American Journal of Psychiatry*, 148, 586–591.

Holland, T., & Gosden, C. (1990). A balance chromosomal translocation partially segregating with psychiatric illness in a family. *Psychiatry Research*, 32, 1–8.

Horwitz, A. V., & Wakefield, J. C. (2007). *The loss of sadness*. New York: Oxford University Press.

Hutchins, H., & Kirk, S. A. (1997). *Making us crazy: DSM: The psychiatric Bible and the creation of mental disorders*. New York: Free Press.

Jablon, S., Neel, J. V., Gershowitz, H., & Atkinson, G. F. (1967). The NAS-NRC twin panel. *American Journal of Human Genetics*, 19, 133–161.

Juel-Nielsen, N., & Videbech, T. (1970). A twin study of suicide. *Acta Geneticae Medicae et Gemellologiae*, 19, 307–310.

Juel-Nielsen, N. (1979). Suicide risk in manic-depressive disorders. In M. Schou & E. Stromgren (Eds.), *Origin, prevention and treatment of affective disorders*, pp. 269–276. New York: Academic.

Kallman, F. J. (1952). Twin and sibship study of overt male homosexuality. *American Journal of Human Genetics*, 4, 136–146.

Kallman, F. J. (1953). *Heredity in health and mental disorder*. New York: Norton.

Kallman, F. J., & Anastasio, M. (1947). Twin studies on the psychopathology of suicide. *Journal of Heredity*, 37, 171–180.

Kallman, F. J., & Anastasio, M. (1947). Twin studies on the psychopathology of suicide. *Journal of Nervous & Mental Disease*, 105, 40–55.

Kallman, F. J., De Porte, J., & Feingold, L. (1949). Suicide in twins and only children. *American Journal of Human Genetics*, 1, 113–126.

Kendler, K. S. (1993). Twin studies of psychiatric illness. *Archives of General Psychiatry*, 50, 905–914.

Kessler, R. C., Borges, G., & Walters, E. E. (1999). Prevalence of and risk factors for lifetime suicide attempts in the National Comorbidity Survey. *Archives of General Psychiatry*, 56, 617–626.

Khan, A., Leventhal, R. M., Khan, S., & Brown, W. A. (2002). Suicide risk in patients with anxiety disorders. *Journal of Affective Disorders*, 68, 183–190.

Kringlen, E. (1986). Genetic studies of schizophrenia. In G. D. Burrows, T. R. Norman & G. Rubinstein (Eds.), *Handbook of studies on schizophrenia*, pp. 45–69. New York: Elsevier.

Lester, D. (1968). Note on the inheritance of suicide. *Psychological Reports*, 22, 320.

Lykken, D. T., McGue, M., & Tellegen, A. (1987). Recruitment bias in twin research. *Behavior Genetics*, 17, 343–362.

Marhsall, R. D., Olfson, M., Hellman, F., Blanco, C., Guardino, M., & Struening, E. (2001). Comorbidity, impairment, and suicidality in subthreshold PTSD. *American Journal of Psychiatry*, 158, 1467–1473.

Mazza, J. J. (2000). The relationship between posttraumatic stress symptomatology and suicidal behavior in school-based adolescents. *Suicide & Life-Threatening Behavior*, 30, 91–103.

McGuffin, P., Marusic, A., & Farmer, A. (2001). What can psychiatric genetics offer suicidology? *Crisis*, 22, 61–65.

Murphy, S. A., Tapper, V. J., Johnson, L. C., & Lohan, J. (2003). Suicide ideation among parents bereaved by the violent deaths of their children. *Issues in Mental Health Nursing*, 24, 5–25.

Oquendo, M. A., Friend, J. M., Halberstam, B., Brodsky, B.S., Burke, A. K., Grunebaum, M. F., Malone, K. M., & Mann, J. J. (2003). Association of comorbid posttraumatic stress disorder and major depression with greater risk for suicidal behavior. *American Journal of Psychiatry*, 160, 580–582.

Persons, J. B. (1986). The advantages of studying psychological phenomena rather than psychiatric diagnoses. *American Psychologist*, 41, 1252–1260.

Petrie, A. (1967). *Individuality in pain and suffering.* Chicago: University of Chicago Press.

Pollin, W., & Stabenau, R. (1968). Biological, psychological and historical differences in a series of monozygotic twins for schizophrenia. In D. Rosenthal & S. Kety (Eds.), *The transmission of schizophrenia*, pp. 317–332. New York: Pergamon.

Pompili, M., Galeandro, P. M., Lester, D., & Tatarelli, R.(2006). Suicidal behavior in surviving co-twins. *Twin Research & Human Genetics*, 9, 642–645.

Roy, A. (1992). Genetics, biology, and suicide in the family. In R. W. Maris, A. L. Berman, J. T. Maltsberger & R. I. Yufit (Eds.), *Assessment and prediction of suicide*, pp. 574–588. New York: Guilford.

Roy, A., & Segal, N. L. (2001). Suicidal behavior in twins. *Journal of Affective Disorders*, 66, 71–74.

Roy, A., Segal, N. L., & Sarchiapone, M. (1995). Attempted suicide among living co-twins of twin suicide victims. *American Journal of Psychiatry*, 152, 1075–1076.

Roy, A., Segal, N. L., Centerwall, B. S., & Robinette, C. D. (1991). Suicide in twins. *Archives of General Psychiatry*, 48, 29–32.

Rudd, D. M., Dahm, P. F., & Rajab, M. H. (1993). Diagnostic comorbidity in persons with suicidal ideation and behavior. *American Journal of Psychiatry*, 150, 928–934.

Scarr-Salapatek, S., Carter-Saltzman, L., & Katz, S., & Barker, W. (1979). *Twin method.* Mahwah, NJ: Lawrence Erlbaum.

Schachter, S. (1971). *Emotions, obesity and crime.* New York: Academic.

Segal, N. L., & Bouchard, T. J. (1993). Grief intensity following the loss of a twin and other close relatives. *Human Biology*, 65, 87–105.

Slater, E. (1968). A review of earlier evidence on genetic factors in schizophrenia. In D. Rosthenal & S. Kety (Eds.), *The transmission of schizophrenia*, pp. 15–26. London: Pergamon.

Statham, D. J., Heath, A. C., Madden, P. A. F., Bucholz, K. K., Bierut, L., Dinwiddie, S. H., Slutske, W. S., Dunne, M. P., & Martin, N. G. (1998). Suicidal behaviour. *Psychological Medicine*, 28, 839–855.

Thompson, M. P., Kaslow, N. J., Kingree, J. B., Thompson, N., & Meadows, L. A. (1999). Partner abuse and posttraumatic stress disorder as risk factors for suicide attempts in a sample of low-income, inner-city women. *Journal of Traumatic Stress*, 12, 59–72.

Ullman, S. E., & Brecklin, L. R. (2002). Sexual assault history and suicidal behavior in a national sample of women. *Suicide & Life-Threatening Behavior*, 32, 117–130.

Voracek, M., & Loibl, L. M. (2007). Genetics of suicide. *Wiener Klinische Wochenschrift*, 119, 463–475.

Wilson, P. T. (1931). A study of twins with special reference to heredity as a factor determining differences in environment. *Human Biology*, 6, 324–354.

Zaw, K. M. (1981). A suicidal family. *British Journal of Psychiatry*, 139, 68–69.

Table 4.1. Summary Of The Studies On Twins

		MZ	DZ	p˜
Completed Suicide				
Haberlandt (1967)	Males	0 of 2	0 of 2	–
	Females	0 of 2		
ˆJuel-Nielsen &	Males	3 of 14	0 of 42	.003
Videbech (1970)	Females	1 of 5	0 of 16	
ˆJuel-Nielsen (1979)	Males	2 of 6		
	Females	1 of 4		
ˆHarvald & Hauge	Unknown	4 of 21	0 of 38	
(1965)	same-sex		0 of 37	
	opposite			
Kallman & Anastasio	Male	0 of 1	0 of 3	
(1946, 1947)	Female	0 of 2	0 of 3	–
	Opposite		0 of 2	
Kallman et al. (1949)	Male	0 of 4		
	Female	0 of 4		–
	Unknown		0 of 16	
#Kallman (1953) *	Unknown	1 of 18	0 of 21	.46
Roy et al. (1991)	Males	5 of 53	2 of 112	
	Males	2 of 5		
	Females	0 of 4	0 of 1	.80
	Opposite		0 of 1	
Suicidality				
Kallman (1953)	Unknown	4 of 18 (CS-AS/SI)	0 if 21	.04
Roy et al. (1995)	Males	2 of 13 (CS-AS)	0 of 1	
	Females		0 of 4	.12
	Opposite	8 of 13 (CS-AS)	0 of 4	
Roy and Segal (2001)	mixed	4 of 13	0 of 13	.03
Statham et al. (1998)	Males	164 of 401 (SI-SI)	73 of 235	<.001
	Females		140 of 540	
	Opposite	412 of 936 (SI-SI)	0 of 604	
Cho et al. (2006)	Same sex	7 of 53 (SI)	2 of 45	< .20
	Opposite		5 of 32	
Cho et al. (2006)	Same sex	3 of 13 (AS)	2 of 14	> .30
	Opposite		0 of 7	

* The concordant pair was male

Each later report from Kallman and his colleagues includes the twins from the earlier reports

ˆ Most of these pairs were included in Juel-Nielsen and Videbech (1970) report

+ The concordance is for "serious" attempts

˜ The probabilities were calculated by the present authors omitting opposite sex twin pairs. For small samples Fisher's exact test was used, for large samples the chi-square test

5

The Sociological Study of Suicide

In an essay in a commemorative volume on Emile Durkheim celebrating the one hundredth anniversary of the publication of *Le Suicide* (Lester, 1994), Gibbs (1994) entitled his contribution "Durkheim's Heavy Hand in the Sociological Study of Suicide." Gibbs noted that "the remembrance of ancestors dooms a field," and he urged that ".....sociologists should rightly proclaim Durkheim to have been a genius, and then get on with it" (p. 30).

In this critique of the sociological study of suicide, we will begin by commenting on the problems in the field caused by the devotion to Durkheim's theory *as he wrote it*.

Durkheim's Theory Of Suicide

Durkheim's (1897) theory of suicide maintains its role over one hundred years after its initial formulation as the major sociological theory of suicide. Durkheim argued that the social suicide rate was determined by two broad social characteristics: the degree of social integration (that is, the extent to which the members of the society are bound together in social networks) and the degree of social regulation (that is, the degree to which the emotions, desires and behaviors of people are governed by the norms and customs of the society). Suicide rates will be higher when the level of social integration is too high (leading to altruistic suicide) or too low (leading to egoistic suicide) and when the level of social regulation is too high (leading to fatalistic suicide) or too low (leading to anomic suicide). Thus, curvilinear relationships are predicted between suicide rates and the levels of social integration and regulation.

Despite many claims by researchers to be testing Durkheim's theory of suicide in their empirical studies, the extent research suffers from inadequate specification of the theoretical constructs. For example, Durkheim proposed two social dimensions – societies can be high, moderate or low in each of the two dimensions, and this produces a 3-by-3 table of possibilities – see Table 5.1.

As indicated in Table 5.1, Durkheim's theory would predict highest suicide rates for societies in cells A, C, G, and I, moderate rates in cells B, D, F and H, and lowest rates in cell E. We might note, however, that suicides in each cell are hard to classify. Suicides in cell B, for example, are fatalistic since social integration is high and social regulation moderate. However, suicides in cell A are fatalistic/altruistic since both social regulation and social integration are high. It is clear that Durkheim's four types of suicide do not adequately fit the nine cells demanded by his theory.

A few older studies have tested Durkheim's theory adequately. Rootman (1973) studied in between fifty five nonliterate societies. Drawing upon other researchers' ratings of these societies, Rootman identified two measures which he thought assessed social integration and social regulation. One measure included scores for the permanency of residence, constancy of food supply, and group life versus atomism – Rootman felt that this would be a good measure of social integration. A second measure included scores for power vested in a chief, an organized priesthood, and codified laws – Rootman felt that this would be a good measure of social regulation.

Interestingly, scores on the two factors were not strongly correlated, suggesting that the two social characteristics could be measured separately. For the nine groupings of societies possible, Rootman found the mean suicide rate estimates shown in Table 5.2. (Note that these are not conventional rates per 100,000 per year, but rather subjective estimates of frequency. Judges read the reports of anthropologists and other visitors to these societies and tired to estimate the frequency of suicide from those accounts. The estimates are not based on actual counts of suicides.)

Rootman carried out no statistical analyses of his results. However, we can see that the societies with moderate levels of both social integration and social regulation did have the lowest suicide rate (1.2). Those societies with high or low levels of one variable and moderate levels of the other variable had higher suicide rates (the mean of the four cells is 1.95). Those societies with high and/or low levels of both social variables had the highest suicide rates (the mean of the four cells is 2.1). However, Lester (1992) repeated this study using appropriate statistical tests of significance and failed to find significant differences between the estimated suicide rates of the cells.

In a follow-up study to Rootman's study, Lester (1989) studied suicide in 53 nations of the world in 1980. Several measures of social regulation were included in the data set: a political rights index and a civil rights index, and measures of political freedom, religious liberty for Christians, and a political freedom index. The marriage rate and the birth rate were used as measures of social integration. The seven measures were subjected a principal components analysis (with a varimax rotation), resulting in two orthogonal (i.e., independent) components (see Table 5.3).

As indicated in Table 5.3, Component I appears to tap social regulation while Component II may tap social integration. However, a high birth rate (which was expected to increase social integration since it would lead to a large number of children and larger families) was loaded on both components. This illustrates the necessity for empirical investigation of the relationship of social indicators to the concepts supposedly underlying them. It should be noted that the component scores were completely independent (Pearson $r = 0.00$). Thus, it was again possible to assess the two concepts (social regulation and social integration) separately and independently.

Using these same data, the nations were divided into three groups on each component score – high, moderate and low. The nations were then sorted into the nine cells (see Table 5.4), and their suicide rates examined. Categorized in this format, these data provide some support for Durkheim's theory – that is, nations high on both dimensions and low on both did have the highest suicide rates. Those nations moderate on both had low suicide rates. However the data illustrate an asymmetry. *Low* social regulation and *high* social integration appear to be the more powerful correlates of suicide rates.

Recommendation 5.1: Tests of Durkheim's theory of suicide must consider all combinations of levels of social integration and social regulation and test for curvilinear relationships rather than assuming linearity.

The Problem Of Type Of Suicide

Similar to the lack of specificity reflected in the extant research related to Durkheim's two dimensional model based on the broad social characteristics of integration and regulation, purported tests of his typology have also been problematic. For example, Durkheim did not propose that *suicide* would be more common when the level of social integration, for example, was too low. Rather, he proposed that *egoistic suicide* would be more common.

Since Durkheim defined four types of suicide (egoistic, altruistic, anomic and fatalistic), a test of Durkheim's theory requires that suicide rates be estimated for each of these four types of suicide. No researcher has ever done this. All researchers have used the overall suicide rate of a society (or subgroup of the society) as the measure of the dependent variable. As a result, *none* of the research has provided and adequate test of Durkheim's theory as stated.

It is, however, possible to classify individual suicides using Durkheim's typology. For example, Reynolds and Berman (1995) took a sample of 404 completed suicides and were able to classify 71 percent into Durkheim's typology with 79 percent agreement between judges.

Recommendation 5.2: Tests of Durkheim's theory of suicide must classify suicides by type and calculate four rates of suicide – egoistic, anomic, fatalistic and altruistic.

What Does The Expert Sociologist Know?

In psychological research, when a measure of some variable is proposed, the researcher always has to justify the use of the measure. Is it reliable (is it a consistent measure?[11]) and is it valid (does it measure what it is proposed to measure?) In seeking to measure social integration or social regulation, sociologists tend to propose what they "think" is a relevant variable and assume its validity.

For example, a high divorce rate in a society has always been assumed to imply a lower level of social integration/regulation. However, no researcher has ever produced any evidence that this is so. It is easy to find personal examples of married people whose social interactions and friendships are limited to their immediate family and of divorced people whose social network is huge. Indeed, many unmarried people, because of their isolated state, are motivated to build large social networks and sources

---

[11] Reliability can be (i) test-retest reliability (giving the test on two or more occasions and obtaining the same scores), (ii) parallel forms reliability (examining whether the scores from two parallel measures are similar), and (iii) item-analysis (for example, whether each item in a multi-item test correlates with scores on the remaining items).

of support. The question arises then of whether a high rate of divorce in a society lessens social intgration/regulation or strengthens it (or does neither!). Although there have been studies of the social networks of suicidal and nonsuicidal people, hardly any research purporting to test Durkheim's theory of suicide presents evidence to validate divorce, marriage, birth, inter-region migration, immigration or church membership rates as valid measures of social integration/regulation.

Recommendation 5.3: Researchers must seek to validate their presumed measures of social integration and social regulation.

Barclay Johnson's Theory

There have been many analyses based on Durkheim's work, but one of the more incisive was by Johnson (1965). Johnson argued that it was very difficult to distinguish between social integration and social regulation, and he proposed combining them into one dimension. Johnson also argued that suicide resulting from overly high levels of social integration/regulation was rarely found in modern industrialized societies. Thus, he proposed a more simplified hypothesis, namely that suicide rates would be inversely related to the level of social integration/regulation, a linear relationship. This hypothesis has apparently received a great deal of confirmation from empirical research into the relationship between suicide rates and such sociological variables as divorce, marriage and birth rates (for example, Stack, 1978), presumed social indicators of increased or decreased social integration.

However, what makes Johnson's theory important is that by eliminating fatalistic and altruistic suicide from consideration, the theory predicts a linear rather than a curvilinear relationship. By making social integration and social regulation the same dimension, Johnson's theory also eliminates the need for a two-dimensional array of types (cells in Table 5.1). Thus, Johnson's theory, which is no longer Durkheim's theory, becomes testable by the simple correlational techniques typically used by sociologists.

The Heavy Hand

As mentioned above, Durkheim's theory has had a "heavy hand" effect on the sociological study of suicide. This oppressive influence is obvious in the comments of editors and reviewers of sociological journals. For example, one of us has had an article rejected because it focused on primitive societies, and Durkheim did not study these in his book. Another article was rejected because it focused on suicide *and* homicide, and Durkheim did not study homicide in his book.[12] If other disciplines followed this practice, Einstein would never have got his papers published, and we would still be studying Newtonian physics!

As Gibbs said, let's get on with it!

---

[12] Both of these papers were eventually published in non-sociology journals.

Recommendation 5.4: Sociologists must move on from an excessive reliance on Durkheim's theory of suicide.

Other Theories

There are other sociological theories of suicide. Two which have received some mention in sociology journals are from Henry and Short (1954) and Gibbs and Martin (1964). However, it is rare for these theories to be mentioned, and few sociologists have explored predictions from these theories.

Henry and Short's Theory

Henry and Short (1954) presented a theory of suicide that departed to a considerable extent from the basic ideas of Durkheim's theory. Henry and Short used the frustration-aggression hypothesis developed by Dollard et al. (1939) for the basic framework of their theory.

Henry and Short first investigated the relationship between the business cycle and suicide and homicide rates. They made two predictions: (a) Suicide rates will rise during times of business depression and fall during times of business prosperity, while crimes of violence against people will rise during business prosperity and fall during business depression; and (b) the correlation between suicide rates and the business cycle will be higher for high status groups than for low status groups, while the correlation between homicide rates and the business cycle will be higher for low status groups than for high status groups. Henry and Short considered that their predictions had been confirmed by the data.

The data presented, however, did not in fact support their predictions. The only status category with data available for both suicide and homicide rates was that of race (White versus Black). The correlations between suicide and homicide rates and the business cycle for Whites were −0.81 and −0.51 respectively, and for Blacks −0.38 and +0.49 respectively (Henry & Short, 1954, pp. 29, 49).

The second prediction (point b above), however, was confirmed. The negative correlation between suicide rates and the business cycle was greater for the high status group (Whites) than it was for the low status group (Blacks), whereas the positive correlation between homicide rates and the business cycle was higher for the low status group (0.49) than for the high status group (−0.51). However, the first prediction (point a above) was not confirmed. The prediction of a positive correlation between homicide rates and the business cycle was not found for Whites. It must be concluded that the data presented do not confirm their predictions in full.

Frustration, Aggression, and the Business Cycle

Henry and Short attempted to interpret their results in terms of the frustration-aggression hypothesis. Their assumptions were (a) aggression is often a consequence of frustration, (b) business cycles produce variations in the hierarchical rankings of persons by status, and (c) frustrations are generated by a failure to maintain a constant or rising position in the status hierarchy relative to the status position of other groups.

The interpretation of their results required two additional assumptions: (a) high status persons lose status relative to low status persons during business contraction while low status persons lose status relative to high status persons during business expansion, and (b) suicide occurs mainly in high status persons while homicide occurs mainly in low status persons.

The statistics presented by Henry and Short in the first part of their book were based on the suicide and homicide rates of societal subgroups, such as White versus Black. However, they extended their thesis by considering high and low class Whites and high and low class Blacks. In so extending their analysis, they went beyond the bounds of their data. Thus their arguments become speculative and not grounded in empirical data.

Consider those who lose income during business contraction. The higher status person has more income to lose and his fall is greater than that of the low status person. The high status person loses status relative to the low status person. The low status person may actually experience a gain in status relative to the high status person. Thus in times of business contraction, high status people lose status relative to low status people and this generates frustration. The aggression consequent to this frustration in high status people is predominantly self-directed aggression, and so suicide rates rise in times of business contraction in high status people. This analysis explains why suicide rates and the business cycle are negatively correlated in whites, a high status group.

If suicide occurs mainly in Whites and in particular in high status Whites, then why should the correlation between the business cycle and suicide rates be larger in Whites than in Blacks? Henry and Short predicted this difference since Whites are of higher status than Blacks and high class Whites are of higher status than low class Whites.

When all of their explanations are considered together, it becomes clear that Henry and Short assume that Whites assess their relative status by comparing themselves to Blacks and vice versa; that high class Whites assess their status relative to low class Whites and vice versa; and that high class Blacks assess their status relative to low class Blacks and vice versa. The first of these assumptions is incompatible with the latter two. Do high class Blacks assess their status relative to low or high class Whites or Blacks? Henry and Short assume, for example, that when a Black is considered as a Black, he assesses his status relative to Whites, but that when he is considered as a high class Black he assesses his status relative to low class Blacks. This makes less than good sense. A person's assessment of himself is independent of how we may choose to label him.[13]

---

[13] A similar problem exists when Henry and Short consider homicide. During business contraction, lower class Whites lose status relative to lower class Blacks. Therefore, they will suffer frustration, and the aggression consequent to this frustration will be homicide since they are low status people. Thus their homicide rate should increase during business contraction. But their status relative to high class Whites rises during business contraction and thus their homicide rates should decrease. Which analysis is correct? Is there a rule for deciding which analysis is correct? No.

In conclusion, Henry and Short have to resort to changing the reference groups for particular groups of individuals in order to account for the particular associations that arise. There is no general rule possible to decide which reference group a particular societal subgroup will choose, whether it will be within racial groups or across racial groups for example. The system becomes, therefore, *post hoc*. The reference groups are deduced after the correlations between the suicide and homicide rates and the business cycle have been determined.

Henry and Short concluded that their data support the notion that suicide and homicide are acts of aggression undifferentiated with respect to their common source in frustration generated by business cycles. Insofar as the predictions of their system were confirmed, such a conclusion may be allowed. Henry and Short noted, however, that it was necessary that their results be checked with other data from other countries, and since no replication study has appeared in print, the necessity of replication must be stressed again here.

Sociological and Psychological Determinants of the Choice: Between Suicide and Homicide

Henry and Short assumed that the basic and primary target of aggression is another person rather than the self. They then attempted to identify the sociological and psychological bases of the legitimization of other-oriented aggression. What enables the child to develop so that his primary response to frustration, that of other-oriented aggression, is seen as legitimate, while other children develop in such a way that this primary response is inhibited and self-directed aggression becomes legitimate?

Sociologically, the strength of external restraint was seen as the primary basis for the legitimization of other-oriented aggression. When behavior is required to conform rigidly to the demands and expectations of others, the share of others in the responsibility for the consequence of the behavior increases, thereby legitimizing other-oriented aggression. When external restraints are weak, the self must bear the responsibility for the frustration generated, and other-oriented aggression fails to be legitimized.

Henry and Short found two psychological correlates of other-oriented aggression in people, low superego strength and low guilt, and a specific type of cardiovascular reaction during stress similar to the effects of norepinephrine. They presented evidence to indicate that in the male child, these two factors are associated with the use of physical punishment as opposed to love-oriented punishment and punishment by the father rather than punishment by the mother. Henry and Short did not address this part of their analysis to female children, a serious omission, especially since their statistical data in the earlier part of the book used suicide and homicide rates for both sexes combined.

Henry and Short then sought to show how experience of love-oriented punishment dealt out by the parent who is the source of nurturance and love leads to the development of tendencies to inhibit the primary other-oriented expression of aggression. The argument centers around the idea that when the source of nurturance and love also administers the punishment, the primary other-oriented expression of aggression threatens to end the flow of love and nurturance. If the child retaliates, he will receive no nurturance. Therefore, the child develops habits of inhibiting this primary other-oriented aggression.

In support of this theory, Henry and Short cited studies correlating discipline experiences with superego strength, guilt, and cardiovascular reactions to stress. They then assumed that the discipline experienced causally determined these other variables. There is, of course, an alternative explanation based on the underlying interpretation of correlation: a correlation between two variables does not imply a causal sequence. For example, children may be predisposed by another (as yet undetermined) factor that leads to low superego strength which, in a sense, encourages or facilitates the use of physical punishment by their parents. Glueck and Glueck (1950) proposed this latter alternative as an explanation of the correlation that they found between delinquency in boys and experience of physical punishment. Unruliness in male children may lead to the father taking a more dominant role in disciplinary matters and, through their behaviour, children may influence negatively the disciplinary practices of their parents.

Henry and Short explored the implications of their ideas for two topics: the suicide rates of the widowed and divorced and the suicide rates of murderers. They argued that the act of divorce is an expression of aggression against the spouse and that prior to the divorce the spouse was a primary source of nurturance and love. Therefore, for the divorced the consequence of aggression was loss of nurturance. For the widowed the loss of love was a consequence of death and independent of aggression against the spouse. (Henry and Short did not acknowledge that the widowed might have harbored hostile wishes against the deceased partner.) Henry and Short predicted, therefore, that the suicide rate should be higher in the divorced than in the widowed. First, it may be noted that the previous analysis was a developmental one, whereas the present analysis is not. The divorced person should have developed patterns of handling aggressive impulses prior to being married and so it is not possible to argue that present loss of nurturance as a result of aggression leads to the development now of habits of directing aggression against the self.

Henry and Short go on to predict that murderers who murder primary sources of love and nurturance will have higher suicide rates than murderers who do not murder such sources. The same objection can be made to the derivation of this prediction as was made in the previous case. The *developmental* analysis may not apply to the present situation.

Further and equally serious objections can be made. Henry and Short set out in their book to show how homicide and suicide are differentially determined. Homicide, for example, was characteristic of low status persons whereas suicide was characteristic of high status persons. Suicide rates varied negatively with the business cycle whereas homicide rates varied positively with the business cycle. Then Henry and Short made predictions about homicide and suicide being committed by the same person. Such a prediction makes nonsense of the whole thesis of the book. If suicide and homicide can be committed by the same person, then it is difficult to assert that these behaviors should show different patterns of associations and correlations. If Henry and Short undertook to show how either habits of other-oriented or self-oriented aggression develop in men, how could they contemplate both habits occurring in the same person? Henry and Short suggested that a basically suicidal person could project his internalized or superego demands on behavior onto the victim and thus the internalized prohibition against the outward expression of aggression is weakened. This will not do. It enables us to conclude that the basic patterns of aggressive habits that develop according to Henry and Short's analysis are of little importance. Secondly, it makes the theory incapable of disproof. Any circumstances can be explained by assuming the existence of projection in this case and denying it in another.

Discussion

The theory of Henry and Short has stimulated much research – for a review see Lester (1989). In addition, the theory is noteworthy for at least three features. First, by contrasting suicide with homicide, Henry and Short broaden the focus of sociological theories to include homicide, and this suggests research strategies for the study of suicide that we would not otherwise have thought of in this context.

Second, by focussing on the external restraints on behavior, Henry and Short are theorizing about what Durkheim called social regulation, and they are alone in giving this concept much attention.

Third, Henry and Short are rare among sociologists and psychologists in their consideration of both sociological and psychological determinants of the choice between suicide and homicide. Thus, their theory bridges the gulf between the two disciplines.

Recommendation 5.5: Henry and Short's theory is worthy of examination and needs modification to overcome its inherent inconsistencies.

Recommendation 5.6: The study of homicide together with suicide can provide important comparisons and contrasts leading to a better understanding of both behaviors.

Gibbs and Martin's Theory

Gibbs and Martin (1964) summarized their theory in five postulates:

(1) The suicide rate of a population varies inversely with the stability and durability of social relationships within that population.

(2) Because of the inadequate state of sociological knowledge regarding social relationships, Gibbs and Martin did not attempt to measure the stability and durability of social relationships directly. Instead, they made use of an idea of Weber's (1947) that a fundamental condition for the maintenance of a social relationship is the requirement of conformity to the demands and expectations of others. Therefore, Gibbs and Martin postulated that the stability and durability of social relationships within a population conform to the patterned and socially sanctioned demands and expectations placed upon people by others.

(3) The demands of others constitute the role of the individual in the society. An individual with a particular status has to conform to a certain role if he wishes to maintain stable and durable social relationships. Conformity to one role is made difficult when an individual occupies several roles. Since people do occupy several statuses at any time, the individual is often faced with a conflict between the roles and, therefore, as to how he should behave. It is when conformity to one role interferes with confor-

mity to another role that the individual has difficulty in maintaining his social relationships. Thus the extent to which individuals in a population conform to patterned and socially sanctioned demands and expectations placed upon them by others varies inversely with the extent to which individuals in that population are confronted with role conflicts.

(4) Gibbs and Martin defined a status as a social identification. Every member of society is socially identified by inclusion in recognized categories: man, husband, laborer, and so on. If conforming to the role of one status conflicts with conforming to the role of another status, then the statuses are incompatible. Two statuses with conflicting roles are incompatible only when they are occupied simultaneously. Therefore, the extent to which individuals in a population are confronted with role conflicts varies directly with the extent to which individuals occupy incompatible statuses in that population.

(5) Gibbs and Martin assumed that if two statuses have conflicting roles, making them incompatible statuses when occupied simultaneously, then they will be less frequently occupied simultaneously then will two statuses with roles that do not conflict. The relative frequency with which a status configuration is occupied is labelled the degree of integration among the statuses in the configuration or, simply, the degree of status integration. The fifth postulate is, therefore, that the extent to which individuals occupy incompatible statuses in a population varies inversely with the degree of status integration in that population.

Combining these five postulates leads to the major thesis: the suicide rate of a population varies inversely with the degree of status integration in that population.

How is status integration measured? Gibbs and Martin noted that the measures that they chose were arbitrary. At the one-dimensional level, the degree of status integration is simply proportional to the percentage of individuals in a particular category. Thus, for the categories single, married, divorced, and widowed, the degrees of status integration are proportional to the percentage of individuals in each category. This measure has meaning, of course, only when the groups under investigation are homogeneous on all other statuses. Multi-dimensional categorizations are preferred (Gibbs & Martin, 1964, pp. 36–40).

To illustrate a typical test of the thesis, for the six categories of race by sex in the United States (White–Black–other/male–female), Gibbs and Martin used the proportions of each in each of the eleven occupational categories to calculate the status integration of each of the race by sex categories. The correlation between the suicide rate and the status integration scores was –0.94, indicating that as status integration increases, the suicide rate decreases.

One problem in the theory is the arbitrariness in the choice of status categories. Gibbs and Martin at one point in their book examined status integration for males and females of different ages in Bengal, India, in 1911, using marital categories. For the United States they used occupational categories. They argued that it may not be appropriate to use particular categories for particular countries. However, this raises the issue of arbitrariness. What if the use of marital statuses gave a different set of results than those obtained when occupational statuses were used to derive the measures of status integration? Which one is to be used? Are there any rules for determining this?

Gibbs and Martin illustrated this problem. They looked at the ratio of the suicide rate for males and females in the 14 districts of West Bengal, India, 1951. They also presented data on the ratio of the measures for status integration using both occupational statuses and marital statuses. (The status integration measures were much closer for males and females in the case of occupational categories than in the case of marital categories, reflecting the greater homogeneity of occupational categories in less developed countries.) Where the suicide rate was higher for males than for females, the status integration measure should have been less for males than for females and vice versa. Using status integration measures from marital categories, this prediction was confirmed in eight of the fourteen districts, whereas using status integration measures from occupational categories it was confirmed in six of the fourteen districts. The agreement between the ratio of the male and female status integration measures for the two different measure of status integration was low: in seven districts they agreed and in seven districts they disagreed. Thus there appeared to be little reliability in the measures of status integration, and Gibbs and Martin noted this. There was also little agreement with the predictions for either measure of status integration. Gibbs and Martin calculated what proportion of their tests were in the predicted direction, and they reported that this number was greater than would be expected if chance factors alone were operating.

Criticisms of the Theory

Most commentators have not approved of the measure of status integration proposed by Gibbs and Martin. For example, Douglas (1967) expressed doubts over the operational measure of status integration. He suggested that a status configuration might be occupied infrequently, not because of a role conflict once an individual occupies it, but rather because society restricts entry into that particular status configuration. Douglas's argument does not, however argue against there being conflict if one did acquire a particular status configuration.

Naroll (1965) also objected to the measure of status integration. He noted that it was a measure of status association. The most popular combinations of statuses were the most integrated. He noted that commonly associated statuses may involve conflicts. For example, the status configurations of wife and mother are frequently associated, but the roles involve important role conflicts, as noted by Hendin (1965) in the case of Norwegian mothers.

Naroll felt that the association found by Gibbs and Martin might result since the most frequently occupied statuses might be the most desired (if the statuses are open to individual choice). Therefore, statuses that are satisfying are likely to be popular, which will make them highly associated and will lead to low suicide rates in those occupying them.

Discussion

It is clear that the operational definition of status integration used by Gibbs and Martin does seem inadequate. The success of the tests correlating the measure with suicide rates is proven, but the measure does not seem, at an intuitive level perhaps, to operationalize the concepts of status integration, role conflict, or the stability of social relationships. However, this uneasiness must remain only a feeling until useful alternatives can be proposed for the operational definition. These have not yet been forthcoming.

To illustrate the problems with the measure of status integration, let us present some data from a recent paper by Gibbs and his colleagues (Stafford and Gibbs, 1988). They present hypothetical measures of marital integration in a social unit.

	Society A	Society B
proportion single	0.912	0.247
proportion married	0.063	0.252
proportion widowed	0.010	0.251
proportion divorced	0.015	0.250
status integration (sum proportions squared)	0.836	0.250

This means that a society with everyone in the same status has more status integration than one with equal proportions in all four marital statuses and, therefore, should have a lower suicide rate. This does not make sense to evaluators of the theory since the stability and durability of social relationships, the demands placed on others, the role conflicts and the occupation of incompatible statuses, all critical elements in Gibbs and Martin's theory do not, a priori, appear to differ in the two societies. They certainly have not been shown to differ. Yet these are the measures used by Stafford and Gibbs in their paper.[14]

Recommendation 5.7: Alternative measures of status integration need to be devised for adequate tests of Gibbs and Martin's status integration theory.

Minor Theories

There are also many minor theories. Holinger's (1987) cohort theory (based on Easterlin's [1980] ideas) proposed that the suicide rate (and the homicide rate) of the youth age group would depend on its relative size in the population. Based on the ideas of Wechsler and Pugh (1967), Lester (1987) proposed a social deviancy theory which hypothesized that any demographic group which is relatively rare in a region would have a higher rate of suicide. There are many competing theories of criminal behavior in the discipline of criminology. Lester (1990) explored how these could be extended to explaining suicide, and he proposed a classical theory, a positivist individualistic theory, a social structure theory, a learning theory, a social control theory, a social reaction theory and a social conflict theory of suicide. However, even these theorists have been lax in not generating hypotheses for study and testing them themselves. All too often, the theory is proposed and simply left there for others to explore (e.g., Lester, 1990).

---

[14] For further discussion of Gibbs and Martin's theory, see Lester (1989).

Furthermore, rarely are two theories explored for situations in which they would make conflicting predictions so that we can see which theory performs better.

One exception to this is an analysis by Bijou Yang (in Lester & Yang 1997) of three theories concerning the relationship between economic contractions and expansions on the suicide rate. She showed that Durkheim's (1897) theory predicts a U-shaped relationship, Henry and Short's (1954) theory a downward sloping relationship and Ginsberg's (1966) theory an upward sloping relationship, clearly competing and incompatible predictions.

Recommendation 5.8: Alternative sociological theories of suicide need to be explored, and those proposed need to be explored for competing predictions which can then be tested empirically.

The Study of Non-Fatal Suicidal Behavior

It has been noted that attempted suicide deserves study by sociologists. Wilkins (1967) argued that current sociological theories of suicide are, in fact, misleading since they exclude attempted suicide and suicidal ideation from the realm of behaviors to be explained. Sociological theories attempt to account for the rare behavior of completed suicide, rare since there are estimated to be 25 suicide attempts for every completed suicide (Farberow and Shneidman, 1961). Wilkins argued that:

> An improved theory of suicide would (1) deal with conditions that predispose to suicide – as the theoretical portions of current works would have us believe that they do – but with due recognition that these predispositions may be halted in their course; and (2) deal with those conditions under which a distinct and particular minority of such persons are permitted to complete their intentions. (Wilkins, 1967, p. 297)

American sociologists may have been hindered in their efforts to study attempted suicide by the fact that not very many epidemiological studies of suicidal attempts and ideation have been conducted. But such studies do now exist. For example, Schwab et al., (1972) surveyed a community in Florida and found that 2.7 percent of those surveyed had previously attempted suicide. Females, Whites, the young, those separated and those who were poor had a higher incidence of attempted suicide. These investigators also found that sixteen percent of those surveyed had previously contemplated suicide. Whites, the richer, the younger and those who were single reported a higher incidence, but there was no gender difference.

A comparison of completed suicides and attempted suicides coming to the attention of authorities in Los Angeles in 1957 was conducted by Farberow and Shneidman (1961). They reported on differences for such variables as the month of the year and the day of the week of the suicidal act, the method used for suicide, and the apparent reason for the suicide. Studies such as these can provide rates of suicide attempts and suicidal ideation for various social groups so that sociologists can be informed of the phenomenon that their theories must explain.

In other countries, ecological data on attempted suicide have been collected. For example, Edinburgh has had a reasonably complete accounting of attempts at suicide, especially self-poisoning (at least, those attempts serious enough to require medical attention) for several decades. Thus, reseachers there have been able to calculate rates of attempted suicide for each of the twenty three electoral wards of the city.

McCulloch and Philip (1970) have reported ecological correlates of rates of completed suicide and of attempted suicide over these electoral wards. Rates of both completed suicide and attempted suicide were associated with a high population density, many divorced persons, more cruelty to children, and a high rate of juvenile delinquency.

McCulloch and Philip were not concerned with differentiating the correlates of these two types of suicidal behavior. However, even in this early research, they made an effort to avoid the ecological fallacy by investigating whether the correlates of attempted suicide identified in their ecological study over regions were also associated with attempted suicide in individuals. (The variables identified in the ecological study did indeed differentiate the attempted suicides from nonsuicidal individuals.)

Thus, in conclusion, not only do attempted suicide and suicidal ideation deserve sociological scrutiny, but researchers have demonstrated convincingly that the requisite data for such scrutiny are available and can be collected in a form amenable for research.

More recently, Manuel, Gunnell, van der Hoek, Dawson, Wijeratne, and Konradsen (2008) measured the incidence of self-poisoning in 189 administrative divisions in a small rural area of Sri Lanka. The overall rate of self-poisoning in the year 2002 was 315 per 100,000, and the correlates of the rate over the divisions included education, agricultural population and housing quality (based on such indicators as plumbing and electricity access). They also found that the correlates of self-poisoning differed for pesticides as the agent versus non-pesticides. For example, unemployment rates correlated with non-pesticide self-poisoning but not with pesticide self-poisoning.

Recommendation 5.9: Sociological theories of suicidal behavior and research must include both fatal and nonfatal suicidal behavior.

Discussion

Four themes have emerged in this chapter. First, Durkheim has had too great an influence on the sociological study of suicide. His "heavy hand" has impeded the development of creative theory and research in the field. Furthermore, magnificent as his book was in 1897, his theoretical presentation is flawed, and subsequent research and theory have failed to advance his work.

Secondly, other sociological theories of suicide have been neglected, and many of these theories have been explored *only* by those who proposed them. These theories merit more extensive exploration.

Thirdly, sociologists have neglected to examine the validity of the measures they have employed to operationalize sociological concepts. "Expert opinion" is not sufficient to provide evidence of validity. For example, it was noted that no suicidologist has provided evidence that divorced and married people differ in their degree of social integration.

Finally, the study of non-lethal suicidal behavior has been neglected by sociologists, even though now adequate data do exist in some countries. If sociologists were to focus more on these non-lethal forms of suicidal behavior, then public health agencies might be more motivated to collect data on these behaviors.

References

Douglas, J. D. (1967). *The social meanings of suicide*. Princeton: Princeton University Press.

Durkheim, E. (1897). *Le suicide*. Paris: Felix Alcan.

Easterlin, R. A. (1980). *Birth and fortune*. New York: Basic Books.

Farberow, N. L., & Shneidman, E. S. (1961). *The cry for help*. New York: McGraw-Hill.

Gibbs, J. P. (1994). Durkheim's heavy hand in the sociological study of suicide. In D. Lester (Ed.), *Emile Durkheim Le Suicide 100 years later*, pp. 30–74. Philadelphia: Charles Press.

Gibbs, J. P., & Martin, W. T. (1964). *Status integration and suicide*. Eugene, OR: University of Oregon.

Ginsberg, R. B. (1966). Anomie and aspirations. *Dissertation Abstracts*, 27A, 3945–3946.

Henry, A. F., & Short, J. F. (1954). *Suicide and homicide*. New York: Free Press.

Holinger, P. C. (1987). *Violent deaths in the United States*. New York: Guilford.

Johnson, B. D. (1965). Durkheim's one cause of suicide. *American Sociological Review*, 30, 875–886.

Lester, D. (1987). Social deviancy and suicidal behavior. *Journal of Social Psychology*, 127, 339–340.

Lester, D. (1989). *Suicide from a sociological perspective*. Springfield, IL: Charles Thomas.

Lester, D. (1990). *Understanding and preventing suicide*. Springfield, IL: Charles Thomas.

Lester, D. (1992). A test of Durkheim's theory of suicide in primitive societies. *Suicide & Life-Threatening Behavior*, 22, 388–395.

Lester, D. (1994). *Emile Durkheim Le Suicide 100 years later*. Philadelphia: Charles Press.

Manuel, C., Gunnell, D. J., van der Hoek, W., Dawson, A., Wijeratne, I. K., & Konradsen, F. (2008). Self-poisoning in rural Sri Lanka. *BMC Public Health*, 8, #26.

McCulloch, J. W., & Philip, A. E. (1970). *Suicidal behaviour*. New York: Pergamon.

Naroll, R. (1965). Status integration or status association? Unpublished. Northwestern University.

Reynolds, F. M. T., & Berman, A. L. (1995). An empirical typology of suicide. *Archives of Suicide Research*, 1, 97–109.

Rootman, I. (1973). A cross-cultural note on Durkheim's theory of suicide. *Life-Threatening Behavior*, 3, 83–94.

Schwab, J., Warheit, G., & Holzer, C. (1972). Suicidal ideation and behavior in a general population. *Diseases of the Nervous System*, 33, 745–748.

Stack, S. (1978). Suicide. *Social Forces*, 57, 644–653.

Stafford, M. C., & Gibbs, J. P. (1988). Changes in the relation between marital integration and suicide rates. *Social Forces*, 66, 1060–1079.

Weber, M. (1947). *The theory of social and economic organizations*. New York: Oxford University Press.

Wechsler, H., & Pugh, T. F. (1967). Fit of individual and community characteristics and rates of psychiatric hospitalisation. *American Journal of Sociology*, 73, 331–338.

Wilkins, J. (1967). Suicidal behavior. *American Sociological Review*, 32, 286–298.

Table 5.1. The Full Durkheimian Array

		Social Integration		
		High	**Moderate**	**Low**
Social Regulation	**High**	A	B	C
	Moderate	D	E	F
	Low	G	H	I

Table 5.2. Rootman's Estimates Of Suicide Rates For Primitive Societies

		Social Integration		
		Low	**Moderate**	**High**
Social Regulation	**Low**	1.4	1.7	1.7
	Moderate	1.9	1.2	2.9
	High	2.7	1.3	2.6

Table 5.3. Lester's Factor Analysis Of Social Indicators For Nations (from Lester, 1989)
(Lester did not provide the variances accounted for by each factor)

	Factor	
	I	**II**
Political rights index	0.95*	−0.06
Civil rights index	0.97*	−0.04
Political freedom	0.90*	0.01
Religious liberty	0.71*	0.24
Political freedom index	−0.97*	0.09
Birth rate	0.46*	−0.66*
Marriage rate	0.28	0.83*

* Factor loading > 0.40

Table 5.4. Suicide Rates Of Nations With Varying Levels Of Social Regulation And Social Integration

Social Integration	*Social Regulation*		
	High	**Moderate**	**Low**
High	Bulgaria 13.5 Czechoslovakia 19.9 Egypt 0.1 Hungary 45.0 Korea, South 20.6 Poland 11.7 Singapore 9.8 Yugoslavia 14.8 ──── *Mean 16.9*	Israel 6.0 Japan 17.6 Portugal 8.3 Sri Lanka 29.2 USA 12.0 ──── *Mean 14.6*	Australia 11.3 Canada 14.1 New Zealand 10.2 UK 8.6 ──── *Mean 11.0*
Moderate	Argentina 7.1 Brazil 3.4 Chile 5.5 Syria 0.4 ──── *Mean 4.1*	Greece 3.2 Spain 4.4 Trinidad & Tobago 4.8 ──── *Mean 4.1*	Austria 26.0 Belgium 21.8 Costa Rica 4.4 Denmark 29.1 Finland 24.7 France 19.2 Germany, West 21.4 Ireland 6.2 Italy 7.1 Netherlands 10.2 Norway 12.4 ──── *Mean 16.6*
Low	Honduras 1.2 Jordan 2.8 Mexico 1.6 Panama 1.9 Philippines 8.3 ──── *Mean 3.2*	Colombia 3.5 Dominican Republic 2.0 Ecuador 3.2 El Salvador 12.1 Guatemala 1.0 Paraguay 2.7 Peru 1.2 Thailand 7.1 Turkey 1.8 Venezuela 4.6 ──── *Mean 3.9*	Sweden 19.1 Switzerland 24.7 ──── *Mean 21.9*

6

Anthropology and Suicide

Anthropology has been defined as "the study of humankind everywhere" (Haviland, 1993), and most anthropologists admit that anthropology is a diverse field, difficult to define precisely. In general, "culture" is the focus of study, but the term "culture" is also hard to define. Haviland (1993, p. 30) has defined culture as "a set of rules or standards shared by members of a society which, when acted upon by the members, produce behavior that falls within a range of variation the members consider proper and acceptable."

There are, however, several clearly defined fields within anthropology. *Physical anthropology* is concerned with the differences in physical and physiological traits between people from different cultures and with the evolution of humans. *Cultural anthropology* explores the cultures that people establish, that is, the standards and norms for behavior and the customs that guide the behavior in the culture. One branch of cultural anthropology, *archaeology*, studies the material remains of cultures in order to gain clues as to how ancient civilizations lived. Another branch, *linguistic anthropology*, studies the languages that different cultures employ. Finally, *ethnography* focuses on the study of present-day cultures by means of first-hand observation. Physical anthropology, archaeology and linguistic anthropology have little to say about suicidal behavior; ethnography is the field which has insights to offer about suicidal behavior.

Ethnography has been characterized by the study of primitive societies (sometimes called nonliterate societies) in which the anthropologist becomes a participant observer in the culture. In contrast, sociology involves the study of modern societies in recent times, usually with quantitative data and well-designed research methodology. In recent years, however, the distinction between these two disciplines has become blurred. Anthropologists have applied their techniques of study to cultural (and subcultural) customs in modern societies, and they have introduced quantitative techniques, usually based on formal codings of aspects of culture and behavior in samples of primitive societies. Sociologists, on the other hand, have acted as participant observers, a field that has come to be called ethnomethodology.

The aim of this chapter is to present a brief overview of some of the topics and issues which are present in the interaction of suicide and culture, to explore what anthropologists and others have written about these topics, and to make recommendations for the future.

In a series of books, Lester (2000) reviewed the scholar literature on suicide from 1897 to 1997. In order to prepare this chapter, we looked at *Abstracts in Anthropology* from 1998–2004.[15] There were 58 abstracts for articles on suicide in these volumes,

---

[15] The library we were using did not possess these abstracts for 2005–2007.

most of which were from journals such as *American Journal of Psychiatry* and *American Journal of Forensic Medicine and Pathology*. Only one abstract out of the 58 was for an article on suicide in an anthropology journal (De Alcântra, Doula & Rocha, 1999–2000). From this review, it seems clear that anthropologists find the topic of suicide in different cultures of little interest.

Of course, some of the articles listed in *Abstracts in Anthropology* from psychiatric and sociology journals were on suicide in other nations. For example, Utriainen and Honkaralo (1996) studied suicide notes from women in Finland, while Di Nunno (2001) reported on suicides by hara-kiri, a Japanese style for committing suicide. But these reports were not from anthropologists.

Recommendation 6.1: Anthropologists should devote more thought and research to the topic of suicidal behavior than they do at the present time.

Culture, Linguistics and Suicide

As Douglas (1967) pointed out, a shared linguistic terminology for suicidal behavior is associated with shared meanings of the behavior, and there are also shared associated terms and phrases, such as despair, hopelessness, and "life isn't worth living." Douglas emphasized that these terms are not the phenomenon itself but rather are adopted by members of the culture (or subculture) to construct meanings for suicidal behavior. However, since the terms are rarely clearly defined or detailed and since there is often disagreement among commentators on their meaning, it follows that the meaning of suicide is ambiguous. Furthermore, since the terms are used to construct meanings for suicidal behavior, then estimates of the incidence and circumstances of suicidal behavior are in part a social construction.

For example, according to the Mohave, a Native American tribe in the southwest of the United States, a fetus which presents itself in the transverse position for birth, leading to its own death and that of its mother, is viewed as having intended to commit suicide and to murder its mother so that they can be together in the spirit world (Devereux, 1961). Medical examiners and coroners in the rest of the United States would not view such a still-born infant as a suicide.

Counts (1980), who has studied the suicidal behavior of women in the Kaliai district of Papua New Guinea, noted that, in the past, elderly widows sometimes immolated themselves on their husband's funeral pyre. The German and Australian colonial governors considered this behavior to be a form of ritual murder rather than suicide, and they outlawed it. Counts, however, saw neither term (suicide or murder) as appropriate for this custom since it differed so much from what North Americans and Europeans regard as either suicide or murder. Neither term describes the behavior, the interpersonal relationships involved, or the attitudes toward the widow and those assisting in her death, nor do they predict how the community will respond to her death.

Recently, some scholars, especially in Europe, have expressed doubts that people engaging in nonfatal suicidal behavior have self-destruction as their aim, and they have moved to calling the behavior "parasuicide" (Kreitman, 1976), "self-poisoning" or "self-injury" (e.g., Ramon, 1980) and, most recently, "deliberate self-harm" (Maden, Chamberlain & Gunn, 2000). The semantic implication is that nonfatal suicidal behavior is not "suicide." Since in most cultures women engage in more nonfatal suicidal actions than do men, this renaming of nonfatal suicidal behavior as self-injury makes "suicidal behavior" less common in women than it was hitherto.

Other suicidologists on the other hand, include a wider range of behaviors under the rubric of "suicidal behavior." For example, Menninger (1938) classified such behaviors as alcoholism, drug abuse and anorexia as *chronic suicide* since such individuals were shortening their lives by their behaviors. Menninger also classified such behaviors such as polysurgery, self-castration, and self-mutilation as *focal suicide*, acts in which the self-destructive impulse is focused on one part of the body. These behaviors are often gender-linked. For example, anorexia is more common in women whereas illicit drug abuse is more common in men. Canetto (1991) has speculated that adolescents may respond differentially when under stress, with girls choosing nonfatal suicidal behavior more while boys choose drug abuse more. The use of Menninger's categories would change greatly the relative incidence of nonfatal suicidal behavior in women and men.

Recommendation 6.2: Anthropologists should identify and document the definitions of suicide in different cultures.

Culture and The Individual Suicide

Suicidal behavior may be quite differently determined and have different meanings in different cultures. The classic comparative study which demonstrated this was Hendin's (1964) study of suicide in Scandinavia. In Denmark, Hendin noted that guilt arousal was a major discipline technique used by Danish mothers, especially to control aggression, resulting in extremely strong dependency in their sons. This marked dependency was the root of depression and suicidality after adult experiences of loss or separation, and reunion fantasies were common in suicides.

In Sweden, there was a strong emphasis on performance and success by parents, resulting in ambitious children for who work was central to their lives. Suicide typically followed failure in performance which had damaged the men's self-esteem. In Norway where, when Hendin conducted his study, the suicide rate was much lower than the rates in Denmark and Sweden, he found a strong dependency of the sons on their mothers. Norwegian children were less passive and more aggressive than Danish children. Alcohol abuse was more common, and Norwegian men were more open about their feelings – able to laugh at themselves and cry more openly. Norwegian boys please their mothers by causing no trouble, and they do not worry unduly about failure, typically blaming others and retreating into alcohol abuse.

Counts (1988) illustrated the ways in which a culture can determine the meaning of the individual suicidal act in her account of suicide among females in Kaliai in Papua-New Guinea. Here, female suicide is a culturally-recognized way of imposing social sanctions, with political implications for the surviving kin and for those held responsible for the events driving the woman to suicide. In one instance, the suicide of a rejected fiancée led to sanctions being imposed on the family which had rejected her. Counts noted that the woman's suicide was a political act which took her from a position of powerlessness to one of power.

Closer to home, it has been argued that part of the explanation for the low suicide rate in African Americans as compared to white Americans is that suicide is a less acceptable behavior for African Americans. Homicide rates are much higher in African Americans, both as murderers and as victims, and a large proportion of murders are victim-precipitated, that is, the victim played some role (conscious or unconscious) in precipitating his or her own demise. Perhaps African American culture deems a victim-precipitated murder as a more acceptable method of dying than suicide (Gibbs, 1988)?

Recommendation 6.3: Anthropologists should document the *meanings* and psychodynamics of suicidal behavior in different cultures.

Cultural Anthropology's Role in Challenging Myths

Many theories of human behavior, including suicidal behavior, are based on physiological factors. For example, the role of estrogen in attempted suicide is sometimes stressed since the incidence of attempted suicide in women does appear to vary over the menstrual cycle. Cultural anthropology helps challenge such theories by showing, for example, that behaviors which we consider gender-specific are not found in every culture. As we have noted above, in the United States and in European nations, nonfatal suicidal behavior appears to occur at a higher rate in women than in men; as a result it is has come to be viewed as a "feminine" behavior by the general public (Linehan, 1973) and by suicidologists as well. Other cultures, however, provide examples where non-fatal suicidal behavior, often carried out in front of others, is more common in men rather than women. The Nahane (or Kaska), a Native Canadian tribe located in British Columbia and the Yukon, provide a good example of this.

> .....observations and communications agree that attempted suicide by men is of frequent occurrence and very likely to appear during intoxication. There is a general pattern for such attempted self-destruction. In the two cases of the sort observed during field work, the weapon selected was a rifle. As he brandishes the weapon the would be suicide announces his intention in an emotional outburst. This becomes the signal for interference to block the deed. One or more men leap forward to wrest the gun from the intended suicide's possession and toss it out of sight. The would be victim is now usually emotionally overwhelmed by his behavior. This pattern is illustrated by Louis Maza's behavior during intoxication. Several times during the afternoon, Louis had manifested aggression toward himself, crying: "I don't care if I'm killed. I don't care my life." After several hours of such emotional outbursts interspersed with quarrelling and aggression toward his companions, he seized his large caliber rifle and threatened to kill himself. Old Man threw

himself on the gun and as the two men grappled for the weapon, Louis succeeded in fir-
ing one wild shot. John Kean and the ethnographer ran to the camp and together
wrenched the gun from the drunken man. John fired the shells in the chamber and Old
Man tossed the gun half-way down the cutbank. No punishment or other discrimination is
reserved for attempted suicides. The individual is comforted and in the future, while in-
toxicated, he is watched lest he repeat the attempt. (Honigmann, 1949, p. 204)

Among the Washo, located in Nevada and California, nonfatal suicidal behavior seems
to be equally common in men and women.

In one case, a man had been having difficulty with his wife; she was interested in another
man. The husband ate wild parsnip, but was saved. As a result his sons brought pressure
on the wife and made her behave. The couple stayed together until the husband
died.....Pete also says that men attempt suicide more than women, who just leave home
when interpersonal difficulties arise. The destruction of the self is an ultimate, and the
fact that men are more likely to invoke it than women indicates a lack of male authority
in Washo culture (D'Azevedo et al., 1963, p. 50–51).

The Washo man is described as lacking authority and lacking in self-confidence, perhaps
because the Washo man has had more difficulty adapting to the changing culture in this
century than has the Washo woman. Interestingly, the explanation provided by these
Western anthropologists for the occurrence of nonfatal suicidal behavior among Washo
men may be generalizable to societies where nonfatal suicidal behavior is more common
in women. It may be that nonfatal suicidal behavior is not simply a "feminine" behavior,
but rather a behavior found more commonly in those who are oppressed in a society,
perhaps because the oppressed have fewer options for expressing their discontent.

**Recommendation 6.4: Anthropologists should document the phenomenon of sui-
cidal behavior in cultures to identify which aspects of the phenomenon are culture specific and which are found across all cultures.**

Culture Conflict

Cultures often come into conflict. For example, the conflict between the traditional Native American culture and the dominant American culture has often been viewed as play-
ing a major role in precipitating Native American suicide. May and Dizmang (1974)
noted that there were three major sociological theories which have been proposed for explaining the Native American suicide rate. One theory focuses on *social disorganization*.
The dominance of the Anglo-American culture has forced Native American culture to
change and has eroded traditional cultural systems and values. This changes the level of
social regulation and social integration, important causal factors for suicide in Durkheim's (1897) theory of suicide.

A second theory focuses on *cultural conflict* itself. The pressure, especially from the
educational system and mass media, on Native Americans, especially the youth, to ac-
culturate, a pressure which is opposed by their elders, leads to great stress for the youths.

A third theory focuses on the *breakdown of the family* in Native American tribes. Parents are often unemployed, substance abusers and in trouble with the law. Additionally, divorce and desertion of the family by one or more parent is common.

Acculturation occurs when a culture encounters a dominant alternative culture. The resulting pressure from the dominant culture leads to a variety of changes in the non-dominant culture (Berry, 1990): physical changes (such as type of housing, urbanization and increasing population density), biological changes (resulting from changing diet and exposure to new diseases), political changes (such as loss of autonomy for the non-dominant culture), economic changes (such as changes in type of employment), cultural changes (in language, religion, education and the arts), social relationships (both within the culture and between the two cultures), and psychological changes at the individual level (in behavior, values, attitudes and motives).

Berry noted that four possibilities are open to the non-dominant culture: *integration* – maintaining relations with the dominant culture while maintaining cultural identity; *assimilation* – maintaining relations with the dominant culture but not maintaining cultural identity; *separation* – not maintaining relations with the dominant culture but maintaining cultural identity; and *marginalization* – not maintaining relations with the dominant culture and not maintaining cultural identity.

Bagley (1991) looked at the suicide rate of Canadian Indian males aged 15 to 34 on the 26 most populated reservations in Alberta, Canada, and found that the more isolated reservations had the higher suicide rates. In contrast, Garro (1988) found that the suicide rates in the more isolated communities in Manitoba were lower than in the more accessible communities. Thus, these Canadian results appear to be in conflict.

It would be of great interest to categorize the different indigenous cultures in the world as to which strategy appears to have been chosen and to examine the different consequences for the society and for the individuals in the society.[16]

Recommendation 6.5: Anthropological research should focus on the role of cultural conflict in suicidal behavior and the effect of different styles of coping with the conflict on suicidal behavior.

Anthropological Theories of Suicide

Although many anthropologists have, of course, discussed suicide in the societies which they have studied, only one anthropologist has proposed a general theory of suicide. Naroll (1963, 1969) proposed that suicide was more likely in those who were *socially disoriented*, that is, in those who lack or lose basic social ties (such as those who are single or divorced). Since not all socially disoriented people commit suicide, there must be a psychological factor which makes suicide a more likely choice when a person is

---

[16] Bachman (1992) examined the correlates of the suicide rate in 120 counties in the United States which are partially or totally located on reservation land and found that economic deprivation, rather than acculturation, seemed to be the strongest correlate of Native American suicide rates.

socially disoriented, and Naroll suggested was that it was the person's reaction to *thwarting disorientation contexts*. Such contexts involve a weakening of the person's social ties as a result of the actions of other people or oneself (but not as a result of impersonal, natural or cultural events). Being divorced by a spouse and murdering one's spouse are examples of such contexts, whereas storm damage to your property or losing a spouse to cancer are not representative. In thwarting disorientation contexts, some people commit *protest suicide*, which Naroll defined as voluntary suicide committed in such a way as to come to public notice (and, therefore, excludes unconsciously motivated suicides and culturally-motivated suicides such as suttee). Naroll tested his theory using data from primitive cultures.

Lester (1995) noted the similarity of this theory to the classic sociological theories of suicide proposed by Durkheim and by Henry and Short (see Chapter 5), but he also noted that Naroll's theory had different implications. For example, Durkheim's theory of suicide refers more to steady state characteristics of the society as major explanatory variables, whereas Naroll's theory suggests the role of sudden, acute changes in a society. Furthermore, Naroll's theory is phrased in a way which makes it more validly applicable to individuals as well as societies as a whole.

Although anthropologists often use psychological theories (such as psychoanalytic theory) and sociological theories (such as those of Emile Durkheim) to guide their research, it would be stimulating if anthropologists would more often follow the lead of Naroll and devise their own theories based on their experience with cultures from around the world.

Recommendation 6.6: Anthropologists should endeavor to devise theories of suicide based on their studies of cultures rather than attempt to fit anthropological data within psychological and sociological theories.

Indigenous Groups in Developed Nations

In some nations there has been a good deal of research on and speculation about suicidal behavior in indigenous peoples, sometimes called aborigines. A great deal of research has been conducted on Native Americans in the United States, and some on aborigines in Australia and Taiwan and on the Inuit in Canada and Greenland.

What is noteworthy, however, is that many nations have indigenous peoples, yet we hear little about their suicidality and other self-destructive behaviors. For example, in Central and South America, almost every nation has an indigenous population: 71% in Bolivia, 66% in Guatemala, 47% in Peru, 38% in Ecuador, 14% in Mexico, 8% in Chile, 2% in Colombia, 1.5% in Paraguay, 1% in Venezuela, and 0.4% in Brazil (Anon, 2004). In recent years, these indigenous peoples have become organized politically. They have begun to protest against the governments of their nations, often toppling governments (as in Bolivia and Ecuador) and in rare cases assuming power (as in Bolivia and Peru).

Even in developed nations, the oldest inhabitants are often ignored. In suicide statistics from the United Kingdom, data from England and Wales are reported together.

A recent report on suicide in Wales (Lester, 1994c) was rejected by reviewers for the *British Journal of Psychiatry* as being of no interest![17] The United Kingdom has ethnic groups in Wales and the county of Cornwall who predate the Roman, Danish and French invaders and who have their own languages and ethnic identity. Yet their suicidal behavior has received no attention.

In Africa, the situation is odd in a different way. Setting aside the remnants of the European colonialists, all of the peoples there can be considered indigenous. Yet, when data on suicide are reported, they are reported for the artificial nations that the colonial rulers established with no regard for the tribal groups in each country. For example, suicide rates have been reported for Zimbabwe (Rittey & Castle, 1972; Lester & Wilson, 1988), yet Zimbabwe has two major ethic groups, the Shona (the dominant ethnic group) and the Ndebele. It would make much more sense to explore and compare suicide in these two ethnic groups.

Some nations are only now beginning to organize their mortality-reporting procedures and structures. In many of these, it will be important to take into account the various indigenous groups in the country, such as China which has a multitude of ethnicities within its borders.

In a couple of nations, it has been possible to compare different ethnic groups within a nation. Lester (1997a) reviewed all of the studies on Native American suicide and summarized the suicide rates by tribe and by era. There was a slight tendency for the suicide rates to rise during the 20th Century and for the tribes to differ greatly in their suicide rate, ranging in the 1970s from 149 per 100,000 per year in the Kwakiutl and 73 in the Sioux to 7 in the Pima and 9 in the Lumbee.

Cheng (1995, 1997) compared suicide in Taiwan in two aboriginal groups (the Atayal and the Ami) with suicide in the dominant Han Chinese. The Atayal had a suicide rate of 68.2 per 100,000 per year, the Ami 15.6 and the Han Chinese 18.0. The suicides in all three groups had a similarly high incidence of psychiatric disorder, and the high suicide rate in the Atayal was attributed to their high rate of alcoholism and earlier onset of major depressive disorders.

We need many more studies comparing the different groups of indigenous peoples within a nation – not simply the crude suicide rates, but also the circumstances, motives and meanings of suicide in these different groups.

Recommendation 6.7: Anthropologists should study suicidal behavior in the different ethnic groups within developed nations, groups which have been ignored by suicidologists hitherto.

Cultural Invariance

Studies by Lester on suicidal behavior in Chinese illustrates the role of culture, a culture of particular interest because the Chinese are native to many nations (such as mainland China and Hong Kong) and have emigrated in large numbers to nations such as America.

---

[17] It is no wonder that there is a Welsh liberation movement.

Lester (1994a) examined the epidemiology of suicide in Chinese in Hong Kong, Singapore, Taiwan, mainland China, Hawaii and the United States as a whole. A couple of examples here will illustrate the results. The ratio of the male to female suicide rates in 1980 was 1.2 for Chinese Americans, 1.2 for Hong Kong residents, 1.2 for Taiwanese residents and 1.2 for Singapore Chinese, identical gender ratios. Suicide rates peaked in the elderly in all the nations: for those 65 and older in Chinese Americans, 75 and older in Hong Kong and Taiwan and 70 and older in Singapore Chinese.[18]

However, the suicide rates differed: in 1980 the suicide rates were 13.5 per 100,000 per year in Singapore and Hong Kong Chinese, 10.0 in Taiwan and 8.3 for Chinese Americans. Furthermore, the methods used for suicide differed for the different groups of Chinese: jumping was more common in the Chinese in Singapore and Hong Kong, hanging in Chinese Americans and poisons in Taiwan, probably a result of the difference between the nations in the availability of methods for suicide. For example, Lester (1994b) showed that the used of jumping for suicide in Singapore was strongly associated with the development of high rise apartments.

Thus, gender and age patterns in Chinese suicide seem to be affected strongly by culture, while the absolute suicide rates and methods used are affected by the nation in which the Chinese dwell.

Recommendation 6.8: Anthropologists should endeavor in their research to identify which aspects of suicidal behavior are (relatively) culturally invariant and which vary with culture.

The Human Relations Area Files

There is a superb source of data on indigenous peoples in the Human Relations Area Files (HRAF). The headquarters for this project are at Yale University, but microfiche copies of the results of the project are available at other major universities in the United States and around the world. The staff of the project have collected reports from visitors to these cultures as far back as they can and from all kinds of visitors (such as missionaries, colonial administrators and anthropologists). The content of the reports is coded for topic, and, for example, to see what has been written about suicide in these cultures, the code for suicide is ascertained from the codebook (it is 762), and then the section for 762 can be located for each culture in the HRAF. There are about 330 cultures represented in the HRAF. The files are now becoming available on a CD-ROM and online (www.yale.edu/hraf/collections.htm).

The files are updated and enlarged continually. To give some examples of the source material, in 1994, the Ainu in Japan had 1,573 text pages from 11 sources that had been coded, the Lapps in Finland 3,284 text pages from 16 sources, the Yoruba in Nigeria 1,637 text pages from 45 sources, and Delaware Indians in the United States 1,733 text pages from 15 sources.

The HRAF can be used in many ways to advance the study of suicidal behavior.

---

[18] The nations used different classifications by age.

For example, Masumura (1977) had two judges rate 35 nations for the frequency of suicide by having them read the suicide entries in the HRAF, and his ratings are shown in Table 6.1.[19] From this group of cultures, it would appear that, among Native American groups, the Kwakiutl have a relatively high suicide rate and the Pomo a relatively low suicide rate. In a research study on this sample, Masumura found that the estimated suicide rate was *positively* associated with a measure of social integration in opposition to a prediction from Durkheim's (1897) classic sociological theory of suicide.

Ember and Ember (1992) drew attention to the fact that the materials on suicides in the HRAF come from very different time periods. Therefore, they urged that it was important to specify the year from which the data were derived. For example, they rated the Creek suicide rate as 1.74 (on a scale of 0–8) *in 1800* and the Omaha as 1 *in 1860*.

Recommendation 6.9: The entries for suicide for all cultures in the Human Relations Area Files need to be gathered together, rated by independent judges so that inter-judge reliability can be assessed, specified by era, and explored for cross-cultural correlates.

Indigenous Theories of Suicide

In Western cultures, there has been a great deal of interest in lay theories of psychopathology, several papers have explored the theories of suicide held by lay persons in general (e.g., Knight, Furnham & Lester, 2000) and for different subcultures, such as African-Americans versus white Americans (e.g., Walker, Lester & Joe, 2006). Indigenous cultures also have their theories of mental illness in general and suicide in particular.

Lester (1997b) noted that the Mohave have a clearly specified theory of suicide – namely that suicide in their people is increasingly due to a breakdown in ties to the community and tribe as a whole and to an increasing dependence on a primary relationship with a lover or spouse. Lester tested this hypothesis by examining whether suicide would be common in nations with higher levels of individualism, and the results confirmed this hypothesis.

Recommendation 6.10: Anthropologists should explore indigenous cultures for their theories of suicide and endeavor to test these theories empirically.

---

[19] Each judge rated the suicide rate of each society on a scale of 0–4, and their ratings were summed.

Discussion

It seems that anthropologists have lost interest in suicide as a topic for study, but the reasons for this are not apparent. Anthropologists have a great deal to contribute to our understanding of suicide, not only because they study cultures that are typically ignored by most suicidologists, but also because their methodology engages them personally with the members of the cultures. They study both the psychodynamics of individual suicides and the social contexts in which the suicidal behavior occurs, thereby providing comprehensive accounts of the suicidal behavior. Cultural anthropologists are the true interdisciplinary scholars in the field of suicidology, and their contributions are sorely missed.

References

Anon. (2004). A political awakening. *The Economist, 370(8363)*, 35–37.

Bachman, R. (1992). *Death and violence on the reservation.* New York: Auburn House.

Bagley, C. (1991). Poverty and suicide among Native Canadians. *Psychological Reports*, 69, 149–150.

Berry, J. W. (1990). Acculturation and adaptation. *Arctic Medical Research*, 49, 142–150.

Canetto, S. S. (1991). Gender roles, suicide attempts, and substance abuse. *Journal of Psychology*, 125, 605–620.

Cheng, A. T. A. (1995). Mental illness and suicide. *Archives of General Psychiatry, 52*, 594–603.

Cheng, A. T. A. (1997). Personality disorder and suicide. *British Journal of Psychiatry, 170*, 441–446.

Counts, D. A. (1980). Fighting back is not the way: Suicide and the women on Kaliai. *American Ethnologist*, 7, 332–351.

Counts, D. A. (1988). Ambiguity in the interpretation of suicide. In D. Lester (Ed.), *Why women kill themselves* (pp. 87–109). Springfield, IL: Charles Thomas.

D'Azevedo, W. L., Freed, S. A., Freed, R. S., Leis, P. E., Scotch, N. A., Scotch, F. L., Price, J. A., & Downs, J. F. (1963). *The Washo Indians of California and Nevada.* Salt Lake City, UT: University of Utah.

De Alcântra, M. de L., Doula, S. M., & Rocha, C. M. (1999–2000). Suicides in Guarani culture. *Bulletin of the International Committee for Urgent Anthropology & Ethnographic Research*, 40, 191–196.

Devereux, G. (1961). *Mohave ethnopsychiatry: The psychic disturbances of an Indian tribe.* Washington, DC: Smithsonian Institution.

Di Nunno, N. (2001). Suicide by hara-kiri. *American Journal of Forensic Medicine & Pathology*, 22, 68–72.

Douglas, J. D. (1967). *The social meanings of suicide.* Princeton, NJ: Princeton University Press.

Durkheim, E. (1897). *Le suicide.* Paris: Felix Alcan.

Ember, C. R, & Ember, M. (1992). Warfare, aggression, and resource problems. *Behavior Science Research*, 26, 169–226.

Garro, L. C. (1988). Suicides by status Indians in Manitoba. *Arctic Medical Research*, 47, supplement 1, 590–592.

Gibbs, J. T. (1988). Conceptual, methodological, and sociocultural issues in black youth suicide. *Suicide & Life-Threatening Behavior*, 18, 73–89.

Haviland, W. A. (1993). *Cultural anthropology.* Fort Worth, TX: Harcourt Brace Jovanovich.

Hendin, H. (1964). *Suicide and Scandinavia*. New York: Grune & Stratton.

Honigmann, J. J. (1949). *Culture and ethos of Kaska society*. New Haven, CT: Yale University.

Knight, M. T. D., Furnham, A. F., & Lester, D. (2000). Lay theories of suicide. *Personality & Individual Differences*, 29, 453–457.

Kreitman, N. (1976). Age and parasuicide. *Psychological Medicine*, 6, 113–121.

Lester, D. (1994a). The epidemiology of suicide in Chinese populations in six regions of the world. *Chinese Journal of Mental Health*, 7, 25–36.

Lester, D. (1994b). Suicide by jumping in Singapore as a function of high-rise apartment availability. *Perceptual and Motor Skills*, 79, 74.

Lester, D. (1994c). Predicting the suicide rate in Wales. *Psychological Reports, 75,* 1054.

Lester, D. (1995). Thwarting disorientation and suicide. *Cross-cultural Research*, 29, 14–26.

Lester, D. (1997a). *Suicide in American Indians*. Commack, NY: Nova Science.

Lester, D. (1997b). Note on a Mohave theory of suicide. *Cross-Cultural Research*, 31, 268–272.

Lester, D. (2000). *Why people kill themselves*. Springfield, IL: Charles Thomas.

Lester, D., & Wilson, C. (1988). Suicide in Zimbabwe. *Central African Journal of Medicine, 34,* 147–149.

Linehan, M. (1973). Suicide and attempted suicide. *Perceptual and Motor Skills*, 37, 31–34.

Maden, A., Chamberlain, S., & Gunn, J. (2000). Deliberate self-harm in sentenced male prisoners in England and Wales. *Criminal Behaviour & Mental Health*, 10, 199–204.

Masumura, W. T. (1977). Social integration and suicide. *Behavior Science Research*, 12, 251–269.

May, P. A., & Dizmang, L. H. (1974). Suicide and the American Indian. *Psychiatric Annals*, 4(11), 22–28.

Menninger, K. (1938). *Man against himself*. New York: Harcourt, Brace & World.

Naroll, R. (1963). *Thwarting disorientation and suicide*. Unpublished, Northwestern University.

Naroll, R. (1969). Cultural determinants and the concept of the sick society. In S. C. Plog & R. B. Edgerton (Eds.), *Changing perspectives in mental illness* (pp. 128–155). New York: Holt, Rinehart & Winston.

Ramon, S. (1980). Attitudes of doctors and nurses to self-poisoning patients. *Social Science and Medicine*, 14A, 317–324.

Rittey, D. A. W., & Castle, W. M. (1972). Suicides in Rhodesia. *Central African Journal of Medicine, 18,* 97–100.

Utriainen, T., & Honkaralo, M. L. (1996). Women writing their death and dying. *Semiotica*, 109(3/4), 195–220.

Walker, R. L., Lester, D., & Joe, S. (2006). Lay theories of suicide. *Journal of Black Psychology*, 32, 320–344.

Table 6.1. Estimates Of Relative Suicide Rates For 35 Non-Literate Societies By Masumura (1977)

Group	Suicide Score (range 2–8)
Ainu	6
Andamanese	2
Araucanians	5
Ashanti	6
Bakongo	6
Banks Islanders	7
Bushmen	6
Shippewa	7
Chukchee	8
Creek	6
Crow	6
Dahomeans	6
Fang	6
Hottentot	6
Iban	7
Iroquois	5
Jivaro	7
Kazak	6
Kutenai	4
Kwakiutl	8
Lango	8
Maori	8
Navajo	2
Norsemen	5
Omaha	4
Pomo	2
Rwala	7
Samoans	8
Sema Naga	6
Semang	2
Toda	6
Trobrianders	8
Tuareg	4
Vedda	4
Yahgan	2

Part 2: Illustrative Topics

7

Studies of Attitudes Toward Suicide

with
Liesl L. Glover

The study of attitudes toward suicide has a long history in the field of suicidology. One approach in this arena has been to look at "myths" related to suicide (e.g., Lester, McIntosh, & Rogers, 2005: McIntosh, Hubbard, & Santos, 1985). This research investigated whether beliefs, whether grounded in empirical data or not, might be related to a person's ability to indentify risk for suicide in others and to one's own propensity to consider suicide as a possible solution under difficult circumstances. A more specific attitude-focused approach is grounded in the expectation that there is a relation between attitudes toward suicide and concurrent or subsequent suicidal behaviors (e.g., Rogers & Carney, 1994; Rogers, 1996). The intent of empirical work in this area then has been to identify whether both positive and negative attitudes toward suicide are related to other suicidal behaviors in the hope that those attitudes may translate into preventive interventions, including the assessment of suicidal risk.

Examples of measures of attitudes toward suicide include scales developed by Domino, Moore, Westlake and Gibson (1982), Diekstra and Kerkhof (1989), and Lester and Bean (1992). Additionally, researchers have developed attitude measures based on subsets of items from these scales (e.g., Rogers & DeShon, 1992, 1995) or have assessed attitudes using a limited number of study-specific constructed items (e.g., Singh, Williams, & Ryther, 1986). This chapter first focuses on a consideration of studies of attitudes toward suicide as they relate generally to attitude theory and research and second considers additional measurement issues beyond the psychometric issues identified in Chapter 2.

Attitudes as a Psychological Construct

Attitudes in general have been a focus of psychological research for decades because of their presumed link to behavior (Schwarz, 2007). In predicting behavior, researchers have worked under the assumption that understanding the evaluative nature of a person's judgment related to a behavior or set of behaviors enhances the ability to predict those behaviors. Over time, many theories have emerged about the structure, nature, and usefulness of attitudes in behavioral prediction. For example, considerable work has examined what attitudes really are and attempted to reduce the confusion over how to define and measure them (Krosnick, Judd, & Wittenbrink, 2005). In turn, there have been many theories proposed to describe the structure of attitudes and their relation to behavior. Difficulty in measuring attitudes in general and, specific to suicidology, has been grounded in the lack of consensus regarding the structure of attitudes toward suicide and the application of insufficient methodology for their measurement. Recently, several theories have been proposed that suggest ways to understand the structure of attitudes in general and their connection to behavior, and to identify ways to enhance the measurement of attitudes in order that there is a clearer connection between attitudes and behavior.

One issue that must be addressed by researchers investigating attitudes toward suicide is whether one is adopting a dispositional versus a contextual perspective or an interaction of the two (Schwarz, 2007). These are important underlying distinctions in that a dispositional perspective on attitudes toward suicide suggests that those attitudes are less amenable (if at all) to change. To the extent that attitudes about suicide are conceptualized as dispositional, the goal of research in this area would be understanding attitudes rather than identifying attitudes as risk factors to be targeted for change.

Equally problematic may be adopting a solely contextual perspective. If attitudes toward suicide are context driven, then they are unstable and potentially easily influenced. If this is the case, the psychometric measurement of attitudes becomes extremely difficult because the attitudes could be constantly in flux. Additionally, if suicide attitudes are primarily context driven, while intervention may be possible, the targets for intervention would be constantly shifting, and interventions would be difficult to deliver. On the other hand, if attitudes are a product of an interaction between dispositions and context, addressing risk-related attitudes via prevention and/or intervention activities may be possible by focusing on both the enduring attitudinal components and the situational influences. The importance of the distinctions between these approaches to conceptualizing attitudes leads to our first recommendation in this chapter.

Recommendation 7.1: Researchers investigating attitudes toward suicide and other suicidal behaviors should identify their underlying conceptualization of "attitudes" and consider the implications of that conceptualization since it impacts the methodology and the interpretation of the results of the study.

Beyond the dispositional versus contextual distinction, there are a number of other important issues to consider with regard to attitude research. For example, Fazio (2007) pointed out that attitudes can vary in importance, and this variation can account for differences observed in the relation between measured attitudes and behaviors. For example, Abelson (1988) discussed this issue in terms of "non-attitudes" suggesting that research participants are likely to respond to items on attitude measures whether or not they have thought about the issue under investigation. This probable mix of attitudes and non-attitudes weakens any association between the measures of attitudes and relevant behavior. Rogers (1996) extended the work of Abelson to the area of assessing right-to-die attitudes by encouraging researchers in that area to include not only measures of attitude valence (for or against), but to also assess participants' level of *conviction* to their reported attitudes.

For example, Lester and Bean (1992) explored students' attitudes toward preventing and, separately, for assisting suicide by asking them about their level of commitment. Did they believe in the cause, would they publicly voice their support to friends and family, would they publicly voice their support to strangers, would they donate money for the cause, would they join a public demonstration for the cause and would they work in a center for that cause (a suicide prevention center in the first case and assisting a person to commit suicide in the second case)?

Using Abelson's constructs of *ego preoccupation, emotional commitment,* and *cognitive elaboration,* Rogers (1995) argued that researchers could distinguish between meaningful attitudes and non-attitudes in part based on measures of conviction, using only the former as "predictors" of subsequent behaviors. This same argument can be extended to the assessment of attitudes toward suicide and suicidal behavior, that is, in addition to assessing whether one has a positive or negative attitude toward suicidal individuals or characteristics related to suicidal behavior, comprehensive assessment should include an assessment of the degree to which the person is or has been involved with the topic (i.e., the frequency of thoughts about suicide and/or suicidal people and the importance of the beliefs associated with suicide), the degree of certainty one has toward his or her beliefs, and the ease of access of those attitudes and their connections with other attitudes and beliefs. Accordingly, a more comprehensive assessment model that includes Abelson's conceptualization of conviction for measuring attitudes toward suicide is offered in Figure 7.1.

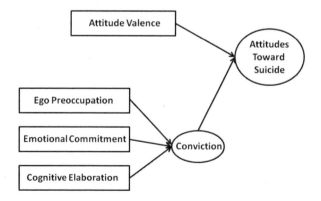

Figure 7.1. Including conviction constructs in assessing attitudes toward suicide.

Recommendation 7.2: Attitude researchers should move beyond a simple assessment of the valence of attitudes and include measurement techniques related to commitment and conviction that can help differentiate between attitudes and non-attitudes.

In addition to Abelson's conceptualization of conviction, Visser, Bizer, and Krosnick (2006) discussed a number of attitude strength-related attributes that are important to consider in assessment because of their impact on attitude salience. These authors suggested that measuring attitude strength can enable researchers to distinguish between attitudes that have an impact on thinking and behavior and those that are relatively inconsequential. Both impactful and inconsequential attitudes toward suicide can be measured, but it is the impactful attitudes that are likely to further an understanding of the link between attitudes and behavior. Attitude strength characteristics identified by Visser et al. include attitude *importance, knowledge, ambivalence, certainty, extremity, accessibility,* and *intensity*, to name a few. They suggest and cite research supporting the claim that "attitudes to which people attach more personal importance are better predictors of behavior" and are "more resistant to change" (p. 2).

Related more specifically to identifying strength-related characteristics relevant to suicide attitude research, Rogers (1996) suggested three individual factors that could reasonably be assessed in attitude research to tap attitude salience. These factors include personal experience, death anxiety, and religiosity. Personal experience would include the experience of being a suicide survivor, experience with others in one's social network who are or have been suicidal, and one's own history with suicidal ideation, feelings, and behaviors. The role of death anxiety in this context might be related to a willingness to engage honestly in the assessment of attitudes, while religiosity may contribute to an assessment of attitude strength by understanding religious/spiritual perspectives related to suicide as well as the potential role of doctrine-associated stigma.

In thinking about the characteristics identified by Abelson (1988) related to the construct of conviction and relevant individual characteristics such as those identified above, it seems reasonable to expect that there would be a reciprocal relation between conviction and individual characteristics. As such, Figure 7.2 represents a general measurement model that would lead to a more meaningful assessment of attitudes toward suicide in that researchers could distinguish between suicide attitudes that may relate to behavior and non-attitudes that are more or less "constructed" on the spot to respond to items on a measure.

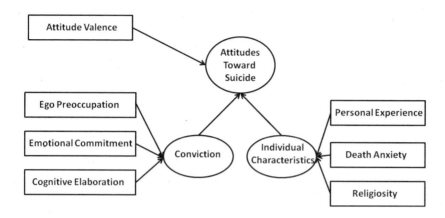

Figure 7.2. Suggested conceptual measurement model for assessing attitudes toward suicide.

Recommendation 7.3: In addition to measures of conviction, suicide attitude re-searchers should include an assessment of relevant individual characteristics in order to interpretation attitude strength.

Additional Measurement Issues

The foremost instrument used in the United States for the assessment of attitudes toward suicide is Domino's Suicide Opinion Questionnaire (Anderson, Lester, & Rogers, 2008). The Suicide Opinion Questionnaire (SOQ; Domino et al., 1982) was developed by the authors as a measure to assess various attitudes toward suicide in general and toward suicidal individuals, specifically. It consists of 100 attitude-related items responded to on a five-point Likert scale with response options ranging from strongly agree to strongly disagree. Because of its extensive use in the research literature, we refer to the SOQ in our discussion of measurement issues. Rather than reiterate our discussion related to differentiating between meaningful attitudes and non-attitudes, we merely note that no published research using the SOQ has included an assessment of respondents' conviction with regard to their attitudes or has utilized data on individual characteristics in order to differentiate responses based on attitude strength. Although the use of the SOQ as a suicide attitude measure is not without controversy related to general psychometric issues (Anderson et al., 2008; Rogers & DeShon, 1992, 1995), here we focus our comments on issues related to item development.

Item development is a critical issue in measurement construction in general. In developing the SOQ, the authors began with approximately 3000 items that were ultimately narrowed down to the 100 items that exist today. Processes for narrowing down an original pool of items include expert judgment, protocol analysis, and the use of a variety of statistical procedures such as exploratory and confirmatory factor analysis and item analysis. Despite employing these various procedures for identifying appropriate items, however, researchers need to be cognizant of the impact of item wording on responses. For example, Schwarz (1999) has provided convincing data indicating that relatively minor differences in the wording of items in survey research can result in dramatically different results. Similarly, Alwin and Krosnick (1991) and Krosnick, Judd and Wittenbrink (2005) have suggested that researchers should be aware of the many ways in which survey questions, wording, and response options may dictate the responses gathered. Thus, it is important for researchers developing or using suicide attitude scales to ensure that potential respondents will interpret the items as intended. An additional issue here is related to potential changes in the meaning and/or relevance of items over time. For example, the 100 items of the SOQ were developed in the early 1980's with no item revisions to date. The likelihood that those 1980 items will prompt the same interpretations from respondents some 25 years later is relatively small given changes in language usage and social understandings of suicide and suicidal behaviors.

Recommendation 7.4: Researchers interested in studying attitudes toward suicide using established measures should consider the possibility that items developed in the past may not reflect current understandings of suicide and suicidal individuals. Thus, it is important to reestablish support for the validity of interpretations intended to be drawn from the scores on the attitude measure.

Recommendation 7.5: In developing new measures to identify attitudes toward suicide, researchers must provide empirical evidence supporting the assumption that items are interpreted by respondents as anticipated and provide sample-specific evidence for the reliability of scores and the validity of interpretations based on those scores.

Conclusions

Extending this discussion regarding attitudes toward suicide to the current literature, it is reasonable to ask, "What do we know about attitudes toward suicide?" Our response would be "very little!" Despite the fact that a recent PsycINFO literature search using "attitudes and suicide" as the search criterion identified over 2000 hits, there is little evidence for a meaningful relation between measured attitudes and suicidal behaviors. In reference specifically to research using the Suicide Opinion Questionnaire, Domino (2005) concluded that, "studies suggest not only that the SOQ is applicable to various cultures, but also suggests that there is diversity in attitudes worldwide." (p. 107). Although parenthetically noting that there are psychometric problems with the SOQ, this conclusion was offered in spite of the empirical reality that, of the various factor or scale structures that have been offered for the interpretation of this measure, none have stood the test of replication either within the United States or cross-culturally.

We encourage researchers drawn to investigating attitudes toward suicide to move beyond the simplistic approaches of the past by working to ensure that they are in fact assessing meaningful attitudes toward suicide and making an effort to exclude the noise created by the inclusion of non-attitudes. To the extent that future research moves in this direction, the role of attitudes toward suicide as an important component of assessment, prevention, and intervention can be clarified.

References

Alwin, D. F., & Krosnick, J. A. (1991). The reliability of survey attitude measurement: The influence of question and respondent attributes. *Sociological Methods & Research, 20*, 139–181.

Anderson, A. L., Lester, D., & Rogers, J. R. (2008). A psychometric investigation of the Suicide Opinion Questionnaire. *Death Studies*, 32, 924–936.

Fazio, R. H. (2007). Attitudes as object-evaluation associations of varying strength. *Social Cognition, 25*, 603–637.

Gawronski, B., & Bodenhausen, G. V. (2007). Unraveling the processes underlying evaluation: Attitudes from the perspective of the APE model. *Social Cognition, 25*, 687–717.

Krosnick, J. A., Judd, C. M., & Wittenbrink, B. (2005). The measurement of attitudes. In D. Albarracin, B. T. Johnson, & M. P. Zanna (Eds.), *The handbook of attitudes,* pp. 21–76. Mahwah, NJ: Lawrence Erlbaum & Associates.

Lester, D., & Bean, J. (1992). Attitudes toward preventing versus assisting suicide. *Journal of Social Psychology*, 132, 125–127.

Lester, D., McIntosh, J., & Rogers, J. R. (2005). Myths about suicide on the Suicide Opinion Questionnaire: An attempt to derive a scale. *Psychological Reports, 96*, 899–900.

Petty, R. E., Briñol, P., & DeMarree, K. G. (2007). The meta-cognitive model (MCM) of attitudes: Implications for attitude measurement, change, and strength.

Rogers, J. R. (1996). Assessing right to die attitudes: A conceptually guided measurement model. *Journal of Social Issues, 52*, 63–84.

Rogers, J. R., & DeShon, R. P. (1995). Cross-validation of the five factor interpretive model of the suicide opinion questionnaire. *Suicide and Life-Threatening Behavior, 25*, 303–309.

Rogers, J. R., & DeShon, R. P. (1992). A reliability investigation of the eight clinical scales of the suicide opinion questionnaire. *Suicide and Life-Threatening Behavior, 22*, 428–441.

Schwarz, N. (2007). Attitude construction: Evaluation in context. *Social Cognition, 25,* 638–656.

Schwarz, N. (1999). Self-Reports: How the questions shape the answers. *American Psychologist, 54,* 93–105.

Sun, J., & Willson, V. L. (2008). Assessing general and specific attitudes in human learning behavior: An activity perspective and multilevel modeling approach. *Education and Psychological Measurement, 58*, 245–261.

Visser, P. S., Bizer, G. Y., & Krosnick, J. A. (2006). Exploring the latent structure of strength-related attitude attributes. *In Advances in Experimental Social Psychology* (pp. 1–68).

8

Studies of Sexual Abuse and Suicidality[20]

In this chapter, we will review and critique the research on a specific problem, namely the link between childhood sexual abuse and suicidality. However, the recommendations we propose apply to the study of the link between almost any antecedent (or current) behavior and suicidality.

General estimates of the prevalence of childhood sexual abuse (CSA) across samples have ranged from 6% to 62% for women and 3% to 31% for men (Peters, Wyatt & Finkelhor, 1986). More recently, Rind, Tromovitch, and Bauserman (1998), in their review of 59 studies investigating the effects of CSA in college samples, have reported prevalence rates of 27% and 14% for women and men, respectively. One result of the discovery of the high prevalence of CSA has been the generation of a considerable amount of research investigating the possible links between a history of CSA and subsequent psychological difficulties (e.g., Lynskey & Fergusson, 1997; Pharris, Resnick & Blum, 1997; Rind et al, 1998). According to Briere and Runtz (1993), "the aggregate of positive findings in this literature has led many researchers and clinicians to conclude that sexual abuse is a significant long-term mental health hazard" (p. 312).

A subset of the general literature of CSA and its psychological effects has included a specific focus on the relationship between a history of CSA and suicidality (e.g., Briere & Runtz, 1986; Coll, Law, Tobias, & Hawton, 1998; Fergusson, Lynskey & Horwood, 1996; Lipschitz et al., 1999; Mullen et al., 1988; Neumann, Houskamp, Pollock, & Briere, 1996; Peters & Range, 1995; Rind et al., 1998). Estimates of the strength of this relationship in the literature vary considerably as a function of sample characteristics. For example, Rind et al. (1998) identified 9 studies that investigated the effects of CSA upon subsequent suicidal behaviors in college students. Their meta-analysis indicated that CSA accounted for less than 1% of the variance in suicidal behavior. In contrast to the relatively small effect size reported by Rind et al. (1998), Neumann et al. (1996) reported a more moderate effect size in standard deviation units of .34 (95% C.I. = .24 –.44) for their subset of 8 studies specifically looking at the relationship between CSA and suicidal behaviors in adult women. Based upon their results, Neumann et al. concluded that CSA is significantly related to suicidality. As with the literature investigating the psychological correlates of CSA in general, the positive findings in the literature on the relationship between CSA and suicidality have led many clinicians

---

[20] An earlier version of this chapter appeared as Rogers (2003). It was reprinted with the permission of the publisher, Taylor & Francis, Ltd (www.tandf.co.uk/journals).

and researchers to conclude that CSA is a significant risk factor for subsequent suicidal ideation, attempts, and completed suicides (Bryant & Range, 1997; Coll et al, 1998; Law, Coll, Tobias & Hawton, 1998; Thompson, Kaslow, Lane & Kingree, 2000).

Despite what appears to be a relatively consistent and interpretable pattern of relationships between CSA and psychological difficulties in general, a number of researchers have questioned this rather straightforward interpretation of the data on methodological grounds (e.g., Bauserman & Rind, 1997; Briere & Runtz, 1993; Kilpatrick, 1987; Rind et al., 1998). For example, Bauserman and Rind (1997) suggested that the literature in this area suffers from the use of overly broad and vague definitions of sexual abuse and a bias toward clinical samples. Similarly, Jumper (1995) highlighted the need in the research to differentiate between the effects of CSA and the effects of events that have occurred post CSA that may impact subsequent psychological difficulties while Beitchman (1992) underscored the difficulty in assessing the psychological effects of CSA independent of the effects of physical abuse. Finally, Rind et al. (1998) also discussed the problems with definitions of CSA in general suggesting that "the construct of CSA, as commonly conceptualized by researchers, is of questionable scientific validity" (p. 46) and that the observed effects of CSA are typically confounded by family environment factors.

Clearly, there are many methodological issues impacting the study of CSA and psychological adjustment. Many of the same methodological issues that inhibit the unambiguous interpretation of the general CSA literature speak to the literature on the relationship between CSA and suicidality as well. In addition to these shared issues, there are some methodological issues that are relatively unique to the study of CSA and suicidality. Thus, the purpose of this chapter is to provide a critical overview of the literature investigating the relationship between CSA and suicidality in order to highlight the major methodological issues that need to be considered when drawing inferences from this body of knowledge. In addition, an awareness of and attention to these methodological issues in research design should allow for a more straightforward interpretation of future research in this area than is possible at this time. Finally, it is not the intent of this review to criticize specific studies since, by its nature, all research is flawed (e.g., Bickman & Rog, 1998; Gelso, 1979). Rather, the goal is to use the existing literature base to identify persistent methodological limitations that need to be addressed in order to advance the research on the relationship between CSA and suicide.

Childhood Sexual Abuse and Suicide

Studies included in this review were identified through computerized data-based searches of Psychinfo from 1967 to September 1999 and ERIC from 1966 to September 1999. Additional articles were identified from the reference lists of the identified studies. Key search terms entered into the data-bases were *sex* or *sexual abuse*, *child* or *childhood sexual abuse*, and *suicide*, *suicide attempts*, or *suicidal behaviors*. This search process resulted in the identification of 18 empirical studies specifically investigating the relationship between sexual abuse and suicide and 11 literature reviews broadly investigating the relationship between a history of sexual abuse and psychological difficulties. The methodological issues to be discussed include (1) lack of consistency in definitions of CSA and suicidality, (2) sample selection, (3) causality, and (4) theoretical grounding.

Definitions of CSA and Suicidality

A major obstacle to drawing conclusions from the body of empirical literature on CSA and suicidality is the lack of consistency across studies in defining the constructs. Because there are no generally accepted and systematically employed operationalized definitions of these terms in the extant literature, the ability to aggregate the empirical results is severely limited and subsequent qualitative inferences must be considered to be tentative, at best.

For example, Coll et al. (1998) and Rind et al. (1998) have discussed the lack of consensus in the empirical literature on the assessment of CSA as representing a major methodological limitation and source of error. As an illustration of this difficulty in the CSA/suicide literature, some authors have utilized single author constructed survey questions to classify respondents as sexually abused (e.g., Darves-Bornoz et al., 1998; Garnefski & Arends, 1998; Pharris et al., 1997). For example, Garnefski and Arends (1998) categorized participants into CSA and non CSA groups based upon responses to the general question, "Have you ever been sexually abused, for example been forced into sexual acts, assaulted or raped?" (p. 101). Some researchers have provided participants with a description of sexually abusive behavior and asked, based upon the description, if the participant considers him or herself as sexually abused (Molnar et al., 1998).

Other authors have utilized formalized assessment measures to identify sexual abuse victims (e.g. Bryant & Range, 1997; Law et al., 1998; Lipschitz et al., 1999; Stepakoff, 1998; de Wilde et al, 1992) as well as open or semi-structured interview formats (e.g., Baral et al., 1998; Calam et al., 1998; Lynskey & Fergusson, 1997; Sansonnet-Hayden, Haley, Marriage & Fine, 1987; Shaunesey, Cohen, Plummer & Berman, 1993; Yoder, 1999) with no emerging consistency in methodology. The study by Bryant and Range (1997) illustrates the use of formalized assessment measures with their use of the Child Sexual Abuse Questionnaire (Bendixen, Muus, & Schei, 1994) as a standardized assessment of CSA. In contrast, Yoder (1999) identified individuals in his sample as sexually abused through the use of open interviews with no clear description of the strategies used to elicit a history of CSA.

Finally, across all of these studies, the predominant method of collecting information with regard to a history of CSA has been through retrospective self-report (e.g., Coll et al., 1998; Lipschitz et al., 1999; Molnar et al., 1998) with this method's inherent strengths and weaknesses (Neumann et al., 1996; Schwarz, 1999). While self-report is often the only way to investigate a history of CSA, the phenomenon of recall bias and contextual cues imbedded in questions challenge the unambiguous interpretation of self-report data.

The differences in the methods of obtaining information related to a history of sexual abuse (i.e., interview versus survey) and the variations in the definitions of sexual abuse suggested above lead to difficulties in interpretation of the literature as a whole. In addition, as indicated by Rind et al. (1998), there may be some important moderators of the CSA experience that need to be systematically included in studies in this area rather than viewing CSA as a dichotomous variable. These moderators include gender, level of consent, degree of force, penetration, frequency and duration, and incest (Rind et al., 1998). As suggested by a number of authors, the assumption that CSA, as it is typically assessed, necessarily leads to negative outcomes has not been borne out in the empirical literature (e.g., Bauserman & Rind, 1997; Constantine, 1981; Jumper, 1995; Kendall-Tackett et al., 1993; Kilpatrick, 1987; Okami, 1991; Rind et al., 1998; Rind & Tromovitch, 1998). Thus the development of a standardized definition of CSA and research attention to moderators may help clarify the impact of CSA on subsequent functioning.

In a similar fashion, the assessment and, by extension, the definitions of suicidality in this body of literature are equally varied. As with CSA, some researchers have used author-developed measures or items (e.g., Garnefski & Arends, 1998; Lynskey & Fergusson, 1997; Molnar et al., 1998; Pharris et al., 1997). Garnefski and Arends (1998), for example, assessed suicidal thoughts by asking participants "During the past 12 months, did you seriously think of killing yourself?" (p. 102) and assessed suicide attempts by asking "Have you ever made a serious attempt to end your life?" (p. 102). In contrast, some authors have used more standardized procedures (e.g., Bryant & Range, 1997; Lipschitz et al., 1999; Stepakoff, 1998) such as Bryant and Range's use of the abbreviated Suicide Behaviors Questionnaire (Linehan & Nielson, 1981).

Finally, some researchers have determined the suicide status of their participants through a review of clinical records (e.g., Baral et al., 1998; Briere & Runtz, 1986; Bryer, Nelson, Miller & Krol, 1987) and through semi-structured (e.g., Briere & Zaidi, 1989; de Wilde et al, 1992) or unspecified interview processes (e.g., Calam et al., 1998; Coll et al., 1998; Law et al., 1998; Sansonnet-Hayden et al, 1987; Shaunesey et al., 1993; Yoder, 1999). Of all of these studies, however, only Shaunessey et al. (1993) clearly indicated any attempt to validate interview self-report information on suicidality with other forms of data. In addition, with the exception of Calam et al's. (1998) prospective study, information related to suicidal behaviors in this body of literature has been based primarily on retrospective self-report.

Thus, the assessment of suicidality across these studies has varied widely and generally relied on retrospective self-reports of suicidal behaviors with few attempts to validate the self-reports with other forms of data. This general lack of consistency in the definition and assessment of suicidality, as with CSA, makes generalizing across studies difficult. Thus, in the specific area of CSA and suicide, the difficulties associated with drawing conclusions from the literature are significantly confounded.

Recommendation 8.1: Researchers must not only be clear about the definitions of the terms that they use, but efforts must also be made to reach consensus of how variables should be measured in a reliable and valid manner.

Recommendation 8.2: The measurement of variables should not be overly simplified. The complex aspects of the variables should be taken into account.

Recommendation 8.3: Because of the reconstructive nature of memory, researchers should attempt to gather corroborating reports of sexual abuse (or other antecedent behavior) and other relevant moderating factors whenever possible in order to overcome possible biases in self-report. While not intending to discount the accuracy and value of self-report information, there are abundant data suggesting the need for independent verification of recalled information (e.g., Pope, 1996). Concern over the reconstructive nature of memory may be especially heightened in clinical samples where co-occurring psychological and psychiatric conditions may substantially impact the memory retrieval process.

Recommendation 8.4: When assessing CSA, researchers should attend to the relevant moderators of the impact of CSA discussed in the literature rather than only asking for the presence of past sexual abuse. The literature is relatively clear that the perception of impact, type, frequency, and duration of the abusive behaviors are important components for assessment as are co-occurring histories of emotional abuse, physical abuse, and neglect. Additionally, attention to significant positive and negative events that may have occurred subsequent to the sexual abuse and prior to the suicidal behaviors would be important. This recommendation applies to the study of other antecedent behaviors.

Sample Selection

Another important consideration in interpreting the literature on CSA and suicide is sample selection. For example, much of the research investigating the association between CSA and suicidality has come from the study of clinical samples (Baral et al., 1998; Briere & Runtz, 1986; Briere & Zaidi, 1989; Bryer et al., 1987; Coll et al., 1998; de Wilde et al., 1992; Law et al., 1998; Lipschitz et al., 1999; Sansonnet-Hayden et al., 1987; Shaunesey et al., 1993), individuals previously identified as CSA victims (Calam et al., 1998; Darves-Bornoz et al., 1998; Pharris et al., 1997), and marginalized community samples such as runaway adolescents (Yoder, 1999) and street youth (Molnar et al., 1998). While a few studies have utilized more general samples such as college undergraduates (Bryant & Range, 1997; Stepakoff, 1998) and community adolescents (Garnefski & Arends, 1998; Lynskey & Fergusson, 1997), the generality of the results beyond specific samples is unknown.

Additionally, the sampling strategies represented in this body of literature clearly underscore the concerns regarding confounds to the interpretation that CSA is a significant risk factor for subsequent suicidal behavior (e.g., Beitchman et al., 1992; Constantine, 1981; Kilpatrick, 1987; Jumper, 1995; Neumann et al., 1995). For example, as suggested by Neumann et al. (1995), studies based on clinical samples are typically biased towards individuals who have been negatively affected by the CSA experience and, therefore, the ability to generalize to a more general population of individuals who have experienced CSA is limited. It can be argued that this same bias may exist also in marginalized samples such as runaways and homeless youth. In addition, a consideration of the possible third factor problem (Neumann et al., 1996) in the study of clinical samples, marginalized samples, and college samples would suggest that researchers must attempt to rule out the impact of factors such as co-occurring psychiatric illnesses, substance abuse, physical abuse, emotional abuse or neglect, family factors, and the effects of other significant experiences that may have occurred since the CSA experience.

Recommendation 8.5: Research on antecedent behaviors and suicidality should be conducted in both clinical and non-clinical samples so that the generality of the research findings can be assessed.

Causality

The majority of the studies identified in this review were correlational in nature. That is, researchers have primarily focused on investigating the co-occurrence of a history of CSA and suicidal behavior by identifying suicidal individuals and inquiring about a sexual abuse history. While correlational designs of this type have typically been used in suicide research to identify risk factors for suicidal behavior (Rogers, 2001), they have limited utility in addressing the issue of causality.

Clearly, the truest test of the effects of CSA on subsequent suicidal behavior would be through the application of longitudinal designs controlling for a variety of third variables such as physical abuse, emotional abuse or neglect, family environment, and experiences that have occurred between the CSA event(s) and the suicidal behaviors. Designs of this sort would allow for the consideration of an interpretation of causality. Unfortunately, the only study identified in this review that employed a longitudinal design was the Lynskey and Fergusson (1997) study of a birth cohort of children followed to age 18. These authors reported that CSA was not a significant predictor of subsequent adjustment difficulties including suicide attempts when delinquent or substance using peer affiliations and the quality of parental relationships were included in the predictive model. As such, the Lynskey and Fergusson results did not provide support for an independent effect of CSA on suicidal behavior and further highlight the need to consider additional factors when investigating the relationship between CSA and suicide.

Recommendation 8.6: Since correlational cross-sectional research does not permit cause-and-effect conclusions to be drawn, more long-term, longitudinal studies should be undertaken so that the causal chains that may be identified are more plausible.

Theory

The importance of theoretically-based research in the social and behavioral sciences was underscored by Pedhazur and Schmelkin (1991) who stated:

> Meaningful hypotheses cannot emerge in a theoretical vacuum. Admittedly, the theory from which a given hypothesis was derived is frequently implicit. The researcher may not even be aware of the theoretical orientation that has led him or her to advance and

test a given hypothesis. Yet it is the theory that renders the hypothesis and the variables that it refers to, relevant to attempts to explain a given phenomenon. Moreover, it is the theory that gives coherence and integration to a set of hypotheses designed to explain a given phenomenon. (p. 185)

With respect to suicide research in general, we have suggested in Chapter 3 that contemporary suicidology has suffered from an over-dependence on atheoretical and pragmatically based research and that this approach has placed limits on the advancement of knowledge in this area.

This same atheoretical approach to the study of suicide in general is evident in the research on CSA and suicide. For example, of the studies identified for this review, only Briere and Runtz (1993) and Yoder (1999) explicitly discussed a theoretical approach as part of their presentation. Of these two, Briere and Runtz discussed theory from a post hoc perspective as part of a discussion of the results of their study, while only Yoder's research was presented as being imbedded in a theoretical perspective and representing a test of theory-derived hypotheses.

Briere and Runtz (1993) investigated the relationship between suicidal thoughts and behaviors and a history of CSA for women clients at a community mental health center. In their discussion section, these authors cast their positive results in terms of impaired self-esteem and blame, powerlessness, and interpersonal dysfunction. Thus, Briere and Runtz suggested that the link between CSA and suicidality may be a function of the effects of the experience of CSA on self-referent evaluations and interpersonal effectiveness. While they provided interesting conjectures with regard to these possible relationships, they did not provide a test of those hypotheses from an a priori theoretical perspective as urged by Pedhazur and Schmelkin (1991).

In contrast, Yoder's (1999) comparison of suicide attempters, ideators, and nonsuicidal homeless and runaway adolescents was conceptualized from the perspective of life-course theory. Thus, Yoder briefly presented the underlying life-course theory and related his research hypotheses to that theory. He then interpreted his results in relationship to his underlying theory. While, in general, both his presentation of the theory and his discussion linking the results back to the theory were rather cursory, the process he used in developing his study appears to reflect the positions of Pedhazur and Schmelkin (1991) with regard to the importance of theory grounded research.

In summary, it appears that very little of the research investigating the relationship between CSA and suicide has been grounded in theory. The atheoretical and pragmatic approach represented in this body of literature inhibits the development of an integrated body of knowledge from which to draw conclusions regarding the relationship between CSA and suicide.

Recommendation 8.7: Research should be conceptualized in an a priori fashion from a theoretical perspective and developed to test theoretically derived hypotheses. Knowing only that there is a relationship between CSA and suicidality is not particularly useful without an explicit consideration of the related mechanism of operation. Prior to the question of whether or not there is a relationship between CSA and suicide, the question of why such a relationship is expected should be asked. This recommendation applies to the study of other antecedent behaviors.

Discussion

The extant literature on the relationship between childhood sexual abuse and suicide is far from conclusive in terms of allowing for a clear interpretation of the impact of CSA. In terms of definitions of the relevant constructs, the assessment of both a history of CSA and suicidal behavior in the literature are inconsistent and may serve to overestimate the relationship through the application of broadly inclusive definitions. Alternatively, the same assessment issues may, in fact, mask the impact of CSA on suicidal behavior by not attending to empirically identified moderators of CSA and by not applying standardized definitions of both CSA and suicidal behavior in research. These definitional problems are significantly exacerbated by the over-representation of clinical samples and the reliance on self-report as the primary, and most often the sole, method of data collection.

As a function of the difficulties associated with the currently used definitions of CSA and suicidality, the over-reliance on self-report methodologies, and the generally restricted sample selection strategies, interpreting causality from the current literature is clearly premature. While CSA and suicidality may be suggested to covary based on current research, there are no clear data to suggest that CSA, independently or in conjunction with other factors, is a "cause" of subsequent suicidal behavior. In fact, with the myriad of possible intervening variables between CSA and later suicidal behavior (not the least of which is the passage of time), identifying CSA and suicidal behavior in a causal relationship will remain a challenging and ambitious endeavor well into the future.

Finally, even if an unambiguous empirical link could be established between CSA and suicidal behavior, the lack of attention to the development of theoretical conceptualizations that would allow for the a priori testing of hypotheses concerning the relationship will continue to hinder progress in suicidology. That is, how would we conceptualize a clear relationship between CSA and suicidal behavior and how would we understand the relationship between a history of CSA and other suspected suicide risk factors? What mechanisms would we hypothesize as explaining the impact of CSA and other risk factors that would account for the fact that some individuals with a history of CSA subsequently engage in suicidal behaviors while others with similar histories do not? Without understanding at the theoretical and conceptual level, how will our knowledge advance suicidology and the treatment of suicidal individuals?

Given these methodological and theoretical issues, we may not know what we think we know about the relationship between sexual abuse and suicide. Based on the existing literature, it is premature to conclude that CSA is a significant risk factor for subsequent suicidal ideation, attempts, or completed suicide. Despite an intuitive sense that this conclusion is valid, the empirical literature does not support it at this point in time. What is clearly needed is the development of research strategies to begin to address the methodological issues that continue to hamper research investigating the relationship between CSA and suicidality.

References

Baral, I., Kora, K., Yuksel, S., & Sezgin, U. (1998). Self-mutilating behavior of sexually abused female adults in Turkey. *Journal of Interpersonal Violence*, 13, 427–437.

Bauserman, R., & Rind, B. (1997). Psychological correlates of male child and adolescent sexual experiences with adults: A review of the nonclinical literature. *Archives of Sexual Behavior*, 26, 105–139.

Beitchman, J. H., Zucker, K. J., Hood, J. E., DaCosta, G. A.., Akman, D., & Cassavia, E. (1992). A review of the long-range effects of child sexual abuse. *Child Abuse & Neglect*, 16, 101–118.

Bendixen, M., Muss, K. M., & Schei, B. (1994). The impact of child sexual abuse: A study of a random sample of Norwegian students. *Child Abuse & Neglect*, 18, 837–847.

Bickman, L., & Rog, D. J. (Eds.). (1998). *Handbook of applied social research methods*. Thousand Oaks, CA: Sage.

Briere, J., & Runtz, M. (1993). Childhood sexual abuse: Long-term sequelae and implications for psychological assessment. *Journal of Interpersonal Violence*, 8, 312–330.

Briere, J., & Zaidi, L.Y. (1989). Sexual abuse histories and sequelae in female psychiatric emergency room patients. *American Journal of Psychiatry*, 146, 1602–1606.

Bryant, S. L., & Range, L. M. (1997). Type and severity of child abuse and college ctudents' lifetime suicidality. *Child Abuse & Neglect*, 21, 1169–1176.

Bryer, J. B., Nelson, B. A., Miller, J. B., & Krol, P. A. (1987). Childhood sexual and physical abuse as factors in adult psychiatric illness. *American Journal of Psychiatry*, 144, 1426–1430.

Calam, R., Horne, L., Glasgow, D., & Cox, A. (1998). Psychological disturbance and child sexual abuse: A follow-up study. *Child Abuse & Neglect*, 22, 901–913.

Coll, X., Law, F., Tobias, A., & Hawton, K. (1998). Child sexual abuse in women who take overdoses: I. A study of prevalence and severity. *Archives of Suicide Research*, 4, 291–306.

Constantine, L. L. (1981). The effects of early sexual experiences: A review and synthesis of research. In Constantine, L. L., & Martinson, F. M. (Eds.), *Children and sex: New findings, new perspectives* (pp. 217–244). Boston: Little Brown & Co.

Darves-Bornoz, J. M., Choquet, M., Ledoux, S., Gasquet, I., & Manfredi, R. (1998). Gender differences in symptoms of adolescents reporting sexual assault. *Social Psychiatry & Psychiatric Epidemiology*, 33, 111–117.

de Wilde, E. J., Kienhorst, I. C., Diekstra, R. F., & Wolters, W. H. (1992). The relationship between adolescent suicidal behavior and life events in childhood and adolescence. *American Journal of Psychiatry*, 149, 45–51.

Fergusson, D. M, Lynskey, M. T., & Horwood, L. J. (1996). Childhood sexual abuse and psychiatric disorder in young adulthood: I. Prevalence of sexual abuse and factors associated with sexual abuse. *Journal of the American Academy of Child & Adolescent Psychiatry*, 35, 1355–1364.

Garnefski, N., & Arends, E. (1998). Sexual abuse and adolescent maladjustment: Differences between male and female victims. *Journal of Adolescence*, 21, 99–107.

Gelso, C. J. (1979). Research in counseling: Methodological and professional issues. *Journal of Counseling Psychology*, 8(3), 7–35.

Jumper, S. A. (1995). A meta-analysis of the relationship of child sexual abuse to adult psychological adjustment. *Child Abuse & Neglect*, 19, 715–728.

Kendall-Tackett, K. A., Williams, L. M., & Finkelhor, D. (1993). Impact of sexual abuse on children: A review and synthesis of recent empirical studies. *Psychological Bulletin*, 113, 164–180.

Kilpatrick, A. C. (1987). Childhood sexual experiences: Problems and issues in studying long-range effects. *Journal of Sex Research*, 23, 173–196.

Law, F., Coll, X., Tobias, A., & Hawton, K. (1998). Child sexual abuse in women who take overdoses: II. A study of prevalence and severity. *Archives of Suicide Research*, 4, 307–327.

Linehan, M. M., & Nielson, S. L. (1981). Assessment of suicide ideation and parasuicide: Hopelessness and social desirability. *Journal of Consulting & Clinical Psychology*, 49, 773–775.

Lipschitz, D. S., Winegar, R. K., Nicolaou, A. L., Hartnick, E., Wolfson, M., & Southwick, S. M. (1999). Perceived abuse and neglect as risk factors for suicidal behavior in adolescent inpatients. *Journal of Nervous & Mental Disease*, 187, 32–39.

Lynskey, M. T., & Fergusson, D. M. (1997). Factors protecting against the development of adjustment difficulties in young adults exposed to childhood sexual abuse. *Child Abuse & Neglect*, 21, 1177–1190.

Molnar, B. E., Shade, S. B., Kral, A. H., Booth, R. E., & Watters, J. K. (1998). Suicidal behavior and sexual/physical abuse among street youth. *Child Abuse & Neglect*, 22, 213–222.

Mullen, P. E., Romans-Clarkson, S. E., Walton, V. A., & Herbison, G. P. (1988). Impact of sexual and physical abuse on women's mental health. *Lancet*, 1, 841–845.

Neumann, D. A., Houskamp, B. M., Pollock, V. E., & Briere, J. (1996). The long-term sequelae of childhood sexual abuse in women: A meta-analytic review. *Child Maltreatment*, 1, 6–16.

Okami, P. (1991). Self-reports of "positive" childhood and adolescent sexual contacts with older persons: An exploratory study. *Archives of Sexual Behavior*, 20, 437–457.

Pedhazur, E. J., & Schmelkin, L. P. (1991). *Measurement, design, and analysis: An integrated approach*. Hillsdale, NJ: Lawrence Erlbaum Associates.

Peters, D. K., & Range, L. M. (1995). Childhood sexual abuse and current suicidality in college women and men. *Child Abuse & Neglect, 19*, 335–341.

Peters, S. D., Wyatt, G. E., & Finkelhor, D. (1986). Prevalence. In D. Finkelhor et al. (Eds.), *A sourcebook on child sexual abuse* (pp. 15–59). Beverly Hills: Sage.

Pharris, M. D., Resnick, M. D., & Blum, R. W. (1997). Protecting against hopelessness and suicidality in sexually abused American Indian adolescents. *Journal of Adolescent Health*, 21, 400–406.

Pope, K. S. (1996). Memory, abuse, and science: Questioning claims about the false memory syndrome epidemic. *American Psychologist*, 51, 957–974.

Rind, B., & Tromovitch, P. (1998). A meta-analytic review of findings from national samples on psychological correlates of child sexual abuse. *Journal of Sex Research*, 34, 237–255.

Rind, B., Tromovitch, P., & Bauserman, R. (1998). A meta-analytic examination of assumed properties of child sexual abuse using college samples. *Psychological Bulletin*, 124, 22–53.

Rogers, J. R. (2001). Theoretical grounding: The "missing link" in suicide research. *Journal of Counseling and Development*, 79, 16–25.

Rogers, J. R. (2003). Sexual abuse and suicide: Why we may not know what we think we know. *Archives of Suicide Research, 7*, 83–91.

Sansonnet-Hayden, H., Haley, G., Marriage, K., & Fine, S. (1987). Sexual abuse and psychopathology in hospitalized adolescents. *Journal of the American Academy of Child & Adolescent Psychiatry*, 26, 753–757.

Schwarz, N. (1999). Self-reports: How the questions shape the answers. *American Psychologist*, 54, 93–105.

Shaunesey, K., Cohen, J. L., Plummer, B., & Berman, A. (1993). Suicidality in hospitalized adolescents: Relationship to prior abuse. *American Journal of Orthopsychiatry*, 63, 113–119.

Stepakoff, S. (1998). Effects of sexual victimization on suicidal ideation and behavior in U.S. college women. *Suicide & Life Threatening Behavior*, 28, 107–126.

Thompson, M. P., Kaslow, N. J., Lane, D. B., & Kingree, J. B. (2000). Childhood maltreatment, PSTD, and suicidal behavior among African-American females. *Journal of Interpersonal Violence*, 15, 3–15.

Watkins B., & Bentovim, A. (1992). Male children and adolescents as victims: A review of current knowledge. In G. C. Mezey & M. B. King (Eds.), *Male victims of sexual assault*, (pp. 27–66). Oxford, U.K.: Oxford University Press.

Yoder, K. A. (1999). Comparing suicide attempters, suicide ideators, and nonsuicidal homeless and runaway adolescents. *Suicide & Life Threatening Behavior*, 29, 25–36.

9

Assessing Suicidal Risk[21]

with
Kimberly M. Oney

The search for suicide assessment measures that can reliably and validly inform the clinical assessment of suicide risk or potential has a long history in suicidology (e.g., Farberow, 1981; Jobes, Eyman & Yufit, 1995; Lester, 1970; Lewinsohn, Garrison, Langhinrichsen, & Marsteller, 1989; Maris, 1992; Range & Knott, 1997; Rothberg & Geer-Williams, 1992; Westefeld, Range, Rogers , Maples, Bromley & Alcom, 2000). While this search over time has led the field away from its prior focus on the prediction of suicide by means of psychological measures to the more reasonable goal of assessment (Maris, 1992), the ability to inform accurately the clinical assessment of suicide risk or potential using suicide assessment scales remains an elusive goal (Westefeld et al., 2000).

Recommendation 9.1: We think that it is premature to abandon the goal of predicting suicide. In addition to the many advances in our understanding of suicidal behaviour in the thirty years since the first efforts to predict suicide, there have been concomitant advances in statistical and mathematical modelling procedures. A move away from simple linear modelling to the application of more complex approached such as models based on chaos and catastrophe theories and self-organized criticality may lead to more successful efforts to predict suicide.

Much of the difficulty in the prediction and assessment of suicidality has been attributed to psychometric weaknesses in suicide assessment scales (e.g., Jobes et al., 1995). Specifically, there has been notable concern regarding the reliability (i.e., stability and replicability) of scale scores and the validity (i.e., meaningfulness, appropriateness and usefulness) of the interpretations of those scores vis á vis suicidal behavior (Maris, 1992; Jobes et al., 1995; Rothberg & Geer-Williams, 1992).

Conspicuously missing from these discussions, however, has been a consideration of the impact of the relational context of assessment on the psychometric characteristics of reliability and validity at the clinical level. In this chapter, we argue that accurate assessment for clinical work involves not only a consideration of the general psychometric properties of assessment measures based on aggregate data, as has been the primary focus in the past, but also attention to the impact of the context of assessment

---

[21] An earlier version of this chapter appeared as Rogers & Oney (2005).

on the reliability and validity of information collected via those measures at the clinical level. Thus, we posit a two-tiered consideration of reliability and validity, with the first tier consisting of an evaluation of those characteristics at the aggregate level and the second tier focused on issues of reliability and validity at the clinical or phenomenological level.

In keeping with this two-tiered model, we first provide a brief overview of three major reviews of suicide assessment scales published in the past ten years focusing on reliability and validity based on group or aggregate data. Next, we present an argument supporting the importance of the relational context as a mechanism for enhancing the reliability and validity of data collected via suicide assessment scales in clinical work. Finally, we offer an example of a clinical assessment protocol that incorporates the relational context in the assessment process and, thereby, increases the potential to derive reliable and valid data from suicide assessment scales at the individual level.

Tier One: Reliability And Validity Based On Aggregate Data

Three major reviews of suicide assessment scales have appeared in the literature over the past decade. Rothberg and Geer-Williams (1992) reviewed 18 published suicide risk scales and evaluated those scales in terms of their psychometric properties. Similarly, Range and Knott (1997) evaluated 20 suicide assessment instruments, and Westefeld et al. (2000) reviewed 12 suicide assessment scales. Authors of these reviews focused primarily on the psychometric issues of scale reliability and validity derived from aggregate data in their evaluations of the scales and subsequent recommendations. As defined by the Joint Committee on Standards for Educational and Psychological Testing (1999), validity is "the degree to which evidence and theory support the interpretations of test scores" (p. 9) while reliability refers to the consistency of measurement when "the testing procedure is repeated on a population of individuals or groups" (p. 25) or the extent to which measurement is free from error (Crocker & Algina, 1986). Thus, from a psychometric perspective the characteristics of validity and reliability are assessed based upon the responses of groups of individuals. This information is then used to evaluate the appropriateness of using those instruments at the individual or clinical level.

Rothberg and Geer-Williams

Rothberg and Geer-Williams (1992) reviewed 18 suicide prediction scales in terms of their psychometric properties. These authors categorized the scales into those relying on the direct self-report of the test-taker (six scales) and those relying on a second party, such as documentation from hospital records as the source of information (12 scales). Seventeen of the scales reviewed by Rothberg and Geer-Williams are presented in Table 9.1 along with their original citations. Because it is imbedded in a projective measure of personality and, therefore, not specifically a suicide assessment measure, the Rorschach Suicide Constellation (Exner & Wylie, 1977) is not included in the table.

In summarizing their review, Rothberg and Geer-Williams lamented the general absence in the literature of attention to the psychometric properties of the suicide assessment scales that they included in their work. In an interesting conclusion to their chapter, however, the authors attempted to apply nine of the second-party scales in their review to five case vignettes characterized as ranging from low risk to high risk for suicide (see Berman, 1992, for case summaries). Their application of the scales to the cases resulted in a wide range of risk estimates across four of the five cases. The one case that was rated in a relatively consistent fashion using the nine scales was uniformly identified as a low risk case. This result suggests that, while the scales may have value in assessing suicide risk as a dichotomous variable (i.e., no risk versus risk), their ability to discriminate across various levels of suicide risk is questionable.

As a result of the dearth of published reliability and validity information on the 18 scales in their review and the lack of agreement among the nine scales used to rate the risk for suicide for four of the five case summaries, the authors refrained from recommending any of the reviewed scales for clinical purposes. Rothberg and Geer-Williams concluded that much more work was needed in developing clinically useful suicide assessment measures, but refrained from making specific recommendations in that regard.

Range and Knott

Range and Knott (1997) published a review of twenty suicide assessment instruments. These 20 instruments were classified as (1) clinician-rated, (2) self-rated, (3) those representing buffers against suicide, (4) assessment measures for adolescents and children, and (5) special purpose scales. The 20 scales reviewed by Range and Knott are also presented in Table 9.1 along with their original citations. Only two of these 20 suicide assessment scales overlapped with those reviewed by Rothberg and Geer-Williams (1992). In fact, Range and Knott purposely excluded many of the second-party informant scales from the earlier review because of their predominant focus on listings of demographic and status variables and the limited reliability and validity information available to support their use.

Range and Knott summarized their review of suicide assessment scales by suggesting that choices between the various instruments should be made on the basis of the (1) the purpose of assessment (i.e., research, screening, intervention), (2) the age of the respondent, (3) time considerations, and (4) the psychometric properties of the instrument. In contrast to Rothberg and Geer-Williams, these authors concluded their review by recommending three instruments above the rest for the clinical assessment of suicidality. Their recommendations were based on a number of criteria including the existing validity and reliability information, conciseness, and ease of administration. The instruments recommended by Range and Knott were the various forms of the Scale for Suicide Ideation (Beck, Kovacs, & Weissman, 1979), the Reasons for Living Inventory (Linehan, Goodstein, Nielson & Chiles, 1983), and the four-item version of Linehan's (1981) Suicide Behavior Questionnaire (Cole, 1988).

Westefeld and Colleagues

As part of their general overview of suicidology, Westefeld et al. (2000) provided a brief review of 12 suicide-specific measures in terms of their psychometric properties. In addition to examining 11 of the 20 suicide assessment measures reviewed by Range and Knott, these authors also provided a brief review of the Suicide Status Form (Jobes, Jacoby, Cimbolic, & Hustead, 1997) which had not been previously reviewed. These scales are listed in Table 9.1.

While Westefeld et al. took a less critical approach to their review of the various measures in terms of reliability and validity as compared with Rothberg and Geer-Williams and avoided making specific recommendations for choosing any one scale over the others as such as those made by Range and Knott, they did suggest that a number of the measures were particularly useful for assessing individuals with regard to specific suicide-related characteristics and for designing interventions. These measures were the Scale for Suicide Ideation (Beck et al., 1979), the Suicidal Ideation Scale (Rudd, 1989), the Suicide Behavior Questionnaire (Cole, 1988; Linehan, 1981), the Reasons for Living Inventory (Linehan et al., 1983), the Suicide Probability Scale (Cull & Gill, 1982), the Suicidal Ideation Questionnaire (Reynolds, 1987), the Multiattitude Suicide Tendency Scale (Orbach, Milstein, Har-Even, Apter, Tiano & Elizur, 1991), the Fairy Tales Test (Orbach, Feshback, Carlson, Glaubman, & Gross, 1983), and the Suicide Status Form (Jobes et al., 1997). Thus, Westefeld et al. seemed to have a more positive view of the clinical utility of suicide assessment measures as compared to the views of Rotherberg and Geer-Williams and Range and Knott.

Summary

Over the three reviews, the trend for suicide assessment scales had been to move from measures completed by clinicians based predominantly on demographic and status variables to measures either completed by the potentially suicidal individual or completed by the clinician based on self-reported information obtained through a clinical interview. Additionally, it appears that there has been an appropriate increase in focus on the psychometric issues of reliability and validity in the more current literature. As the first tier, suicide assessment scales that meet acceptable levels of psychometric reliability and validity at the aggregate level[22] can be considered for clinical use.

Recommendation 9.2: Examination of the reliability, validity, specificity and sensitivity of suicide assessment scales is paramount and ongoing as these characteristics tend to vary over time and across groups and settings. Therefore, suicide assessment scales, whether used for prediction or assessment, should be examined for their applicability to men and women, people of different ages and cultures/ethnicities and in different settings. For example, it is foolish to expect the

---

[22] See Crocker & Algina (1986) and Joint Committee on Standards for Education and Psychological Testing (1999) for a thorough discussion of these issues.

same scales to be useful in all settings whether a telephone crisis counselling service or a prison.

Consistent across the reviews offered by Rothberg and Geer-Williams (1992), Range and Knott, and Westefeld et al. (2000), however, has been a general lack of attention to the context of suicide assessment and the potential impact of that context with regard to the validity and reliability of self-report responses at the clinical level. Although Rothberg and Geer-Williams attempted to move somewhat beyond the aggregate evaluation of validity and reliability to consider the validity of selected suicide assessment scales at the clinical level, the analogue nature of their analysis and the lack of inter-rater reliability information regarding the application of the scales to the case summaries limits the usefulness of their results.

Ultimately, the validity of interpretations of scale scores vis á vis suicide risk or suicide potential at the clinical level must be affected by the context of assessment, and more specifically, the quality of the relationship in which assessment occurs. For example, Shea (1998, 1999) has discussed techniques aimed at improving the quality of the information garnered through the clinical interview by reducing client resistance around suicidal communications, and Finn and Tonsager (1992, 1997) have presented their therapeutic assessment model based on the premise that a collaborative approach to assessment can improve the accuracy and subsequent usefulness of the information collected via psychological measures. The conceptualizations of Shea and of Finn and Tonsager are presented below as we see them related to the application of psychometrically sound suicide assessment measures to clinical work with suicidal individuals.

Tier Two: Reliability And Validity In The Clinical Context

The assessment of risk for suicide most often occurs in the midst of a suicidal crisis: a situation where both the clinician and client are in a heightened state of emotionality. As Bonner (1990) has suggested, suicidal crises represent clinicians' "worst fear, often paralyzing the clinician emotionally and interfering with sound clinical judgment and effective crisis resolution" (p. 232). Training in suicide assessment and intervention is typically based on a crisis intervention model wherein the focus is on a rapid data-based assessment of risk for suicide based predominantly on self-report (Clark, 1998; Rogers, 2001; Rogers, Lewis, & Subich, 2002). Risk assessment then leads to a clinical judgment of suicide potential and a subsequent plan for safety and intervention (Kleespies, Deleppo, Mori, & Niles, 1998). In discussing the differences in interview strategies and purposes with a potentially suicidal client as opposed to a nonemergency client, Kleespies et al. suggested that:

> In the case of the former, the clinician will be preoccupied with assessing the degree of risk and formulating an appropriate response; in the case of the latter, the clinician may be far more interested in the patient's personal and family history and its relationship to the patient's presenting problem. (p. 42)

Thus, the typical context of suicide risk assessment is replete with strong emotional reactions on the part of both the client and clinician, is time-limited and highly structured by the clinician, and is focused on a more narrow range of topics viewed by the clinician as relevant to assessing risk and providing interventions. This is a scenario not particularly conducive to effective and open communication. Just as authors have discussed issues related to the validity of client information solicited in emergency assessment interviews in general (e.g., Kleespies et al., 1998; Shea, 1998), the same concerns exist for information collected via suicide assessment instruments. That is, regardless of appropriate reliability and validity support based on aggregate data, the reliability and validity of self-report information collected in the clinical use of any suicide assessment measure may be compromised as a function of the highly-charged, emotional context and the crisis intervention focus on risk assessment and response as secondary to developing a strong therapeutic relationship.

In the following sections, we discuss two general and interconnected approaches for enhancing the reliability and validity of information collected via suicide assessment measures in the clinical setting. The first approach references the work of Shea (1998, 1999) and Michel et al. (2001) and focuses on overcoming barriers to the open communication of suicide-related content between clinicians and clients within a therapeutic relationship. The development of an effective therapeutic relationship sets the groundwork for scale-based assessment that can be further enhanced by applying practices and principles embedded in Finn and Tonsager's (1992, 1997) therapeutic assessment model and feminist philosophies with regard to assessment (Santos de Barona & Dutton, 1997).

The Therapeutic Context: Setting The Stage For Effective Scale-Based Assessment

Consistent with Kleespies et al's. (1998) observation that clinicians working with suicidal clients are preoccupied with risk assessment and response, Michel et al. (2001) and Shea (1998, 1999) have presented arguments related to the tendency of clinicians working with suicidal clients to minimize attention to the therapeutic relationship. Michel et al. have suggested that a strong therapeutic relationship is a prerequisite for communication regarding suicidal intent to occur, while Shea has argued that the primary obstacle to collecting reliable and valid information via the clinical interview is low engagement on the part of the client in the interview process. Just as the therapeutic relationship is a precursor to effective communication in the clinical interview, it also provides the context for collecting reliable and valid data via self-report suicide assessment measures. Low engagement in the assessment process resulting from a limited therapeutic relationship will negatively impact the reliability and validity of information collected via suicide assessment scales in clinical work. Therefore, the recommendations made by Michel et al. and by Shea to improve the quality of the information garnered through the clinical interview are also relevant to enhancing the reliability and validity of data collected through suicide assessment measures.

Described as sources of resistance, Shea suggests that clients' values and beliefs regarding their own suicidality may include viewing suicide as a sign of weakness, seeing suicide as an immoral or sinful act, feeling that suicide is a taboo subject, concern over being perceived as crazy or fear of being "locked up," and having a true wish to die. Accordingly, these client "resistances," which can negatively impact the quality of the information garnered through the clinical interview, must be addressed in order to develop a productive therapeutic relationship. In much the same way, these resistances undoubtedly serve as obstacles to collecting reliable and valid data using suicide assessment scales. This may be especially true when assessment is conducted outside of the therapeutic relationship. For example, it is not unusual for clients to complete self-report suicide assessment scales as a result of an initial screening process conducted prior to meeting with a clinician. As a result of the potential complications as a function of clients' resistance-based beliefs and values, any interpretation of the assessment results in this scenario in terms of reliability and validity at the clinical level should be suspect.

In addition to the potential negative impact of client beliefs and values regarding suicidal behavior, unexplored beliefs and values of the clinician regarding suicide can also impede the development of a productive therapeutic relationship between the clinician and client (Shea, 1999). To the extent that clinicians hold and unwittingly communicate beliefs that suicide is a sign of weakness, sinful, unnatural or immoral, or an indication that one is "crazy," the reliability and validity of information collected in the clinical interview as well as from the use of suicide assessment sales will be negatively affected.

In summary, clients may have a number of personal beliefs and values that affect their willingness and ability to provide reliable and valid self-report responses to suicide assessment scales related to their suicidal thoughts, feelings, and behaviors. In addition, the negative impact of these beliefs and values on the reliability and validity of suicide assessment scales may be exacerbated by the crisis context in which suicide risk assessment is typically conducted in clinical work and the potential negative effects of the personal beliefs and values of the clinician on developing a therapeutic context conducive to open communication regarding suicide. In order to enhance the potential to derive reliable responses and valid conclusions from using suicide assessment scales in clinical work, clinicians are encouraged to consider the impact of their own beliefs and values regarding suicide and suicidal behavior, maintain a focus on developing a strong therapeutic relationship despite the "crisis" context, and explore and overcome potential sources of resistance to open communication that clients may bring with them to the assessment session prior to using any suicide assessment scale. Shea (1999) and Michel et al. (2001) provide more specific suggestions to clinicians related to improving the therapeutic relationship with suicidal clients, serving to set the stage for the effective use of suicide assessment scales in clinical work.

Collaborative Assessment Using Suicide Assessment Scales

Within the context of a therapeutic relationship focused on overcoming the obstacles to open communication regarding suicidal content, a collaborative approach to using suicide assessment scales can serve to further enhance their reliability and validity at the clinical level. In this regard, Finn and Tonsager (1992, 1997) have developed a comprehensive model of psychological assessment, commonly referred to as Therapeutic Assessment (TA).

According to these authors, TA is unique to the body of literature in assessment in that it is a model grounded in theory, employs specific techniques, and represents a collaborative approach between client and therapist. Finn and Tonsager suggest that the primary goal of TA is the creation of a transforming and connecting therapeutic experience for the client in the context of the assessment. It is our contention that, based on the underlying philosophies and the model's impact on the therapeutic relationship, the application of the principles of TA with suicidal clients will result in substantial increases in the reliability of self-report information and the validity of the interpretations of scores derived from suicide assessment measures.

Influential to the development of TA were the humanistic movement of the 1950's and 1960's and the dissonance believed to be associated with the traditional rigid, mechanistic, and impersonal approach to assessment in more recent times. These influences on assessment fostered their conceptualization of the assessment process as one that could be therapeutic and beneficial to the client as opposed to being structured solely to provide data for the clinician. Thus, the TA model is viewed by Finn and Tonsager as representing a shift from traditional information-gathering assessment strategies toward more client-centered, collaborative, and therapeutic assessment. Newman and Greenway (1997) described the common processes of the TA model of assessment as beginning with a collaboration between the clinician and the client on the assessment question or questions. Following the assessment, the clinician provides feedback to the client in thematic form, and the client is asked to summarize and validate what he or she has heard from the clinician regarding the assessment information.

In addition to its humanistic influences, the TA model is also consistent with recommendations for change in traditional assessment that have emerged from feminist perspectives. For example, Santos de Barona and Dutton (1997) suggest that assessment grounded in feminist theory would embody a process striving to empower the client and should be collaborative in nature. Thus, assessment from a feminist perspective, much like TA, begins with collaboratively established hypotheses and goals and includes client participation in the collection and interpretation of assessment data, as well as in the recommendations drawn from the assessment. Both TA and feminist assessment philosophies strive to create a therapeutic experience for the client within the assessment process that accentuates collaboration and mutuality.

Although research on therapeutic assessment models is generally sparse, a few empirical studies have focused on Finn and Tonsager's TA model and have found supporting evidence for the efficacy of therapeutic assessment. Finn and Tonsager (1992) for example, examined the effect of MMPI-2 test feedback on a group of college students on a counseling center waiting-list. Those participants who heard their test results showed a decline in symptomatic distress and an increase in self-esteem and hope regarding their problems, and experienced a more positive impression of their experience than a group taking the MMPI-2 without feedback. These self-reported benefits continued to be present at a two-week follow-up.

Further evidence of the efficacy of MMPI-2 feedback as an intervention was demonstrated in Newman and Greenway's (1997) replication study of Finn and Tonsager's (1992) earlier work. Newman and Greenway found symptom relief and gains in self-esteem in a group of university students seeking counseling when compared to a control group. Finally, Ackerman, Hilsenroth, Baity, and Blagys (2000) compared a TA model to a basic information-gathering model in an ecologically-valid study of counseling dyads at a university counseling center. The authors' findings again suggested the value of TA as evidenced by an increase in adherence to treatment and in the quality of the therapeutic alliance.

Summary

Despite the potential psychometric strengths of any suicide assessment scale in the aggregate, its application at the clinical level may or may not produce reliable data leading to valid interpretations. The primary determining factor in this regard is the ability of the client to share his or her suicidal thoughts, feelings, and behaviors with the clinician through item responses. The potential that the client may openly share suicide-related content can be enhanced through a therapeutic relationship focused on minimizing the limiting effects of the crisis situation and addressing sources of client resistances to the communication of that content. In addition, a mutual and collaborative approach to using any suicide assessment scale as embedded in the TA and feminist philosophies should serve to optimize the potential for collecting reliable self-report data and making appropriate interpretations regarding suicidal risk at the clinical level.

Recommendation 9.3: In developing suicide risk assessment measures and protocols, research should be undertaken to examine the impact of the clinician, the client, and their interaction.

Recommendation 9.4: Additional models and approaches, which may hold potential for improving the quality of the assessment relationship and the resulting judgment of risk, should be explored. Beyond the therapeutic assessment and feminist models explored here, alternative methods based on age, gender, and culture/ethnic perspectives should be considered.

One suicide assessment scale that specifically attempts to address these relationship-based issues as part of its administration protocol is the Suicide Status Form (Jobes, 2006). Thus, we next provide an overview of this scale and its intended application as an example of how reliability and validity may be enhanced through greater attention to the therapeutic relationship.

A Therapeutically-Based Model For Using A Suicide Assessment Scale

While the TA model has not been specifically applied to suicide risk assessment, Jobes (2006), Jobes, Jacoby, Cimbolic, and Hustead (1997) and Jobes et al. (2000) have presented an assessment model that employs many of the TA and feminist principles. This model, termed the Collaborative Assessment and Management of Suicidality (CAMS) approach was developed specifically for work with suicidal clients. The assessment instrument used in CAMS is the Suicide Status Form (SSF), a self-report measure of the client's potential for self-harm. According to the authors, the CAMS approach including the SSF has been influenced by many theoretical models, including the work of Beck, Rush, Shaw and Emery (1979), Shneidman (1993), and Baumeister (1990), and emphasizes the assessment of suicidality within the therapeutic relationship. Similar to the TA and feminist models, the SSF is used in the context of the therapeutic relationship and with the intention of working from a shared perspective between client and clinician. It is, therefore, completed in a collaborative and interactive fashion to provide insight into the underlying variables related to the client's suicidality. Jobes et al. suggest that the unique outcome of the application of the CAMS model is the development of a therapeutic alliance through the process of assessing suicidality, an outcome which is foregone to the mechanistic gathering of data in traditional information-gathering models.

As the cornerstone of the CAMS approach, the SSF is a suicide assessment measure that consists of five theoretically-based items self-rated by the client on a five-point rating scale. Three of the items are grounded in Shneidman's (1987) cubic model of suicide (i.e., pain, press and perturbation), one item is a rating of hopelessness based in the work of Beck et al. (1979), and one item is a rating of self-hate (Neuringer, 1974). The SSF also includes a self-rating of overall suicide risk to complete its six basic items. Auxiliary items include those related to the client's desire to live, desire to die, and items addressing the relationship between suicidal thoughts and thoughts and feelings related to ones self and to others. In addition to these rated items, the SSF prompts the suicidal individual to list and rank order in terms of importance, up to five reasons for living and five reasons for dying (based on the work of Linehan et al., 1983).

Preliminary psychometric evidence for the six basic items of the SSF has been generally supportive of the use of the measure based upon aggregate data (Jobes et al., 1997). For example, two-week test-retest reliability coefficients for the five theoretically-based items and the overall rating of risk have ranged from .35 to .69. Although, in a traditional sense, these coefficients are relatively low, given the theoretical conceptualizations of the six basic items as transient and amenable to intervention, this range of coefficients has been interpreted by the authors as reflecting a moderate level of score reliability (Jobes et al., 1997). Construct-related validity evidence for the interpretation of the six SSF items has been supported through convergent procedures. Convergent validity analyses have resulted in validity coefficients ranging from .25 to .74 and claims for the criterion-related validity of the interpretations of the items have been made as a function of the ability of the six items to differentiate statistically between suicidal clients and nonsuicidal college students.

Consistent with the principles of TA and feminist assessment, Jobes (2006) outlined procedures for using the SSF that are intended to promote collaboration between the clinician and the client, augment the therapeutic relationship, and from our perspective, enhance the reliability of the self-ratings on the SSF and the validity of subsequent interpretations of the scale in relationship to suicide risk. The procedures outlined by Jobes et al. include a thorough discussion of the purposes of the assessment, an open discussion of the client's responses in the context of a warm, accepting and non-judgmental relationship, and a collaborative interpretation of the results of the assessment including the meaning of the results for continued assessment and intervention.

While CAMS provides a generally clear and systematic example of how a suicide assessment scale (i.e., the SSF) can be imbedded into a therapeutic context in order to enhance the reliability of the responses and the validity of subsequent interpretations, similar processes can be used with any psychometrically-sound suicide assessment scale. Thus, rather than administer suicide assessment measures outside of the therapeutic relationship where responses may be contaminated by client resistances (based on communication-limiting personal values) and beliefs and by clinician-centered interpretations of the results, exploring possible resistances prior to assessment and administering suicide assessment scales in a collaborative manner is likely to result in increased reliability of client responses and more meaningful, appropriate, and useful interpretations in relationship to client suicidality.

Recommendation 9.5: While collaborative and other empowerment models may make intuitive sense with regard to their potential to increase the validity and reliability of risk assessment data, appropriate effectiveness and efficacy research needs to be conducted to support their usefulness.

Conclusion

Past reviews of suicide assessment scales have focused almost exclusively on the psychometric characteristics of scale reliability and validity determined from group or aggregate data. Across these reviews, it has been recommended that scales meeting minimal standards of reliability and validity may be considered for use in the clinical assessment of suicidal individuals. Missing from these recommendations, however, has been a consideration of the impact of the assessment setting and various client and clinician values and beliefs regarding suicide that may negatively impact the reliability and validity of suicide assessment scales at the clinical level, despite the strength of their psychometric properties at the aggregate level.

In this chapter, we have argued that the broad consideration of reliability and validity represents only the first tier in decisions regarding suicide assessment scales in clinical work and that the second tier should be a consideration of contributions to the reliability and validity of suicide assessment scale responses of the assessment setting, the personal beliefs and values of the suicidal client regarding suicide and suicidal individuals, and the personal beliefs of the clinician regarding suicide and suicidal individuals. Grounded in the work of Shea (1998, 1999) and Michel et al. (2001), we have suggested that pre-assessment attention to these issues through the therapeutic relationship will improve the quality of the response to suicide assessment scales. Additionally, we have argued that the clinical use of a collaborative and mutual therapeutic assessment process as outlined by Finn and Tonsager (1997) and supported by feminist assessment philosophies (Santos de Barona & Dutton, 1997) and extended to suicide assessment by Jobes et al. (2000) will further enhance the reliability of item responses and the validity of interpretations of those responses in the clinical work with suicidal individuals.

While we acknowledge the fact that empirical research in support of these concepts is currently limited, we encourage scientist-practitioners to broaden their approach to investigating the reliability and validity of suicide assessment scales to incorporate a consideration of a clinically-based approach to enhancing the usefulness of these scales. To the extent that this occurs, the long held goal in suicidology to reliably and validly inform the clinical assessment of suicidal individuals via suicide assessment scales may yet be achieved.

References

Ackerman, S. J., Hilsenroth, M. J., Baity, M. R., & Blagys, M. D. (2000). Interaction of therapeutic process and alliance during psychological assessment. *Journal of Personality Assessment,* 75(1), 82–109.

Baumeister, R. F. (1990). Suicide as escape from self. *Psychological Review,* 97, 90–113.

Beck, A. T., Kovacs, M., & Weissman, A. (1979). Assessment of suicidal ideation: The scale for suicide ideation. *Journal of Consulting & Clinical Psychology,* 47, 343–352.

Beck, A. T., Resnik, H. L., & Lettieri, D. J. (Eds.). (1974). *The prediction of suicide.* Bowie, MD: Charles Press.

Beck, A. T., Rush, A. J., Shaw, B. F., & Emery, G. (1979). *Cognitive therapy of depression.* New York: Guilford.

Beck, A. T., Schuyler, D., & Herman, I. (1974). Development of suicidal intent scales. In A. T. Beck, H. L. P. Resnik, & D. J. Lettieri (Eds.), *The prediction of suicide,* pp. 45–56. Bowie, MD: Charles Press.

Beck, A., Steer, R., & Ranieri, W. (1998). Scale for Suicide Ideation: Psychometric properties of a self-report version. *Journal of Clinical Psychology,* 44, 499–505.

Beck, A. T., Weissman, A., Lester, D., & Trexler, L. (1974). The measurement of pessimism: The Hopelessness Scale. *Journal of Consulting & Clinical Psychology,* 42, 861–865.

Berman, A. L. (1992). Five potential suicide cases. In R. W. Maris, A. L. Berman, J. T. Maltsberger, & R. I. Yufit (Eds.), *Assessment and prediction of suicide,* pp. 235–254. New York: Guilford.

Bonner, R. L. (1990). A "M.A.P." to the clinical assessment of suicide risk. *Journal of Mental Health Counseling,* 12, 232–236.

Buglas, D., & Horton, J. (1974). A scale for predicting subsequent suicidal behavior. *British Journal of Psychiatry,* 124, 573–578.

Clark, D. C. (1998). The evaluation and management of the suicidal patient. In P. M. Kleespies (Ed.), *Emergencies in mental health practice: Evaluation and management,* pp. 75–94. New York: Guilford.

Cohen, E., Motto, J. A., & Seiden, R. H. (1966). An instrument for evaluating suicide potential: A preliminary study. *American Journal of Psychiatry,* 122, 886–891.

Cole, D. A. (1988). Hopelessness, social desirability, depression and parasuicide in two college student samples. *Journal of Consulting & Clinical Psychology*, 56, 131–136.

Cotton, C. R., & Range, L. M. (1993). Suicidality, hopelessness and attitudes toward life and death in children. *Death Studies*, 16, 79–86.

Crocker, L., & Algina, J. (1986). *Introduction to classical and modern test theory.* Orlando, FL: Holt, Rinehart & Winston.

Cull, J. G., & Gill, W. S. (1982). *Suicide Probability Scale manual.* Los Angeles: Western Psychological Services.

Dean, R. A., Miskimins, W., DeCook, R., Wilson, L. T., & Maley, R. F. (1967). Prediction of suicide in a psychiatric hospital. *Journal of Clinical Psychology*, 23, 296–301.

Domino, G., Moore, D., Westlake, I., & Gibson, L. (1982). Attitudes toward suicide: A factor analytic approach. *Journal of Clinical Psychology*, 38, 257–262.

Exner, J. E., & Wylie, J. (1977). Some Rorschach data concerning suicide. *Journal of Personality Assessment*, 41, 339–348.

Farberow, N. L. (1981). Assessment of suicide. In P. McReynolds (Ed.), *Advances in psychological assessment, Volume 5*, pp. 124–190. San Francisco: Jossey-Bass.

Farberow, N. L., & MacKinnon, D. R. (1974a). A suicide prediction schedule for neuropsychiatric hospital patients. *Journal of Nervous & Mental Disease*, 158, 408–419.

Farberow, N. L., & MacKinnon, D. R. (1974b). Prediction of suicide in neuropsychiatric hospital patients. In C. Neuringer (Ed.), *Psychological assessment of suicidal risk*, pp. 186–224. Springfield, IL: Charles C. Thomas.

Finn, S. E., & Tonsager, M. E. (1992). Therapeutic effects of providing MMPI-2 test feedback to college students awaiting therapy. *Psychological Assessment*, 4(3), 278–287.

Finn, S. E., & Tonsager, M. E. (1997). Information-gathering and therapeutic models of assessment: Complementary paradigms. *Psychological Assessment*, 9, 374–385.

Holmes, C. B., & Howard, M. E. (1980). Recognition of suicide lethality factors by physicians, mental health professionals, ministers, and college students. *Journal of Consulting & Clinical Psychology*, 48, 383–387.

Ivanoff, A., & Jang, S. J. (1991). The role of hopelessness and social desirability in predicting suicidal behavior: A study of prison inmates. *Journal of Consulting & Clinical Psychology*, 59, 394–399.

Ivanoff, A., Jang, S. J., Smyth, N. F., & Linehan, M. M. (1994). Fewer reasons for staying alive when you are thinking of killing yourself: The Brief Reasons for Living Inventory. *Journal of Psychopathology & Behavioral Assessment*, 16, 1–13.

Jobes, D. A., (2006). *Managing suicidal risk: A collaborative approach.* New York: Guilford.

Jobes, D. A., Eyman, J. R., & Yufit, R. I. (1995). How clinicians assess suicide risk in adolescents & adults. *Crisis Intervention*, 2, 1–12.

Jobes, D. A., Jacoby, A., Cimbolic, P., & Hustead, L. (1997). Assessment and treatment of suicidal clients in a university counseling center. *Journal of Counseling Psychology*, 44, 368–377.

Jobes, D. A., Luoma, J. B., Jacoby, A. M., & Mann, R. E. (2000). Manual for the collaborative assessment and management of suicidality (CAMS). Unpublished manuscript, Catholic University, Washington, DC.

Joint Committee on Standards for Educational and Psychological Testing (1999). *The standards for educational and psychological testing.* Washington, DC: American Educational Research Association.

Kleespies, P. M., Deleppo, J. D., Mori, D. L., & Niles, B. L. (1998). The emergency interview. In Kleespies, P. M. (Ed.), *Emergencies in mental health practice: Evaluation and management*, pp. 75–94. New York: Guilford.

Kowalchuk, B., & King, J. D. (1998). Life Orientation Inventory: A method of assessing suicide risk. Austin, TX: Pro-ed.

Lester, D. (1970). Attempts to predict suicidal risk using psychological tests. *Psychological Bulletin*, 74, 1–17.

Lettieri, D. J. (1974). Research issues in developing prediction scales. In C. Neuringer (Ed.), *Psychological assessment of suicidal risk*, pp. 43–73. Springfield, IL: Charles C. Thomas.

Lewinsohn, P. M., Garrison, C. z., Langhinrichsen, J., & Marsteller, F. (1989). *The assessment of suicidal behavior in adolescents*. Rockville, MD: National Institute of Mental Health. (Contract Report No. 316774–76, Child and Adolescent disorders Research Branch)

Linehan, M. M. (1981). Suicidal behaviors questionnaire. Unpublished inventory, University of Washington, Seattle.

Linehan, M., Goodstein, J., Nielsen, S., & Chiles, J. (1983). Reasons for staying alive when you are thinking of killing yourself: The Reasons for Living Inventory. *Journal of Consulting & Clinical Psychology*, 51, 276–286.

Maris, R. W. (1992). Overview of the study of suicide assessment and prediction. In R. W. Maris, A. L. Berman, J. T. Maltsberger & R. I. Yufit (Eds.), *Assessment and prediction of suicide*, pp. 3–22. New York: Guilford.

Michel, K., Leenaars, A. A., Jobes, D. A., Orbach, I., Valach, L., Young, R. A., Dey, P., & Bostwick, M. (2001). Meeting the suicidal person: New perspectives for the clinician. Retrieved November 12, 2002, from http://www.aeschiconference.unibe.ch/index.html.

Miller, I. W., Norman, W. H., Bishop, S. B., & Dow, M. G. (1986). The Modified Scale for Suicide Ideation: Reliability and validity. *Journal of Consulting & Clinical Psychology*, 54, 724–725.

Motto, J. A., Heilbron, D. C., & Juster, R. P. (1985). Development of a clinical instrument to estimate suicide risk. *American Journal of Psychiatry*, 142, 680–686

Neimeyer, R. A., & MacInnes, W. D. (1981). Assessing paraprofessional competence with the Suicide Intervention Response Inventory. *Journal of Counseling Psychology*, 28, 176–179.

Neuringer, C. (1974). Attitudes toward self in suicidal individuals. *Life-Threatening Behavior*, 4, 96–106.

Newman, M. L., & Greenway, P. (1997). Therapeutic effects of providing feedback to clients at a university counseling service: A collaborative approach. *Psychological Assessment*, 9(2), 122–131.

Orbach, I., Feshbach, S., Carlson, G., Glaubman, H., & Gross, Y. (1983). Attraction and repulsion by life and death in suicidal and normal children. *Journal of Consulting & Clinical Psychology*, 51, 661–670.

Orbach, I., Milstein, I., Har-Even, D., Apter, A., Tiano, S., & Elizur, A. (1991). A Multi-Attitude Suicide Tendency Scale for adolescents. *Journal of Consulting & Clinical Psychology*, 3, 398–404.

Pallis, D. J., Barraclough, B. M., Levey, A. B., Jenkins, J. S., & Sainsbury, P. (1982). Estimating suicide risk among attempted suicides: I. The development of new clinical scales. *British Journal of Psychiatry*, 141, 37–44.

Patterson, W. M., Dohn, H. H., Bird, J., & Patterson, G. A. (1983). Evaluation of suicide patients: The SAD PERSONS scale. *Psychosomatics*, 24, 343–352.

Pierce, D. W. (1977). Suicidal intent in self-injury. *British Journal of Psychiatry*, 130, 377–385.

Plutchik, R., van Praag, H. M., Conte, H. R., & Picard, S. (1989). Correlates of suicide and violence risk: 1. The Suicide Risk Measure. *Comprehensive Psychiatry*, 30, 296–302.

Range, L. M., & Knott, E. C. (1997). Twenty suicide assessment instruments: Evaluation and recommendations. *Death Studies*, 21, 25–58.

Reynolds, W. M. (1987). *Suicide Ideation Questionnaire: Professional manual*. Odessa, FL: Psychological Assessment Resources.

Rogers, J. R. (2001). Suicide risk assessment. In E. R. Welfel & R. E. Ingersoll (Eds.), *The mental health desk reference*, pp. 259–264. New York: John Wiley & Sons.

Rogers, J. R., Lewis, M. M., & Subich, L. M. (2002). Validity of the Suicide Assessment Checklist in an emergency crisis center. *Journal of Counseling & Development*, 80, 493–502.

Rogers, J. R., & Oney, K. M. (2005). Clinical use of suicide assessment scales: Enhancing reliability and validity through the therapeutic relationship. In R. I. Yufit and D. Lester (Eds.), *Assessment, Treatment, and Prevention of Suicidal Behavior*, pp. 7–27. Hoboken, NJ: John Wiley & Sons, Inc.

Rothberg, J. M., & Geer-Williams, C. (1992). A comparison and review of suicide prediction scales. In R. W. Maris, A. L. Berman, J. T. Maltsberger & R. I. Yufit, (Eds.), *Assessment and prediction of suicide*, pp. 202–217. New York: Guilford.

Rudd, M. D. (1989). The prevalence of suicidal ideation among college students. *Suicide & Life-Threatening Behavior*, 19, 173–183.

Santos de Barona, M., & Dutton, M. A. (1997). Feminist perspectives on assessment. In J. Worell & N. G. Johnson (Eds.), *Shaping the Future of Feminist Psychology: Education, Research, and Practice*, pp. 37–56. Washington, DC: American Psychological Association.

Shea, S. C. (1999). *The practical art of suicide assessment*. New York: John Wiley.

Shea, S. C. (1998). *Psychiatric Interviewing: The art of understanding (2nd Edition)*. Philadelphia: Saunders.

Shneidman, E. S. (1987). A psychological approach to suicide. In G. R. Vandenbos & B. K. Bryant (Eds.), *Cataclysms, crises, and catastrophes*, pp. 151–183. Washington, DC: American Psychological Association.

Shneidman, E. S. (1993). *Suicide as psychache: A clinical approach to self-destructive behavior*. Northvale, NJ: Jason Aronson.

Smith, K., Conroy, R. W., & Ehler, B. D. (1984). Lethality of Suicide Attempt Rating Scale. *Suicide & Life-Threatening Behavior*, 14, 215–242.

Tuckman, J., & Youngman, W. F. (1968). Assessment of suicide risk in attempted suicides. In H. L. Resnik (Ed.), *Suicidal behaviors: Diagnosis and management*, pp. 190–197. Boston: Little, Brown.

Westefeld, J. S., Badura, A., Kiel, J. T., & Scheel, K. (1996a). The College Student Reasons for Living Inventory: Additional psychometric data. *Journal of College Student Development*, 37, 348–351.

Westefeld, J. S., Badura, A., Kiel, J. T., & Scheel, K. (1996b). Development of the College Student Reasons for Living Inventory with African Americans. *Journal of College Student Psychotherapy*, 10, 61–65.

Westefeld, J. S., Cardin, D., & Deaton, W. (1992). Development of the College Student Reasons for Living Inventory. *Suicide & Life-Threatening Behavior*, 22, 442–452.

Westefeld, J. S., Scheel, K., & Maples, M. R. (1998). Psychometric analysis of the College Student Reasons for Living Inventory utilizing a clinical population. *Measurement and Evaluation in Counseling & Development*, 31, 86–94.

Westefeld, J. S., Range, L. M., Rogers, J. R., Maples, M. R., Bromley, J. L., & Alcorn, J. (2000). Suicide: An overview. *The Counseling Psych*ologist, 28(4), 445–510.

Zung, W. W. K., & Moore, J. (1976). Suicide potential in a normal adult population. *Psychosomatics*, 17(1), 37–41.

Table 9.1. Reviews of Suicide Assessment Scales

Title of Measure	*Original Citation*
Suicide Measures:	
Hopelessness Scale[a,c]	Beck et al., 1974
Brief Reasons for Living Inventory (RFL-B)[b,c]	Ivanoff et al., 1994
Clinical Instrument to Estimate Suicide Risk (CIESR)[a]	Motto et al., 1985
College Student Reasons for Living Inventory (CSRLI)[b,c]	Westefeld et al., 1992, 1996, 1998
Fairy Tales Test (FT) aka Life and Death Attitude Scale or Suicidal Tendencies Test[b,c]	Orbach et al., 1983
Index of Potential Suicide[a]	Zung, 1974
Instrument for the Evaluation of Suicide Potential (IESP)[a]	Cohen et al., 1966
Intent Scale[a]	Pierce, 1977
Lethality of Suicide Attempt Rating Scale (LSARS)[b]	Smith et al., 1984
Life Orientation Inventory (LOI)[b]	Kowalchuk & King, 1988
Los Angeles Suicide Prevention Center Scale (LASPC)[a]	Beck et al., 1974
Modified Scale for Suicide Tendency Scale (MAST)[b,c]	Miller et al., 1986
Multiattitude Suicide Tendency Scale (MAST)[b,c]	Orbach et al., 1991
Neuropsychiatric Hospital Suicide Prediction Schedule[a]	Farberow & MacKinnon, 1974
Prison Suicidal Behaviors Interview (PSBI)[b]	Ivanoff & Jang, 1991
Reasons for Living Inventory (RFL)[a,b,c]	Linehan et al., 1983
SAD Persons (SP)[a]	Patterson et al., 1983
Scale for Assessing Suicide Risk[a]	Tuckman & Youngman, 1968
Scale for Predicting Suicidal Behavior (SPSB)[a]	Buglas & Horton, 1974
Scale for Suicide Ideation (SSI)[b,c]	Beck et al., 1979
Self-Related Scale for Suicide Ideation (SSI-SR)[b]	Beck et al., 1988
Short Risk Scale (SRS)[a]	Pallis et al., 1982
Suicid al Death Prediction Scale, Long (SDPS-L) and Short Forms (SDPS-S)[a]	Lettieri 1974
Suicidal Ideation Questionnaire (SIQ)[b,c]	Reynolds, 1987
Suicidal Ideation Scale (SIS)[b,c]	Rudd, 1989
Suicide Behaviors Questionnaire (SBQ)[b,c]	Linehan, 1981
Suicide Behaviors Questionnaire for Children (SBQ-C)[b]	Cotton & Range, 1993
Suicide Intent Scale aka Suicidal Intent Scale (SNS)[a,b]	Beck et al., 1974
Suicide Intervention Response Inventory (SIRI)[b,c]	Neimeyer & MacInnes, 1981
Suicide Lethality Scale aka Lethality Scale or Suicide Potential Rating Scale (SLS)[b]	Holmes & Howard, 1980
Suicide Opinion Questionnaire (SOQ)[b]	Domino et al., 1982
Suicide Potential Scale (SPS)[a]	Dean et al., 1967
Suicide Probability Scale (SPS)[a,b,c]	Cull & Gill, 1982
Suicide Risk Measure[a]	Plutchik et al., 1989
Suicide Status Form (SSF)[c]	Jobes et al., 1997

[a]Rothberg & Geer-Williams, 1992
[b]Range & Knott, 1997
[c]Westefeld et al., 2000

10

Fads in Research: Sex Differences in Suicidal Behavior

The popular notion of research in any field is that it plods along, adding brick after brick, until a magnificent edifice is constructed. Sometimes that steady progress is halted because a seemingly insurmountable obstacle is encountered. Once that problem is solved, the steady progress can be resumed. A good example in the field of energy is nuclear fusion reactors, which is the 1960s seemed to be the energy source of the future. But it was difficult (and expensive) to contain the atoms to be fused at a sufficiently high temperature. In the 1990s, the possibility of "cold fusion" was raised, but this seemed to be a false lead. Today, nuclear fusion is once again a possibility and research is continuing.

At the present time, a better way to describe the state of suicidology is with the concept of "fads." Topics gain attention, and there is a flurry of research on them. Then, without any of the basic questions being answered, interest in the topic dies, and it is not clear whether interest will ever return. Many examples can be given. In the 1970s and 1980s, there were many studies in several countries to evaluate the effectiveness of suicide prevention centers, but very little research on this was conducted, if any, in the 21st Century. Research on contagion effects similarly crested and then declined to a small trickle.

This purpose of the present chapter is take one of these "fads," explore its genesis, growth and decline, and draw some recommendations from this history. The fad chosen is that of sex differences in suicidal behavior.

Sex Differences In Suicidal Behavior[23]

The interest in sex differences in suicidal in women began in the 1980s, with books appearing by Neuringer and Lettieri (1982) and Lester (1988), and continued into the 1990s when a book by Canetto and Lester (1995) appeared. Thereafter, interest receded until the discovery that women in China had a higher suicide rate than men, whereupon a slew of papers appeared speculating on the reasons for this, but virtually no research was conducted. Since then, there has been silence.

A similar trend exists in "feminist" approaches to suicidal behavior. Initial articles by Lester (1989) and Canetto and Lester (1998) were accompanied by an edited book

---

[23] The following sections are not intended to be an exhaustive review of the research on this topic.

from Canetto and Lester (1995), but no unique feminist theory of suicidal behavior has ever appeared.

Let us first briefly review the major research and theoretical issues in this field.

Sex Differences in Completed and Attempted Suicide

One of the most consistent findings from research into suicidal behavior is that males kill themselves more than females. In contrast, females attempt suicide more than males. This sex difference has been found in almost all nations, in almost all eras, and in almost all subgroups of the population of a given nation (for example, in white and black Americans, in the single, widowed, married, and divorced, and in all age groups).

It is very difficult to trace all completed and attempted suicides in a community, but three early efforts were made to do this. Farberow and Shneidman (1961) in Los Angeles in 1957 found 540 men but only 228 women who completed suicide. In contrast, they located 1824 women but only 828 men who had attempted suicide. Yap (1958) in Hong Kong located 145 men but only 118 women who had completed suicide, whereas he located 508 women but only 386 men who had attempted suicide. In the Netherlands, de Graaf and Kruyt (1976) located 731 male and 478 female completed suicides as compared to 1562 male and 2551 female attempted suicides.

More recently, Shichor and Bergman (1979) found 452 male and 345 female completed suicides in Israel in 1962–1968, along with 1241 male and 1975 female attempted suicides. The sex difference was not found in those 65 years of age and older. Koczan and Ozsvath (1990) calculated rates of suicidal behavior in one Hungarian county for 1984–1986. The completed suicide rate for men was 87 per 100,000 per year and for women 28; the attempted suicide rate for men was 261 and for women 348.

Sex Ratios in Completed Suicide

Data for completed suicides are more easily obtained since these deaths are officially recorded with somewhat reasonable accuracy. Looking at mortality statistics male suicide rates exceed female suicide rates both across the United States and across the world. In the latest figures for the 21st Century from the World Health Organization (www.who.int/mental_health/prevention/suicide_rates/en/print.html)[24], the ratio of the male suicide rate to the female suicide ranged from 1.4 in Albania (in 2003) to 8.4 in Belize (in 2001).

Lester (1990c) looked at the male/female completed suicide rate ratio for 31 nations. The ratio was lower in wealthier nations for older adults, but higher in wealthier nations for younger adults, suggesting that the sex ratio may be differently determined in young and older adults. Comparing 23 nations in 1974 and 1986, Pritchard (1990) concluded that the trend was for the male/female suicide rate ratio to widen, and Lester (1993a) found the male/female suicide rate ratio increased in the majority of nations

---

[24] Accessed December 13th, 2008.

from 1970 to 1984. The ratio in the nations in 1970 was not associated with gender equality.

Javanainen (1990) looked at the male/female suicide rate ratio for completed suicide in Finland and found that it was lower in the more educated, the upper social class and in urban regions. The ratio was lower in the richer Finns, primarily due to a relatively lower suicide rate in the richer men.

Why does this ratio differ in these different groups?

Sex Ratios in Attempted Suicide

Kessler and McRae (1983) reviewed forty-five studies of attempted suicides from 1940 to 1980 and found that the female/male ratio increased up to 1970, where it peaked, and decreased thereafter.

Why did this ratio increase during the period of 1940 to 1980 and what has happened since 1980?

Attempted Suicide/Completed Suicide Ratios

A popular measure in research on suicide in psychiatric disorders is the attempted to completed suicide ratio. For example, this ratio ranges from 20:1 to 40:1 in the general population, whereas this ratio is about 3:1 in patients with bipolar disorder (Baldessarini et al., 2006). It would be of interest to examine this ratio in different groups of women and men, but no studies have yet appeared on this variable.

Variations and Changes in These Ratios

It is important to document how all of these ratios vary over different groups of the population (by age, ethnicity, marital status, and so on), over regions of countries and the world, and over time and how they vary by personal characteristics (such as psychiatric disorder). Once the variations in ratios as a function of these different classifications are identified, hypotheses as to why ratios vary as they do need to be formulated and tested.

Recommendation 10.1: Identifying the existence of sex ratios in death by suicide and non-lethal suicidal behavior should be viewed as only the preliminary step for research in this area. Beyond identifying broad social/economic differences, research should focus on identifying underlying reasons for both the general consistency in sex differences in suicidal behavior as well as exploring the factors that contribute to differences.

Suicide in Professional Women

Among professionals, the sex difference in suicide is much less. In some studies, females have been found to have a higher suicide rate than males. For example, female physicians have a higher suicide rate than male physicians (Ross, 1973). In other occupations, such as nurses, chemists, and psychologists, the female suicide rate is greater than for the general female population, though still less than the male suicide rate for those occupations. This increased suicide rate among female professionals may be caused in part by the role conflicts created for females when they work. Furthermore, professional females may experience greater stress in their work (as a result of sexism) than do males. It also appears that stressors from a career may be more suicidogenic than stressors from other sources.

Research on this issue has been hindered by the reluctance of professional organizations to note the cause of death in the obituary lists in their journals and magazines. In the 1970s, the cause of death was often listed, and this facilitated research on the topic. The omission of cause of death may reflect the stigma that is still associated with suicide. However, several states do document the occupation of those dying, and Stack has conducted several studies of suicide in different occupational groups but, although he controls for sex in the multivariate analyses (e.g., Stack, 1996), he has not yet studied the differential rates by occupation in men and women in detail.

Marital Status and Suicidal Behavior

Gove (1972, 1979) explored the relationship between marital status and completed suicide for males and females. After World War II, females had higher rates of mental illness in the United States, and in particular, married women have higher rates of mental illness than married men. In contrast, never-married men have higher rates of mental illness than never-married women. Gove concluded that marriage reduces psychiatric stress for males but increases psychiatric stress for females. Marriage is more advantageous for men than for women.

Gove examined the ratio of the suicide rate for never-married to married individuals, an index called by Durkheim (1897) the coefficient of preservation. If Gove's hypothesis is correct this ratio should be higher for males than for females. For the U.S. for 1959–61 the ratio for males aged 26–64 years of age was 2.0 and for females it was 1.5. Single males were 97 percent more likely to complete suicide than married males, while single females were 47 percent more likely to complete suicide than married females. (Divorce and widowhood also seems to be more disadvantageous for males than for females.) Gove also presented data to show that this same pattern appeared when rates of threatened and attempted suicide were examined. Durkheim's coefficient of preservation was consistently higher for males than for females. According to Gove, "there have been changes in the women's role that have been detrimental to (married) women and that, as marital roles are presently constituted in our society, marriage is more advantageous to men than to women while being single (widowed, divorced) is more disadvantageous" (Gove, 1972, pp. 211–212).

Although Daeid (1997) confirmed in Ireland that marriage had a greater protective effect on suicide rates for men than for women, this differential protective effect of marriage has not been studied over time and in different countries and in different subgroups of the population (differing by age, ethnicity, social class, etc.).

Recommendation 10.2: Observed aggregate differences in suicidal behaviors related to professional and marital status provide little information with regard to understanding suicidal behavior. As we discuss again in Chapter 11, most married men and women do not engage in suicidal behaviors nor do most professional women. What is needed is for research in this area to move forward by beginning to identify specific characteristics of marriages and professions that may interact with individual characteristics to lead to suicidal behavior.

Explanations for the Sex Difference

Methods for Suicide

Women use different methods for suicide than those used by men. Some have suggested that this difference occurs because men prefer "active" (or violent) methods such as hanging and shooting while women prefer "passive" methods such as drugs and poisons. However, more subtle differences exist. For example, when suicide is committed by firearms, men are more likely to shoot themselves in the head. Stone's (1990) research in Dallas based on data from 1985–1988 indicated that male and female completed suicides using long guns shot themselves in the body (versus the head) equally often. Among those using handguns, however, women were more likely than men to shoot themselves in the body (31% versus 16%).

Lester (1969) has speculated that women are more concerned with their physical appearance after death and so choose less disfiguring methods for suicide. Evidence exists for this notion in a study conducted by Diggory and Rothman (1961) on the consequences of death feared most. Women reported more concern with their physical appearance after death than did men. No further research has appeared on this possible difference in attitudes toward death.

Thus, one explanation for the sex difference in suicidal behavior is that women choose methods for suicide that are less likely to kill. You are more likely to survive a shot in the body than one in the head, and you are more likely to survive a drug overdose than a bullet wound.

Lester (1969) noted that this explanation, though possibly correct in part, was insufficient because within any method men die more often than women. For example, in Los Angeles in 1957, of 24 men who jumped to their death 16 died, whereas of 27 women who used jumping only nine resulted in death. Related to this, Lester (1990b) analyzed suicidal injury data from men and women jumping from 6 to 12 meters. The sexes did not differ in injury severity when jumping from similar heights. Thus, there is no evidence that women die from suicidal acts less often than men simply because they injure less easily (or are physiologically hardier).

Choice of method may be affected by socialization. For example, Marks and Stokes (1976) surveyed male and female students and found that males had much more familiarity with firearms when growing up than did females. Southern students had more early experience with firearms than northern students, and this was reflected in the finding that suicide was committed most often using firearms in the South, for both males and females. Perhaps these differences in socialization experiences affect the choice of a method for suicide?

Since the 1980s, firearms have become a more popular method for suicide in American women (Rogers, 1990). Has the socialization of men and women with respect to firearms changed in recent years? No research on this has appeared.

Recommendation 10.3: Many hypotheses have been offered in an attempt to understand differences in choice of method for suicide. Testing these different hypotheses have the potential to increase our understanding of this important aspect of suicidal behavior and are long overdue.

Physiological Explanations

Several studies have explored the relationship between the incidence of suicidal behavior and the phase of the menstrual cycle. Lester (1990a) carried out a meta-analysis of the studies on attempted and completed suicide over the menstrual cycle. The only significant variation was for attempted suicide to decline in the third week of the cycle. It appears, therefore, that the incidence of completed suicide does not vary significantly over the menstrual cycle, but that attempted suicide is more common during the premenstrual and menstrual phases (Lester, 1979). Thus, it is possible that the higher incidence of attempted suicide in women is due to an excess of attempts made during these two phases of the menstrual cycle. (However, we must remember that we do not know whether there is an excess during these two phases or a deficit at the other phases of the menstrual cycle.) This has led to the suggestion that the level of the circulating sex hormones affects the incidence of suicidal behavior.

Only two studies on completed suicide over the menstrual cycle were available for inclusion in Lester's (1990a) meta-analysis, on samples of only eleven and 38 suicides. Since that paper was published, only one further study has appeared – by Dogra et al. (2007) on 217 female completed suicides.

Lester (1993b) argued that the sex difference in suicide rates was accounted for solely by the use of violent methods. In 25 nations, he showed that men and women have similar rates of suicide by nonviolent methods. Lester suggested that testosterone was responsible for the high rate of violent suicide by men.

Zhang (2000) endeavored to test whether physiological differences might account for sex differences in suicide rates in China, where women reportedly have a higher suicide rate than men. Unable to utilize physiological measures in men and women, Zhang looked at the national athletic records of Chinese men and women relative to those of Americans. In track and field and in swimming, the difference in the performances of men and women was less for Chinese athletes than for American athletes in

27 of 29 events studied. For example, in the 10,000 meter running event, the Chinese male record was 264 seconds higher than that for American males, whereas the Chinese female record was only 140 seconds higher. Thus, Chinese men perform relatively less well than American men as compared to women in both nations. Does this mean that Chinese women are more "masculine" (or Chinese men less "masculine") than their American counterparts? Zhang suggested that hormonal studies would be of great interest to pursue this line of investigation.

It is easy to assess the levels of testosterone in individuals. A simple salvia assay is available and has been used extensively in research (e.g., Fanin & Dabbs, 2003). Despite this, testosterone levels have never been used to explore sex difference in suicidal behavior.

These reports by no means prove that the levels of circulating sex hormones affect the incidence of suicidal behavior in women. Psychological explanations of the associations can easily be provided. However, the reports do raise the possibility of a physiological influence on the suicidal behavior of women.

Psychosis and Mental Illness as an Explanation

Lester (1970) noted that psychotics have higher rates for completed suicide while neurotics have higher rates for attempted suicide. A recent community survey the United States (Kessler & Üstün, 2008) found similar rates of any DSM-IV disorder in women and men. Women had higher incidences of anxiety and mood disorders, whereas men had higher rates of impulse control and substance disorders.

Men and women who complete suicide are typically found to have different psychiatric disorders. For example, Henriksson et al. (1993) found that female suicides in Finland were less often diagnosed as alcohol abusers and more often as having depressive disorders and borderline personality disorders than were male suicides. Comorbidity was common in both groups, but more so among the men. Wolfersdorf et al. (1993) found that female completed suicides were more often diagnosed with a depressive disorder while male suicides were more often diagnosed with a personality disorder and alcoholism.

Male and female attempted suicides are also found to differ in psychiatric disorder. For example, Spirito et al. (1993) compared adolescent male and female attempters. The males more often had a conduct disorder and the females an adjustment reaction. They did not differ in age, race, social class, living with parents, prior attempts, prior psychiatric contacts, risk-rescue scores, suicidal intent, depression, hopelessness or the characteristics of the attempt. Suominen et al. (1996) found that male attempted suicides were more clinically depressed and more often had an antisocial personality disorder whereas female attempted suicides more often had depressive syndromes and borderline personality disorder.

Thus, women and men may differ in the lethality of their suicidal behavior because of differences in their incidence of particular psychiatric disorders. No adequate test of this hypothesis has yet appeared.

Societal Explanations

There is one explanation of the sex difference in suicidal behavior that has particular importance for a discussion of sex roles and suicidal behavior. Linehan (1973) felt that an important determinant of what happens when a person is in crisis is what alternatives are socially acceptable. She felt that attempted suicide was seen in our society as a weak and feminine behavior, and less available to males. Males, therefore, may be less able to communicate mild levels of distress, suppressing their self-destructive impulses until they are so strong as to precipitate a lethal suicide action.

Linehan tested her ideas by presenting to undergraduate students case studies involving males and females in crisis and varying the characteristics of the patients so that some were portrayed as "masculine" while others were portrayed as "feminine." She found that the students predicted suicide as an outcome more often for males than for females, and also that suicide was the predicted outcome more often for masculine patients than for feminine patients. The students predicted suicide 71 percent of the time for the masculine males, 62 percent of the time for masculine females, 43 percent of the time for feminine males, and 22 percent of the time for feminine females.

This suggests that social sex role stereotypes, which are probably based in part on differences in the social roles and the behavior of males and females in the society, serve to perpetuate those stereotyped roles. No replication or extension of Linehan's classic study have appeared to explore these stereotypes in other eras, cultures and nationalities.

Intent to Die

It has been suggested that women choose less lethal methods for suicide because they are less intent on dying. However, an explanation of why women attempt suicide more than men in terms of "intent to die" is really nothing more than a tautology.

Masculinity/Femininity

A number of interesting issues in this area have been neglected. For example, is the personality dimension of masculinity/femininity relevant? Waeld et al. (1994) found that current suicidal ideation in college students was predicted by masculinity scores (but not femininity scores) for both women and men. Street and Kromrey (1995) found that prior suicidality was less common in androgynous men and women and masculine men and more common in feminine men and masculine women.

Recommendation 10.4: Despite claims in the field of suicidology that suicidal behavior is multidetermined, research continues to be primarily discipline myopic. The limited data on physiological aspects of suicidal behavior suggests that a fuller understanding of suicide should result from research that includes attention to social, psychological, psychiatric and physiological factors related to suicidal behavior.

Discussion

It not easy to make general recommendations for this chapter as it has been in other chapters. It is easy to make recommendations for research on sex differences in suicidal behavior, and several have been made throughout this chapter, but these would not be relevant to other "fads" in suicidology, such as contagion effects. Perhaps a general recommendation can be made here.

Recommendation 10.5: Suicidologists should not abandon research issues until a thorough examination of the phenomena has been undertaken and before hypotheses proposed for explaining the phenomena have been tested.

Examples relevant to this recommendation have been made throughout this chapter.

Recommendation 10.6: Suicidologists should cooperate with researchers grounded in other academic disciplines to form collaborative relationships to explore suicidal phenomena.

The example given above about testing testosterone levels is relevant here.

Research in any field is governed by many factors, including the availability of research funds (from government agencies and private foundations) and the pressure on academic researchers to publish or perish (which pushes them toward research with short-term gains rather than long projects whose results may be delayed for years). In the field of mental health (including suicide), the government emphasis has been on physiologically based studies which support the "medical model" of psychiatric disorder (namely, that psychiatric disorders are caused by genetic and neurophysiological defects and dysfunctions) and on programs to prevent and treat psychiatric disorders. Current research is also affected by the reluctance of researchers to examine the literature on suicide from more than ten years past, possibly a result of the online literature searches that are prevalent today (see Chapter 2 above).

However, what is noteworthy in the field of sex differences is, first, the lack of follow-up of ideas and hypotheses. For example, no recent study has pursued Linehan's hypothesis that social stereotypes affect the choice of suicidal behavior. Since Lester's review in 1990 of suicidal behavior and the menstrual cycle, only one study has appeared on completed suicides. No study has appeared on whether the appearance of the body after death has an impact on the choice of method for suicide in women.

Second, there is rarely any application of research from other fields to suicide research. For example, Nolen-Hoeksema et al. (1999) has documented the differences in depression between women and men, noting that rumination is much more common in depressed women than in depressed men and that women and men experience different stressors in life, as well as differing in coping styles, self-concept and biological responses to stressors. Findings such as these provide possibilities for explaining the sex differences in suicidal behavior.

Thirdly, although scholars argue that a feminist perspective is important, there has been an absence of new theories of suicide generated from a feminist perspective, just as there has been an absence of theories generated from different ethnic and cultural perspectives.

Fourth, there is often an absence of research on particular issues. For example, the finding some 15 years ago that women in mainland China have a higher suicide rate than men resulted in many papers that speculated on the reasons for this (e.g., Pearson, 1995), analysis of the official statistics that exist (e.g., Liu & Yip, 2008), but no research that focuses on an explanation of this difference.

Finally, almost no research has been conducted on the interpersonal relationships of those who complete suicide. Collection of data from completed suicides is difficult. Interviews with the friends and relatives of the deceased person (often called psychological autopsies) yield some information, but it is generally unreliable. Informants often have a distorted perception of the deceased's behavior and personality, and their reports are not an adequate substitute for objective psychological test scores or the observations of expert clinicians. Thus, most of the information on the interpersonal relationships of suicidal individuals has been collected from studies of those who attempt suicide, and many suicidologists have argued that the study of attempted suicide can tell us little that is relevant to completed suicides (see Chapter 2).

At a microscopic level of analysis, where we explore the relation between actual behavioral roles and the frequency and kind of suicidal behavior in individual people, we find little systematic research. It is, of course, easier to study distal variables (such as marital status) than to study proximal variables (such as the nature of an individual's role). Data on distal variables are more readily available, and can be operationally defined more easily than proximal variables. The result is that we have some interesting possibilities as to how and why sex roles might be related to suicidal behavior. But we have little concrete evidence from studies of individuals that sex roles *per se* are (or are not) related to suicidal behavior.

References

Baldessarini, R. J., Tondo, L., Davis, P., Pompili, M., Goodwin, F. K., & Hennn, J. (2006). Decreases risk of suicides and attempts during long-term lithium treatment. *Bipolar Disorders*, 8, 625–639.

Canetto, S. S., & Lester, D. (1998). Gender, culture, and suicidal behavior. *Transcultural Psychiatry*, 35, 163–190.

Canetto, S. S., & Lester, D. (Eds.). (1995). *Women and suicidal behavior*. New York: Springer.

Daeid, N. N. (1997). Suicide in Ireland, 1982 to 1992. *Archives of Suicide Research*, 3, 31–42.

de Graaf, A. C., & Kruyt, C. S.: (1976). Some results of the response to a national survey of suicide and attempted suicide in the Netherlands. In *Suicide and attempted suicide in young people*. Copenhagen: World Health Organization.

Diggory, J. C., & Rothman, D. (1961). Values destroyed by death. *Journal of Abnormal & Social Psychology*, 63, 205–210.

Dogra, T. D., Leenaars, A. A., Raintji, R., Lalwani, S., Girdhar, S., Wenckstern, S., & Lester, D. (2007). Menstruation and suicide. *Psychological Reports*, 101, 430–434.

Durkheim, E. (1897). *Suicide*. Paris: Felix Alcan.

Fanin, N., & Dabbs, J. M. (2003). Testosterone and the work of firefighters. *Journal of Research in Personality*, 37, 107–115.

Farberow, N. L., & Shneidman, E. S. (1961). *The cry for help*. New York: McGraw-Hill.

Gove, W. (1972). Sex, marital status and suicide. *Journal of Health & Social Behavior*, 13, 204–213.

Gove, W. (1979). Sex differences in the epidemiology of mental disorder. In E. S. Gomberg & V. Franks (Eds.), *Gender and disordered behavior*, pp. 23–68. New York: Brunner/Mazel.

Henriksson, M. M., Aro, H. M., Marttunen, M. J., Heikkinen, M. E., Isometsa, E. T., Kuoppasalmi, K. I., & Lonnqvist, J. K. (1993). Mental disorders and comorbidity in suicide. *American Journal of Psychiatry*, 150, 935–940.

Javanainen, M. (1990). Sex ratio in suicide mortality in Finland. In G. Ferrari, M. Bellini & P. Crepet (Eds.), *Suicidal behavior and risk factors*, pp. 95–99. Bologna: Monduzzi-Editore.

Kessler, R. C., & McRae, J. (1983). Trends in the relationship between sex and attempted suicide. *Journal of Health & Social Behavior*, 24, 98–110.

Kessler, R. C., & Üstün, T. B. (2008). *The WHO mental health surveys*. New York: Cambridge University Press.

Koczan, G., & Ozsvath, K. (1990). Suicide events in county Baranja 1984–1987. In G. Ferrari, M. Bellini & P. Crepet (Eds.), *Suicidal behavior and risk factors*, pp. 113–118. Bologna: Monduzzi-Editore.

Lester, D. (1969). Suicidal behavior in men and women. *Mental Hygiene*, 53, 340–345.

Lester, D. (1970). Suicide, sex and mental disorder. *Psychological Reports*, 27, 61–62.

Lester, D. (1972). *Why people kill themselves*. Springfield, IL: Charles C. Thomas.

Lester, D. (1979). Sex differences in suicidal behavior. In E. S. Gomberg & V. Franks (Eds.), *Gender and disordered behavior*, pp. 287–300. New York: Brunner/Mazel.

Lester, D. (1988). *Why women kill themselves*. Springfield, IL: Charles Thomas.

Lester, D. (1989). The study of suicide from a feminist perspective. *Crisis*, 11, 38–43.

Lester, D. (1990a). Suicide and the menstrual cycle. *Medical Hypotheses*, 31, 197–199.

Lester, D. (1990b). Sex differences in severity of injury of attempted suicides who jump. *Perceptual & Motor Skills*, 71, 176.

Lester, D. (1990c). The sex distribution of suicides by age in nations of the world. *Social Psychiatry & Psychiatric Epidemiology*, 25, 87–88.

146   Fads in Research: Sex Differences in Suicidal Behavior

Lester, D. (1993a). The changing sex ratio in suicidal and homicidal deaths. *Italian Journal of Suicidology*, 3, 33–35.

Lester, D. (1993b). Testosterone and suicide. *Personality & Individual Differences*, 15, 347–348.

Linehan, M. (1973). Suicide and attempted suicide. *Perceptual & Motor Skills*, 37, 31–34.

Liu, K. Y., & Yip, P. S. F. (2008). Mainland China. In P S. F. Yip (Ed.), *Suicide in Asia*, pp. 31–48. Hong Kong: Hong Kong University Press.

Marks, A., & Stokes, C. (1976). Socialization, firearms and suicide. *Social Problems*, 23, 622–629.

Neuringer, C., & Lettieri, D. J. (1982). *Suicidal women*. New York: Gardner Press.

Nolen-Hoeksema, S., Larson, J., & Grayson, C. (1999). Explaining gender difference sin depression. *Journal of Personality & Social Psychology*, 77, 1061–1072.

Pearson, V. (1995). Goods on which one loses: Women and mental health in China. *Social Science & Medicine*, 41, 1159–1173.

Pritchard, C. (1990). Suicide, unemployment and gender variations in the Western World 1964–1986. *Social Psychiatry & Psychiatric Epidemiology*, 25, 73–80.

Rogers, J. R. (1990). Female suicide: The trend toward increased lethality in method of choice and its implications. *Journal of Counseling & Development, 69*, 37–38.

Ross, M. (1973). Suicide among physicians. *Diseases of the Nervous System*, 34, 145–150.

Shichor, D., & Bergman, S. (1979). Patterns of suicide among the elderly in Israel. *Gerontology*, 19, 487–495.

Spirito, A., Bond, A., Kurkjian, J., Devost, L., Bosworth, T., & Brown, L. K. (1993). Gender differences among adolescent suicide attempters. *Crisis*, 14, 178–184.

Stack, S. (1996). Gender and suicide risk among artists. *Suicide & Life-Threatening Behavior*, 26, 374–379.

Stone, I. C. (1990). Observations and statistics relating to suicide weapons. *Journal of Forensic Sciences*, 35, 10–12.

Street, S., & Kromrey, J. D. (1995). Gender roles and suicidal behavior. *Journal of College Student Psychotherapy*, 9(3), 41–56.

Waeld, L. C., Silvern, L., & Hodges, W. F. Stressful life events. *Sex Roles*, 1994, 30, 1–22.

Wolfersdorf, M., Faust, V., Brehm, M., Moser, K., Holzer, R., & Hole, G. (1993). Suicide in the Ravensburg area. In K. Bohme, R. Freytag, C. Wachtler & H. Wedler (Eds.), *Suicidal behavior*, pp. 890–895. Regensburg, Germany: S. Roderer.

Yap, P. (1958). Suicide in Hong Kong. *Journal of Mental Science*, 104, 266–301.

Zhang, J. (2000). Gender differences in athletic performance and their implications in gender ratios of suicide. *Omega*, 41, 117–123.

11

Studies of Social Relationships

with
Molly J. Drilling

In this chapter, we consider the study of the role of social relationships as they relate to suicide and suicidal behaviors. Areas of study under this broad rubric include studies of the relations between the perceived quality of social support and suicide and social learning research. Social learning research tends to center around Bandura's (1991) modeling paradigm and includes the concept of suicide contagion or more colloquially identified as "copy-cat" suicides. For the purposes of this chapter, we focus broadly on the areas of social relationships and social learning in order to illustrate what we see as general limitations in the research and ways research investigating the association between social relationships and suicide can be improved to further our understandings of suicide.

Social Relationships and Suicide

Marital Status

Marriage is an important aspect of social relationships that has been studied to determine its relation to suicide and suicidal behavior. Many studies related to the role of marital status and death by suicide have been conducted based on census data and often from the perspective that marital status is an indicator of social integration. For example, based on the work of Durkheim (1951), Kposowa, McElvain and Breault (2008) considered marriage as an indicator of a high level of integration and being divorced as an indicator of the lowest level of integration. The results of their study indicated that the odds of dying by suicide for single, divorced and separated individuals were approximately 2.5 times that of married individuals. Thus, these results suggested to the authors that being single, divorced or separated is a risk factor for suicide.

Similarly a recent European study by Lorant, Kunst, Huisman, Bopp, Mackenbach, and the EU Working Group (2005) also used marital status as a proxy for social integration. These authors analyzed census data from eight European countries. They interpreted their results as indicating that being married is a "protective" factor or "buffer" against suicide for all but elderly individuals (age 65 and older). In Chapter 5, we noted that researchers have never, to the best of our knowledge, produced data or research to validate that married individuals are less socially integrated than non-married individuals.[25] It is easy to propose possible alternative differences between the married and non-married which may account for differences in their behavior. For example, perhaps those who never marry and those who divorce differ in personality and other psychological variables from those who marry and stay married.

On the surface then, research investigating the relation between marital status and suicide seems to suggest that being married is a protective factor, or as suggested by Lorant et al. (2005) a "buffer" against suicide. This protective or buffering effect, to the extent that it exists, has often been attributed to social integration, although an argument may be made for its functioning via a social support mechanism. However, using these as examples, it is clear that the level of analysis employed in these studies provides only gross information that does not necessarily advance our understanding of suicidal behavior either as it relates to the more distal aspect of social integration or the more proximal variable of social support (considered more specifically in the next section). Some married people do die by suicide, and most unmarried (single, divorced, separated) individuals do not. What is needed in this area are more fine-grained analyses to determine qualitative characteristics of marriages that can be used to differentiate between those that may represent risk for suicidal behavior as compared to those that may serve as buffers. Similarly, what are more specific characteristics of being single, divorced, and separated that represent risk versus protective factors? Finally, it is quite likely that there are third variables (i.e., factors associated with both marital status and suicide) that have more explanatory value as risk factors than simple marital status.

Recommendation 11.1: Research investigating the relations between marital status and suicide needs to move beyond the broad epidemiological approach to begin to identify more specific qualitative differences within those statuses that can advance the understanding and prevention of suicide.

Rather than using completed suicide as the criterion in investigating the relation between suicide and marital status, some research in this area has used measures of attitudes toward suicide as a proxy for suicidal behavior. For example, Stack and Wasserman (1995) used the 1972–1990 U.S. General Social Survey data to explore the relation between marital status and what they termed as "pro-suicide ideology." The pro-suicide ideology variable in this case was a summative score on four attitude items identifying scenarios under which someone might consider suicide and asking respondents for their opinion as to approval or disapproval. Based on these data, Stack and Wasserman reported that, for African Americans, being married lowered "pro-suicide ideology" as compared to those who were not married. This result also was observed for Whites in their sample.

The obvious assumption was that the "pro-suicide ideology" reported here could be interpreted as acceptance of suicidal behavior in others (and perhaps for the respondent him or herself), that is, if one has an accepting attitude toward suicide, he or she

---

[25] Indeed, we have several non-married friends whose social networks are far larger than the networks of some married friends.

may be more likely to engage in suicidal behavior and support others similarly considering suicide. However, given previously identified problems with straightforward interpretations of attitude survey data discussed in Chapter 7, that assumption is tenuous at best. This leads to our second recommendation in this chapter.

Recommendation 11.2: Investigations of the relations between suicide attitudes and other social demographic characteristics through the use of epidemiological survey research must move away from the tendency to rely on simplistic approaches to assessing attitudes if meaningful interpretations are to be drawn.

Social support, or more pointedly, perceived or assumed social support represents another area of investigation in terms of social relations research. Suicide research in this area has tended to use self-report of the source (e.g., family, friends), accessibility, of support, and quality (positive versus negative) of social support relations as correlates or predictors of suicidal behavior. The underlying assumption here is that the absence of supportive relations increases the risk for suicidal behavior. General approaches to assessing the role of social support are discussed below.

Social Support

The research related to the relation between social support and suicide has not lead to consistent conclusions for a variety of conceptual and methodological reasons. Although many studies such as those by Kidd, Henrich, Brookmeyer, Davidson, King, and Shahar (2006) Compton, Thompson, and Kaslow (2005), and Thompson, Kaslow, Short, and Wyckoff (2002) have been interpreted to suggest that social support serves as a protective factor for suicidal behavior, Bille-Brahe et al. (1999) concluded that the majority of suicide attempters in their analysis of European data indicated that their social support needs were met prior to engaging in suicidal behavior. A closer look at the primary methodological approach in these studies will lead to our next recommendation.

One of the key problem areas in social support research is the self-report nature of social support assessment. Beyond typical issues involved in interpreting self-report data, the temporal proximity of the assessment of perceived social to a suicide attempt can introduce its own complications. For example, Compton et al. (2005) interpreted their data comparing suicide attempters and controls as suggesting that better family functioning and social support serve protective functions related to suicidal behavior. However, for the suicide attempt group, the time between the attempt and assessment was not specified, leaving the possibility that participants' self-rating of social support was colored by the experience of the suicidal crisis itself. Additionally, the control group for this study was drawn from individuals seeking urgent care in a medical facility. Because of the medical crisis these participants were experiencing, it is likely that their perceptions of social support were positively influenced (e.g., family members tend to be more supporting during medical crises). The statistically significant differences between the suicide attempt and control groups must be interpreted cautiously because of these potential confounds. By contrast, data reported by Bille-Brahe et al. (1999) indicating that the majority of suicide attempters felt that their social support needs were being met was based on an assessment of social support one week after the attempt. Perhaps this time lag between the suicide attempt and assessment of soci-asupport explains some of the inconsistencies in the research results.

In addition to the issue of time lag and control group considerations, Bille-Brahe et al. (1999) concluded their study by highlighting other potential confounds in the study of the relation between social support and suicide. Included in these was the idea that, because of histories of negative childhood experiences, many suicidal individuals may have lowered expectations for social support such that their perceived needs may be easily met. Alternatively, negative past social support experiences may result for some in unrealistic higher expectations for social support. Either of these scenarios would confound the interpretation of the results.

Recommendation 11.3: Researchers need to carefully consider their selection of control group participants and the potential biasing impact of the experience of the suicidal crisis when studying the relation between social support and suicidal behavior to avoid potentially miss-interpreting state influenced ratings of social support as more trait-like evaluations.

Another area where the social support paradigm has been investigated relative to sui-cidal behavior is found in research with gay, lesbian and bisexual individuals. Al-though acknowledging that interpersonal relationships can be demanding regardless of sexual orientation, Saunders and Valente (1987) suggested that they may be even more challenging for gay, lesbian and bisexual persons. Similarly, McBee and Rogers (1997) concluded that "stress related to relationship issues may be exacerbated" (p. 147) for these individuals resulting in lower levels of social support. In part, this in-creased stress due to a lack of social support has been hypothesized as being related to the impact of the coming-out experience on support networks and sanctions against homosexuality in society. A study by Rosario, Schrimshaw and Hunter (2005) serves to highlight some of the challenges in research in this area.

First and foremost, the ability to generalize any results based on studying a sample of participants of gay, lesbian, and bisexual individuals is limited. Because of contin-ued social sanctions regarding homosexuality, research participants are often recruited from gay, lesbian, and bisexual students or community organization, as in the study by Rosario et al. (2005). Thus, questions regarding the representativeness of these sam-ples to a broader population of gay, lesbian and, bisexual individuals is unknown. Sec-ond, there seems to be a broad and unsubstantiated assumption that research measures developed largely on heterosexual individuals, especially in this case related to social support, are appropriate for use for those with other sexual orientations. For example, Rosario et al. utilized a measure of support from family and friends in their research that was developed in 1983 using a general sample of adolescents. The datedness of the measure would exclude any assessment of more currently developed sources of support such as internet-based social networks, and the scale's validity for the gay, lesbian and bisexual sample was never investigated.

A study by McBee and Rogers (2002) demonstrated the problems with the ap-proach of assuming validity in studying gay, lesbian, and bisexual samples. Their research investigated reasons for living in a sample of gay, lesbian and bisexual individuals. Past researchers (Hirsch & Ellis, 1998) had used the Reasons for Living Inventory (Linehan, Goodstein, Nelsen, & Chiles, 1983) with gay, lesbian, and bisexual samples and, under the assumption of validity across the samples, they compared their sample scores on the six subscales of the measures to scores of heterosexuals. Results suggested that gay, lesbian and bisexuals had lower reasons for living as compared to the heterosexual samples. However, the validity of the scale had never been empirically investigated. McBee and Rogers found that the six subscale structure for the Reasons for Living Inventory was not replicated in their sample of gay, lesbian and bisexuals, making interpretations of their reasons for living and comparisons to heterosexual samples inappropriate.

Recommendation 11.4: Although investigating the role of relationship stress as a contributing factor in suicidal behavior by studying gay, lesbian, and bisexual samples may be appropriate given the theoretical expectations that relationship stress may be more significant for these individuals, caution must be used in attempting to generalize study results from samples to populations. Consideration should be given to newer technologically-based sources of relationship support and arguments for the validity of interpretations of measures of social support should be empirically defensible.

Social Learning Research

This section considers the area of social learning research including what is characterized as the Werther or the suggestion-imitation effect (e.g., Hittner, 2005). The social learning paradigm is based on the significant contributions of Bandura (1971, 1977) and is often referenced in the suicide literature as the modeling effect. As the basis for Platt's (1993) research investigating the role of modeling on the acquisition of suicidal behavior, he offered the following:

> The main process by which suicidal behavior may be learned is that of modeling, which of course refers to the acquisition of new patterns of behavior through the observation of the behavior of one or more models. (p. 24)

Although a number of authors have attempted to investigate the "modeling effect" with regard to suicidal behavior, the results have not been either consistent or convincing (e.g., Jonas, 1992; Modestin & Würmle, 1989; Platt, 1993). Often in this research, authors have only been able to look at the phenomenon in a very cursory manner. For example, Hittner (2005) reanalyzed previous data using residualized observed deaths by suicide and compared those with the expected number of suicides following media reports of individuals who died by suicide. Though his analytic strategy was more sophisticated than the original analyses, the variability in death by suicide, in conjunction with the low base-rate of the behavior, makes it difficult to reasonably calculate an "expected" number of suicides for any time period. Additionally, comparing observed from expected suicides following media reports of a death by suicide serves as a very gross test of the modeling effect, leaving many alternative explanations for any observed associations that might result from that approach.

Recommendation 11.5: Tests of the modeling effect related to suicide and suicidal behaviors must move away from simple broad epidemiological analyses to include tests of more specific theoretical relations.

Another approach to investigating the modeling effect as it relates to suicidal behavior can be found in Platt (1993). In this article, Platt attempted test the modeling effect in "parasuicidal" behavior by investigating the prior exposure of participants in his study to others who have engaged in suicidal behavior. Platt appropriately described the modeling paradigm by stating that:

> Experimental evidence suggests that the effect of modeling depends on characteristics of both the observer and the model. The greater the degree of concordance between specific characteristics of the model and the observer, the more plausible is the hypothesis of an imitation or learning by modeling effect. (p. 14)

Additionally, Platt criticized previous research investigating the modeling effect characterizing it as narrowly conceived and inadequate to testing the social learning paradigm. Platt interpreted his data as providing only weak support for a modeling effect and suggested that researchers should move beyond "cultural" (p.31) explanations of suicidal behavior and focus more on characteristics of the individual when studying suicidal behavior.

However, Rogers and Carney's (1994) review of Platt's study identified significant theoretical oversights and methodological weaknesses with regard to testing the modeling effect. Specifically, Rogers and Carney suggested that simple measures of association between prior exposure to individuals engaging in suicidal behaviors and subsequent suicidal behavior (including attitudes) do not provide an adequate test of the model. In order to assess a model's impact on an observer, social learning theory suggests that there needs to be some degree of concordance between the characteristics of the model and characteristics of the observer. According to Bandura (1977), important model characteristics include status, power and competence, with the model possessing more of these attributes than the observer, in addition to age and sex similarities. Similarly, important observer characteristics that influence modeling include dependency, prior reward history for conforming behavior, motivation and self-esteem. Finally, and perhaps one of the most important components of the model has to do with the reward characteristics of the behavior, that is, was the social response to the suicidal model positive (e.g., increased social support) or negative (e.g., anger or avoidance of the model)?

Recommendation 11.6: Investigations of the modeling effect on suicidal behavior must be based on comprehensive model development including attention to both model and observer characteristics and a consideration of the "reward" characteristics for behavioral engagement. Specifically in this regard, social response or

"reward" for engaging in suicidal can be positive (resulting in increased social support and resources) or negative behavior (i.e., social marginalization, anger, frustration). Clearly, a consideration of the reward or consequences resulting from engaging in suicidal behavior will be related to the probability of that behavior being modeled.

Social Interactions

A final comment here is the current focus on distal variables (such as marital status) and easily measured variables (such as self-report inventories) rather than actual observation of the interactions between people. For example, Kumler (1964) examined ten married attempted suicides and noted disruptions in the interaction patterns in the couples, such as rejection of the suicidal partner by the spouse and mutual frustration, rejection, anger, helplessness, guilt and anxiety. Her sample was small, and there was no control group, but Kumler's study (published in a nursing journal) indicates how research might examine interaction patterns in couples, one of which is suicidal.

Hattem (1964) (in an unpublished dissertation) studied couples, one of which was suicidal, and gave both partners a battery of psychological inventories. Each partner had to describe him/herself and the spouse, thereby providing a comparison of how each partner viewed him/herself versus how they were viewed by the other. Lester (1969) found that suicidal students resented those significant others that they also liked and, therefore, had to seek help and support from those whom they resented.

It would be interesting to have families with a suicidal member have discussions, engage in problem-solving tasks, and other interactive activities, while viewed by observers so that the social interactions can be observed and compared with nonsuicidal families.

Recommendation 11.7: Research should move from the study of distal and superficially-measured variables to the study of actual interactive patterns between suicidal individuals and their significant others, observed and coded by the researchers.

Conclusion

As suggested by Bille-Brahe et al. (1999), the role of social relationships in human behavior is a very complex topic. This complexity is further complicated when the behavior of interest is suicide. As we have suggested in this brief review, straightforward interpretations of the research relating social support to suicidal behaviors and studies related to social learning theory are limited by many factors including general methodological issues as identified in Chapter 2, issues related to attitude assessment and self-report as discussed in Chapter 7, and challenges more specific to social support research itself. Not the least of these is determining the extent to which self-reported assessments of the quality of social support are impacted by the experience of suicidality itself. That is, to what extent does suicidality play a contributing role in determining the availability and nature of social support relationships (e.g., via social withdrawal) and color one's evaluation of social support during a suicidal crisis? These are important questions that need to be answered if research in the area of social relationships and suicide are to advance the field in the future.

References

Bagley, C., & Greer, S. (1971). Clinical and social predictors of repeated attempted suicide: A multivariate analysis. *British Journal of Psychiatry, 119*, 515–521.

Bandura, A. (1971). *Psychological Modeling.* Chicago: Adline-Atherton.

Bandura, A. (1977). *Social learning theory.* Englewood Cliffs, NJ: Prentice-Hall.

Bille-Brahe, U., Egebo, H., Crepet, P., De Leo, D., Hjelmeland, H., Kerkhof, A., Lonnqvist, J., Michel, K., Salander Renberg, E., Schmidtke, A., & Wasserman, D. (1999). Social support among European suicide attempters. *Archives of Suicide Research, 5*, 215–231.

Compton, M. T., Thompson, N. J., & Kaslow, N. J. (2005). Social environment factors associated with suicide attempt among low-income African Americans: The protective role of family relationships and social support. *Social Psychiatry & Psychiatric Epidemology, 40*, 175–185.

Durkheim, E. (1951), *Suicide.* Glencoe, IL: The Free Press.

Hattem, J. V. (1964). Precipitating role of discordant interpersonal relationships in suicidal behavior. *Dissertation Abstracts*, 25, 1335–1336.

Hirsch, J. K., & Ellis, J. B. (1998). Reasons for living in homosexual and heterosexual young adults. *Archives of Suicide Research, 4*, 243–248.

Hittner, J. B. (2005). How robust is the Werther effect? A re-examination of the suggestion-imitation model of suicide. *Mortality, 10*, 193–200.

Jonas, K. (1992). Modelling and suicide: A test of the Werther effect. *British Journal of Social Psychology, 31*, 295–306.

Kumler, F. R. (1964) Communication between suicide attempters and significant others. *Nursing Research*, 13, 268–270.

Kidd, S., Henrich, C. C., Brookmeyer, K. A., Davidson, L., King, R. A., & Shahar, G. (2006). The social context of adolescent suicide attempts: Interactive effects of parent, peer, and school social relations. *Suicide & Life-Threatening Behavior, 36*, 386–395.

Kposowa, A. J., McElvain, J. P., & Breault, K. D. (2008). Immigration and suicide: The role of marital status, duration of residence, and social integration. *Archives of Suicide Research, 12*, 82–92.

Lester, D. (1969). Resentment and dependency in the suicidal individual. *Journal of General Psychology*, 81, 137–145.

Linehan, M. M., Goodstein, J. L., Nielsen, S. I., & Chiles, J. A. (1983). Reasons for staying alive when you are thinking of killing yourself: The Reasons for Living Inventory. *Journal of Consulting & Clinical Psychology, 51*, 276–286.

Lorant, V., Kunst, A. E., Huisman, M., Bopp, M., Mackenbach, J., & The EU Working Group. (2005). A European comparative study of marital status and socio-economic inequalities in suicide. *Social Science & Medicine, 60*, 2431–2441.

McBee, S. M., & Rogers, J. R. (1997). Identifying risk factors for gay and lesbian suicidal behavior: Implications for mental health counselors. *Journal of Mental Health Counseling, 19*, 143–155.

McBee-Strayer, S. M., & Rogers, J. R. (2002). Lesbian, gay, and bisexual suicidal behavior: Testing a constructivist model. *Suicide & Life-Threatening Behavior, 32*, 272–283.

Modestin, J., & Wurmle, O. (1989). Role of modeling in in-patient suicide: A lack of supporting evidence. *British Journal of Psychiatry, 155*, 511–514.

Platt, S. (1993). The social transmission of parasuicide: Is there a modeling effect? *Crisis, 14*, 23–31.

Rogers, J. R., & Carney, J. V. (1994). Theoretical and methodological considerations in assessing the "modeling effect" in parasuicidal behavior: A Comment on Platt (1993). *Crisis, 15*, 83–89.

Rosario, M., Schrimshaw, E. W., & Hunter, J. (2005). Psychological distress following suicidality among gay, lesbian, and bisexual youths: Role of social relationships. *Journal of Youth & Adolescence, 34*, 149–161.

Saunders, J. M., & Valente, S. M. (1987). Suicide risk among gay men and lesbians: A review. *Death Studies, 11*, 1–23.

Stack, S., & Wasserman, I. (1995). The effect of marriage, family, and religious ties on African American suicide ideology. *Journal of Marriage & the Family, 57*, 215–222.

Thompson, M. P., Kaslow, N. J., Short, L. M., & Wyckoff, S. (2002). The mediating roles of perceived social support and resources in self-efficacy-suicide attempts relation among African American abused women. *Journal of Consulting & Clinical Psychology, 70*, 942–949.

12

Suicide Notes and Other Personal Narratives

Since suicides leave so little information behind after their death, the study of the suicide notes left by some suicides has assumed great importance in suicidology. This area of research was stimulated by the publication in 1957 of 33 pairs of genuine and simulated suicides published by Shneidman and Farberow (1957). However, the study of suicide notes is plagued by methodological problems.

Note Writers Versus Non-Writers

The first issue is whether those individuals who kill themselves and leave suicide notes differ from those who do not leave notes. There has been some research on this issue, but all of the studies have compared the two groups for simple demographic variables. For example, Tuckman et al. (1960) found no differences between the groups in age, race, sex, employment status, marital status, physical or psychiatric condition or prior suicidality.

No study has compared the two groups for psychological and psychodynamic differences, primarily because such data are hard to obtain for people who complete suicide. However, difficulties in obtaining data should not obscure that fact that studies of suicide notes are primarily of interest because of the insights that they might provide into the psychodynamics of suicide. Thus, a study of the psychodynamic similarities and differences of note writers and non-writers is crucial.

Recommendation 12.1: Investigating differences between suicide note writers and non-writers must move beyond a comparison of simple demographic and status variables to include a consideration of the more relevant psychological and psychodynamic similarities and differences.

Choice Of Comparison Groups

Shneidman and Farberow (1957) published 33 pairs of genuine and simulated notes. The simulated notes were written by people who were not suicidal, but who were asked to pretend that they were about to kill themselves and to write a suicide note. The appearance of these pairs of notes stimulated research on them. For example, Tuckman and

Ziegler (1966) compared the pairs of notes for the use of different pronouns, expecting that the genuine notes would have more self-referents than the simulated notes, indicating less psychological maturity. They found no differences between the genuine and simulated notes in this respect.

Lester (1988) criticized these studies. He argued that such comparisons tell us only about how well nonsuicidal people can fake a suicide note. The study of simulated notes can provide clues to popular conceptions about suicide because the writers will include content that they "think" characterizes suicides. For example, Lester found that women writers of simulated notes more often addressed their simulated note to someone than did men writers of simulated notes and more often apologized and asked for forgiveness. However, simulated notes tell us nothing about genuine suicides.

What is required is that genuine suicide notes be compared with *notes and letters written by these same individuals at an early point in time.* We need to know how their notes changed leading up to and including the moment before their suicide. This task is difficult. Suicide notes are collected quite easily from police departments and from the files of medical examiners. To obtain other notes by the individuals who died by suicide, the relatives would have to be contacted and asked if they would mind searching for and giving to the researchers other notes. This would be difficult and time-consuming, but it is critical for advancing our knowledge of suicide. For example, Spiegel and Neuringer (1963) found that genuine suicide notes were more disorganized than simulated notes. What would be of real interest is whether the genuine suicide notes are more disorganized than notes written by the individuals, say, one year earlier.

Recommendation 12.2: In order to make appropriate comparisons and interpretations, genuine suicides notes must be compared with notes written by the same individuals at an earlier point in time.

What Can Be Learned From Studies Of Suicide Notes?

Since no studies of suicide notes have utilized the appropriate control groups, the only studies which are methodologically sound are those of within-group comparisons. Studies have been conducted, for example, comparing genuine notes written by men and women (Leenaars, 1988b), those of different ages (Leenaars, 1989), those using different methods for suicide (Lester, 1971), those dying versus surviving the suicidal action (Brevard & Lester, 1991), and those from different nations (Leenaars, 1992).

These studies require useful coding categories, preferably associated with theories of suicide. For example, Black (1993) devised a set of categories with no theoretical basis, while Leenaars (1988a) devised sets of categories based on ten separate theories of suicide. The latter is preferable, for then a failure to find significant results still has theoretical implications and advances our understanding of suicide more.

Recommendation 12.3: Coding categories for suicide notes and other materials (diaries, poems, etc.) should be devised, preferably based on theories of suicide and theories of personality.

However, in addition to possible psychodynamic content, suicide notes often differ in type. Some are simple wills, others contain instructions, while some try to explain and justify the suicidal act. Jacobs (1967) presented a classification of types of notes, but alternative rival classifications would be of use, and these classifications need to be examined for their reliability (do different judges agree?) and comprehensiveness (what percentage of notes can be classified using the typology?).

Recommendation 12.4: Typologies of suicide notes need to be developed and studied for their inter-judge reliability and comprehensiveness.

Other Personal Documents

Although suicide notes are of great interest in our efforts to understand the psychodynamics of suicidal behavior, other personal documents and narratives exist. For example, the diaries of suicides have occasionally been the focus of study. Lester (2004) was given the diary of a young woman who killed herself, and he obtained the collaboration of several colleagues to analyze the contents of the diary, focusing especially on changes in the months leading up to her death.

Other diaries of individuals who have killed themselves are been published, and brief analyses of their content have been reported (e.g., Leenaars & Maltsberger, 1994; Lester, 2006a). Some analyses have been qualitative (Leenaars & Maltsberger, 1994) while others have been quantitative (Pennebaker & Stone, 2004; Handelman & Lester, 2007). Diaries written by those who have attempted suicide are also of interest, and Lester has recently began the study of a diary from a young woman who has attempted suicide on several occasions (Lester, 2006b). In time, enough diaries may be collected so that a quantitative comparison of samples of diaries may be undertaken.

Barnes, Lawal-Solarin and Lester (2007) have analysed a series of letters written to a friend by a young man who killed himself, none of which constitute a suicide note, to explore how the content changed as the time of his death became closer. Stirman and Pennebaker (2001) have compared poems written by poets who completed suicide with those written by non-suicidal poets.

Recommendation 12.5: Personal documents and narratives of individuals who kill themselves, other than suicide notes, should also be studied in order to further our understanding of the psychodynamics of suicidal behavior.

Discussion

Although there have been many studies of suicide notes, too many have been based on an unsound methodology (a comparison of genuine versus simulated suicide notes) or on superficial characteristics of the note writers. The inclusion of more appropriate control groups and attention to theoretically and empirically identified psychological and psychodynamic characteristics of individuals who kill themselves would result in more informative studies of suicide notes. These studies are possible even though collecting these data may be much more difficult. As in other examples presented in this book, researchers investigating suicidal behavior via the study of suicide notes have too often chosen the quick and easy research design over the difficult but more meaningful research methodologies. In addition, other documents left by suicides (such as letters, poems and diaries) should also be studied for the insights they can provide into the suicidal mind.

References

Barnes, D. H., Lawal-Solarin, F. W., & Lester, D. (2007) Letters from a suicide. *Death Studies*, 31, 671–678.

Black, S. T. (1993). Comparing genuine and simulated suicide notes. *Journal of Consulting & Clinical Psychology*, 61, 699–702.

Brevard, A., & Lester, D. (1991). A comparison of suicide notes written by completed and attempted suicides. *Annals of Clinical Psychiatry*, 3, 43–45.

Handelman, L. D., & Lester, D. (2007). The content of suicides notes from attempters and completers. *Crisis*, 28, 102–104.

Leenaars, A. A. (1988a). *Suicide notes.* New York: Human Sciences.

Leenaars, A. A. (1988b). Are women's suicide really different from men's? *Women & Health*, 14(1), 17–33.

Leenaars, A. A. (1989). Are young adults' suicides psychologically different from those of other adults? *Suicide & Life-Threatening Behavior*, 19, 149–163.

Leenaars, A. A. (1992). Suicide notes from Canada and the United States. *Perceptual & Motor Skills*, 74, 278.

Leenaars, A. A., & Maltsberger, J. T. (1994). The Inman diary. In A. A. Leenaars, J. T. Maltsberger, & R. A. Neimeyer (Eds.), *Treatment of suicidal people*, pp. 227–236. Washington, DC: Taylor & Francis.

Lester, D. (1971). Choice of method for suicide and personality. *Omega*, 2, 76–80.

Lester, D. (1988). What does the study of simulated suicide notes tell us? *Psychological Reports*, 62, 962.

Lester, D. (Ed.). (2004). *Katie's diary: Unlocking the mystery of a suicide.* New York: Brunner-Routledge.

Lester, D. (2006a). Understanding suicide through studied of diaries: The case of Cesare Pavese. *Archives of Suicide Research*, 10, 295–302.

Lester, D. (2006b). Absolutism in diaries of suicides. *Psychological Reports*, 99, 305.

Pennebaker, J. W., & Stone, L. D. (2004). What was she trying to say. In D. Lester (Ed.), *Katie's diary: Unlocking the mystery of a suicide*, pp. 55–79. New York: Brunner-Routledge.

Shneidman, E. S., & Farberow, N. L. (Eds.). (1957). *Clues to suicide.* New York: McGraw-Hill.

Spiegel, D., & Neuringer, C. (1963). Role of dread in suicidal behavior. *Journal of Abnormal & Social Psychology,* 66, 507–511.

Stirman, S. W., & Pennebaker, J. W. (2001). Word use in the poetry of suicidal and non-suicidal poets. *Psychosomatic Medicine,* 63, 517–522.

Tuckman, J., Kleiner, R. J., & Lavell, M. (1960). Credibility of suicide notes. *American Journal of Psychiatry,* 116, 1104–1106.

Tuckman, J., & Ziegler, R. (1966). Language usage and social maturity as related to suicide notes. *Journal of Social Psychology,* 68, 139–142.

13

Studies of the Suicidal Personality

with
Teri L. Madura

Studies of the relations between personality characteristics and suicidal behaviors have focused on a broad array of factors. These have included the characteristics of neuroticism and extroversion, impulsivity, aggression, hostility, self-criticism and perfectionism and psychoticism, to name a few. For illustrative purposes, in this chapter we reference research related to only two of these characteristics, drawing recommendations that may be applied more broadly. However, prior to looking at these specific areas, a brief discussion of state versus trait views as they relate to research on the suicidal personality is in order.

Most of the research on suicide and personality embraces the underlying assumption that personality characteristics are *trait-like*, that is, personality characteristics are viewed as relatively stable, a result of gene-environment interactions, and, while they may evolve over the lifespan, they "may be rooted in childhood temperament and established by 6 years of age" (p. 180; Brezo, Paris, & Turecki, 2006). However, this state model is not the only perspective on personality. An alternative view of personality characteristics supports a more *state-like* understanding wherein personality characteristics are more malleable and change over time (Heatherton & Nichols, 1994).

Adding to the lack of clarity from an empirical point of view, Roberts and Del Vecchio (2000) concluded their meta-analysis of 152 longitudinal studies by stating that personality *traits* become minimally changeable after 50 years of age, while McCrae and Costa (1990) suggested that personality characteristics stabilize around the age of 30 years. Clearly, with estimates for the establishment of personality stability ranging from six to fifty years of age, unambiguously interpreting relations between personality characteristics and suicidal behavior can be challenging.

Perhaps as a function of this ambiguity, researchers either do not specify a trait versus a state model (e.g., Dougherty et al., 2004) or tend to conceptualizing personality characteristics as more trait-like (e.g., Brezo et al., 2006) suggesting a greater level of determinism in behavior and, potentially, less opportunity for intervention with suicidal individuals. On the other hand, if personality is viewed as more state-like, then an assumption that suicidal behavior is preventable is more tenable. This apparent assumption in the literature of a trait approach to understanding personality then leads to the first recommendation.

Recommendation 13.1: It is important for researchers in the area of personality characteristics and suicide to explicitly identify their underlying theoretical position with regard to trait and stable versus malleable issue in personality research.

An additional, but related issue in personality research and suicide is the issue of development and maturation. Even in the context of a trait perspective on personality, there are clearly personality-like characteristics potentially related to suicidal behavior that have developmental components. For instance, impulsivity is a characteristic that may be both developmental, as in the case of adolescent development, and likewise conceptualized as a more enduring personality characteristic. However, the developmental aspect is often not specifically addressed. An observed relationship between impulsivity as a developmental characteristic (that may be moderated by maturation) and suicide may have different implications for understanding and intervention than a relation between characterological impulsivity and suicide. Thus, some personality characteristics may remain relatively stable over time while others change (Buss, 1994), and there may be individual differences in these distinctions. Furthermore, some characteristics may be changeable over a portion of the life span but stable at other points in the life span.

Recommendation 13.2: Beyond the state versus trait distinction, researchers should take into consideration potential developmental influences, especially in studies with adolescents and youths, as they interpret the relationships between personality and suicidal behavior.

For the present chapter, rather than an organization based on individual or groups of personality characteristics that have been the focus of research related to suicidal behavior, we have organized the chapter around methodological issues beyond those identified in Chapter 2 that further limit our interpretations of the relations between personality and suicidal behavior.

Defining Personality Constructs

Method of Self-Report

Not unlike other areas of research related to suicidal behavior, the primary method of data collection in personality research has been self-report inventories. This is true both for the assessment of the various personality characteristics and for suicidal behavior. Although self-report can be an important and useful component of assessment for both of these variables, the use of self-report as the sole means of data collection leaves the interpretation of results open to a variety of alternative explanations. These include issues of recall bias and impression management (Heppner, Wampold & Kivlighan, 2008) that may be addressed using more behaviorally-linked strategies or by including third party information in research designs. Even though the inclusion of additional or alternative data sources can add complexity to research designs, overcoming the mono-method bias in personality research will allow for stronger and more appropriate interpretations of the relationhips.

Although the mono-method bias is most evident in the use of self-report inventories, it is present in other techniques of data collection. For example, Zouk, Tousignant, Sequin, Lessage, and Turecki (2006) employed "informant" reports in their psychological autopsy study. Given that psychological autopsies are often the only available research approach to studying individuals who have died by suicide, it is an important methodological approach. However, researchers still need to be aware that the informant method also suffers from the effects of the self-report method bias.

Also related to self-report, researchers must consider the potential confounding influence of social desirability. Impression management as a component of social desirability can have a substantial and unknown influence on how participants respond to self-report measures (Paulhus, 1994). In providing self-report information, respondents may manipulate their responses to either look better or worse than they actually are depending on what they see may be the outcome of their responses. This can be true for both first-person self-reports as well as for informant reports used in psychological autopsies. Thus, assessing and controlling for social desirability in self-report data should be considered as a matter of course.

Recommendation 13.3: Researchers investigating personality characteristic should develop data collection strategies that do not rely solely on single methods such as self-report (both for the personality variables and for suicidal behavior) and to include an assessment of impression management as part of their research design.

Operational Definitions

This section will use research on perfectionism as an example of issues related to the operational definitions of personality constructs in suicide research. Although we focus here on perfectionism, to various degrees, the discussion relates also to other personality constructs.

Perfectionism, by most, is considered to be a multidimensional personality trait consisting of both personal and social facets. Currently, the two most widely used measures are the Multidimensional Perfectionism Scale by Frost, Marten, Lahart and Rosenblate (1990) and the Multidimensional Perfectionism Scale by Hewitt and Flett (1991), both of which are self-report measures. A systematic review of the literature by O'Connor (2007) concluded that a critical component of perfectionism is self-criticism and that self-criticism is associated with suicidality in adults. In consideration of O'Connor's conclusion, research by Chang, Watkins, and Banks (2004), Hunter and O'Connor (2003) and Beevers and Miller (2004) are used in this section as examples to address the limitations of this claim. These three studies were selected to represent cross-sectional, case-controlled, and longitudinal designs and highlight the problem as it relates to defining the construct from both a theoretical and measurement perspective.

One consistent problem with the studies by Chang et al. (2004), Hunter and O'Connor (2003) and Beevers and Miller (2004) is the variation in the working definitions of perfectionism. Additionally, each study appears to derive the definition of perfectionism from a different theoretical approach, making a comparison of results difficult. For instance, Beevers and Miller (2004) defined perfectionism as a dysfunctional attitude based in cognitive theory. The authors placed perfectionism and depression under the same dysfunctional belief umbrella in order to better understand the etiology of suicide. Their assessment of perfectionism was unidimensional employing the Dysfunctional Attitudes Scale-Perfectionism by Imber, et al. (1990). Hunter and O'Connor, on the other hand, described perfectionism as reflected in achievement and socially-based vulnerabilities. From their description of perfectionism and their use of the Hewitt and Flett's (1991) Multidimensional Perfectionism Scale for its assessment, it can be assumed that they adhered to a multidimensional definition of the construct. However the authors never offered an explicit operational definition of perfectionism. Chang et al. (2007) also did not provide a description or clear definition of perfectionism in their research although they did focus on "adaptive" versus "maladaptive" perfectionism and linked their formulation to a variety of psychological symptoms (e.g., increased symptoms of depression and anxiety). They used a sample-specific two-factor structure for the Frost et al. (1990) Multidimensional Perfectionism Scale to identify adaptive and maladaptive perfectionism.

As demonstrated by these examples, there is little consensus regarding the definition of perfectionism with both unidimensional and multidimensional frameworks being employed. No matter how statistically significant the results of these study may have been, the variations in definitions of perfectionism leave one questioning the meaningfulness of the conclusions regarding the relation between perfectionism and suicidal behavior.

A related issue here is questions about the validity of interpretations drawn from the instruments used to assess perfectionism. For example, Chang et al. (2004) described the Multidimensional Perfectionism Scale used in their study in terms of item response formats and scale reliability, but provided no evidence of the appropriateness of interpreting scores on the scale as indicative of perfectionism. In fact, these authors took the scale, originally developed with six subscales, and reduced it to a two-subscale measure based on a factor analysis of their data. To interpret appropriately this new factor structure as reflecting a two-dimensional model of perfectionism would require cross validation in a new sample. However, the issue of cross-validation of the two-factor structure of the scale was not addressed. Similarly, Beevers and Miller (2004) provided no psychometric evidence for the validity of interpretations drawn from the Dysfunctional Attitude Scale-Perfectionism (Imber et al., 1990). Their claim for support for the measure was that it had been used previously.

Recommendation 13.4: Authors should identify a theoretically linked and psychometrically sound operational definition for personality constructs to ensure clarity of results and allow for replication.

Risk Versus Protective Factors

There has been a recent surge of interest in "protective factors," that is personality traits or states that reduce the risk of suicide in an individual. For example, Alcantara and Gone (2007) listed spirituality, engagement in cultural practices, and social support as possible protective factors for Native American suicide. In an empirical study of attempted suicide in low income, African American men and women, Kaslow et al. (2005) used a measure of social support and labeled it as a protective factor, whereas spouse abuse was labeled as a risk factor. The only apparent difference in these factors is whether a high score or a low score on the measure predicts suicidality.

It is important that researchers seek conceptual clarity here. What is the difference between asserting, for example, that a high hopelessness score on the Beck Hopelessness Scale (Beck, Weissman, Lester & Trexler, 1974) is a risk factor for suicide and asserting that a low score on the scale is a protective factor? From the other perspective, a high score on Linehan's Reasons for Living Scale (Linehan, Goodstein, Nielsen & Chiles, 1983) can be viewed as a protective factor, while a low score can be viewed as a risk factor.

It is not always clear what the polarities are on a self-report inventory. For example, depression may be contrasted with mania (Thalbourne, Delin & Bassett, 1994) or with happiness (McGreal & Joseph, 1993), two scales which make the polarity quite clear, even though they utilize different poles.

Recommendation 13.5: Researchers should clarify the theoretical underpinning for focusing their research on risk factors versus protective factors. In particular, the polarities of the personality traits and states investigated should be made explicit.

Conclusion

Recent systematic reviews of the relations between personality traits and suicide ideation, attempts and death by suicide have suggested links with such characteristics as neuroticism and extroversion, impulsivity and aggression, hostility, self criticism and perfectionism, and psychoticism (e.g., Brezo et al., 2006 & O'Connor, 2007). The predominant theoretical assumption in most of this research has been that these characteristics are trait-like as opposed to state dependent, and little attention has been given to the potential influence of maturation in the samples that have been studied. Additionally, much of the research in this area has been plagued by an overreliance on self-report as the primary data collection method, minimal attention to issues of impression management, and a limited focus on the critical issues of measurement validity. With regard to this latter issue, although most authors report sample-specific reliability for their research measures, the absence of both general and sample-specific evidence for construct-related validity in much of the research places limits on the confidence one can have in the interpretations of the research. As such, we hope that a consideration of the recommendations that we have made in this chapter will help strengthen research on the relations between personality variables and suicide and advance our understanding in this area.

References

Alcantara, C., & Gone, J. P. (2007). Reviewing suicide in Native American communities. *Death Studies*, 31, 457–477.

Beck, A. T., Weissman, A., Lester, D., & Trexler, L. (1974). The measurement of pessimism: The Hopelessness Scale. *Journal of Consulting & Clinical Psychology*, 42, 861–865.

Beevers, C. G., & Miller, I. W. (2004). Perfectionism, cognitive bias, and hopelessness as prospective predictors of suicidal ideation. *Suicide & Life-Threatening Behavior*, 34, 126–137.

Brezo, J., Paris, J., & Turecki, G. (2006). Personality characteristics as correlates of suicidal ideation, suicide attempts, and suicide completions: A systematic review. *Acta Psychiatrica Scandinavia, 113*, 180–206.

Buss, D. M. (1994). Personality evoked: The evolutionary psychology of stability and change. In T. F. Heatherton & J. L. Weinberger (Eds.), *Can personality change?* (pp. 41–57). Washington D.C.: American Psychological Association.

Chang, E. C., Watkins, A. F., & Banks, K. H. (2004). How adaptive and maladaptive perfectionism relate to positive and negative psychological functioning: Testing a stress-mediation model in black and white female college students. *Journal of Counseling Psychology, 51*, 93–102.

Dougherty, D. M., Mathias, C. W., Marsh, D. M., Papageorgiou, T. D., Swann, A. C., & Moeller, F. G. (2004). Laboratory measured behavioral impulsivity relates to suicide attempt history. *Suicide & Life-Threatening Behavior, 34*, 374–385.

Frost, R., Marten, P., Lahart, C., & Rosenblate, R. (1990). The dimensions of perfectionism. *Cognitive Therapy & Research*, 14, 449–468.

Heatherton, T. F., & Nichols, P. A. (1994). Conceptual issues in assessing whether personality can change. In T. F. Heatherton & J. L. Weinberger (Eds.), *Can personality change?* (pp. 3–18). Washington D.C.: American Psychological Association.

Heppner, P. P., Wampold, B. E., & Kivlighan, D. M. (2008). *Research design in counseling (3rd Edition)*. Belmont, CA: Thompson Brooks/Cole.

Hewitt, P. L., & Flett, G. L. (1991). Perfectionism in the self and social contexts: Conceptualization, assessment and association with psychopathology. *Journal of Personality & Social Psychology, 30*, 456–470.

Hunter, E. C., & O'Connor, R. C. (2003). Hopelessness and future thinking in parasuicide: The role of perfectionism. *British Journal of Clinical Psychology, 42*, 355–365.

Imber, S. D., Pilkonis, P. A., Sotsky, S. M., Elkin, I., Watkins, J. T., Collins, J. F., Shea, M. T., Leber, W. R., & Glass, D. R. (1990). Mode-specific effects among three treatments for depression. *Journal of Consulting & Clinical Psychology, 58*, 352–359.

Kaslow, N. J., Sherry, A., Bethea, K., Wyckoff, S., Compton, M. T., Grall, M. B., Scholl, L., Price, A. W., Kellerman, A., Thompson, N., & Parker, R. (2005). Social risk and protective factors for suicide attempts in low income African American men and women. *Suicide & Life-Threatening Behavior*, 35, 400–412.

Linehan, M. M., Goodstein, J., Nielsen, S., & Chiles, J. (1983). Reasons for staying alive when you're thinking of killing yourself. *Journal of Consulting & Clinical Psychology*, 51, 276–286.

McCrae, R. R., & Costa, P. T. (1990). *Personality in adulthood.* New York: Guilford Press.

McGreal, R., & Joseph, S. (1993). The Depression-Happiness Scale. *Psychological Reports*, 73, 1270–1282.

O'Connor, R. C. (2007). The relations between perfectionism and suicidality: A systematic review. *Suicide & Life-Threatening Behavior, 37*, 698–714.

Paulhus, D. L. (1994). *Reference manual for the Balanced Inventory of Desirable Responding-Version Six (BIDR-6)*. Vancouver Canada: University of British Columbia.

Roberts, B. W., & Del Vecchio, W. F. (2000). The rank-order consistency of personality traits from childhood to old age: A qualitative review of longitudinal studies. *Psychological Bulletin 126,* 3–25.

Thalbourne, M. A., Delin, P. S., & Bassett, D. L. (1994). An attempt to construct scales measuring manic-depressive-like experiences and behavior. *British Journal of Clinical Psychology,* 33, 205–207.

Zouk, H., Tousignant, M., Sequin, M., Lesage, A., & Turecki, G. (2006). Characterization of impulsivity in suicide completers: Clinical, behavioral, and psychosocial dimensions. *Journal of Affective Disorders, 92,* 195–204.

14

Typologies[26]

Studies of suicidal behavior, almost without exception, consider samples of either completed suicides or attempted suicides as a whole. For example, in studies that one of us collaborated on (see for example, Lester, Beck & Mitchell, 1979) a consecutive series of attempted suicides admitted to a general hospital was administered tests of depression and hopelessness and followed-up for several years. In that study, there was no attempt to classify the patients into groups on the basis of psychological traits or states.

In two books, Lester (2000, 2008) presented essays on some sixty famous individuals who had completed suicide – at least famous enough so that someone wrote a biography of them or a publisher agreed to publish their autobiography. Lester (2000) concluded:

> One of the more immediate thoughts after reading about the lives of these suicides is that they are a very heterogeneous group. If we were hoping to find a "suicidal profile," we would fail. It is hard to see what, if anything, people as diverse as Alan Turing, Konoe Fumimaro and Robert Clive have in common. It is difficult even to find groups of "clusters" of similar suicides, so that we could describe three or four possible profiles into which we could classify the suicides. (p. 245)[27]

Suicides have been grouped and compared according to obvious characteristics – such as by sex, age and ethnicity, for example. But the major way in which they have been grouped is by psychiatric diagnosis. In Chapter 4, we have discussed the problems with this set of categories, namely that psychiatric diagnosis is a symptom-based classification system rather than a cause-based classification system, and it has poor reliability. It is also far from clear whether grouping individuals by psychiatric diagnosis furthers our understanding of suicide. For example, the best predictors of suicide in schizophrenics are very similar to those with other psychiatric disorders (Pompili et

---

[26] The issue of how to define and label actual suicidal behavior (completed, attempted, ideation, etc.) is discussed in Chapter 2 on general methodological issues.

[27] Alan Turing was an English mathematician who, in the 1930s, described how computers, if they were ever invented, ought to operate. He was arrested and convicted of being a homosexual in the 1950s, forced to take chemical castrating agents, and killed himself soon afterwards. Konoe Funimaro was commissioned as commander by the Emperor of Japan to lead the government during World War Two. He did for a while and then resigned in 1941 and sat out the war. He was scheduled to be tried as a war criminal and committed suicide. Robert Clive led the British forces in India in the 1700s, defeated the French forces and served as Governor General in India for many years. Back in England, he was attacked for corruption while in office and, although he was exonerated, became depressed and killed himself.

al., 2008), such as depression, hopelessness and comorbid substance abuse and, furthermore, those predictors are also similar to the predictors of suicide in the general population.

One of the most famous classification of suicides was that from the sociologist Durkheim (1897) which we discussed in Chapter 5: anomic, egoistic, fatalistic and altruistic. As we saw in Chapter 5, Durkheim based these types on two social dimensions – social integration and social regulation – where high and low values of these dimensions in a society resulted in a particular type of suicide. It is important to bear in mind that Durkheim used these four types of suicide to described societal rates of suicide. For example, societies with a very low level of social regulation would have high rates of anomic suicide. He did not apply the four types to individuals.

Some scholars have discussed whether suicides in some groups of the society might fit Durkheim's typology. For example, Sharma (1978) discussed whether the Indian custom of *suttee*, in which a Hindu widow commits suicide on her husband's funeral pyre, was altruistic suicide. He noted that some widows may have committed suttee because of strong social pressure, and so he saw the behavior as *obligatory altruistic suicide*. Hitchcock (1967) explored the consequences of the shortage of women among the Nauthars in Nepal, leading to arranged marriages being established when the children were young, resulting in very unhappy young women who often killed themselves. Hitchcok viewed these suicides as fatalistic.

The first scholar to apply Durkheim's types to individuals was Faber (1970) who classified some of the suicides in the plays of Euripides as altruistic. For example, in *Alcestis*, Apollo is fond of Alcestis's husband, Admetus. Admetus is fated to die at a young age, and the Fates agree to spare him only if a substitute can be found whereupon Alcestis volunteers to die in his place. Faber saw Alcestis's death as altruistic suicide. Similarly, Kaplan (1987) classified all of the suicides in the plays by Sophocles and Euripides using Durkheim's typology. Jocasta, Oedipus's mother, was an egoistic suicide, as was Haemon's in *Antigone*.

Lester (1994a) took 30 famous suicides he had studied and tried to classify them into Durhkeim's typology. He was able to classify all of them but some seemed to fit into two categories rather than a single category. For example, the suicide of Vincent Van Gogh, the painter, had elements of both egoism and anomie, as did the suicide of Sylvia Plath, the American poet.

Reynolds and Berman (1995) obtained 484 cases of suicide from the offices of medical examiners and had judges classify them into Durkheim's types. The agreement rate between the judges was 79%, and 71% of the suicides could be classified into one of the four types: 57% were judged to be anomic, 9% as fatalistic, 6% as egoistic and none as altruistic.

Despite this enthusiasm for using Durkheim's typology of suicides in society to describe individual suicides, it would be far preferable to have psychologically based typologies.

Psychologically-Based Typologies of Suicide

Recommendation 14.1: It is important to developed meaningful psychology-based typologies of suicidal individuals.

Besides exploring the usefulness of Durkheim's typology for classifying suicides, Reynolds and Berman (1995) looked at nine other typologies. They included the following classification schemes.

(1) Menninger (1938) described three motives for suicide: the wish to be killed (depression and guilt), the wish to kill (anger-out), and the wish to die (the desire to escape). Suicide notes have been studied for the presence of these three motives (e.g., Brevard, Lester & Yang, 1990), and often the notes contain two or all three motives.

(2) Leonard (1967) proposed a categorization for hospitalized patients who completed suicide (dependent-dissatisfied, satisfied-symbiotic and unaccepting) which she saw as based on inadequate differentiation from the mother during the first three years of life.

(3) Mintz (1968) proposed a psychoanalytic motive-based system with 11 categories: (1) hostility directed toward an introjected object, (2) aggression turned inward on the self, (3) retaliation, revenge and the desire to punish, (4) narcissistic or masochistic gratification, (5) atonement for guilt, (6) destruction of intolerable feelings, (7) rebirth, (8) reunion, (9) escape from pain, (10) counterphobic reaction to a fear of death and (11) defensive regression.

(4) Shneidman (1966) classified suicides as psyde-seeker (those who have a conscious suicidal intent), psyde-initiator (those who have a terminal illness and initiate their own death), psyde-ignorer (those who believe in a continued existence or reunion with deceased loved ones) and psyde-chancer (those who risk death in dangerous situations).

(5) Shneidman (1968) described three types of suicides: egotic (the result of an intrapsychic debate), dyadic (deep unfulfilled needs pertaining to a significant other), and ageneratic (losing one's sense of membership of the march of generations).

(6) Shneidman (1980) used Henry Murray's classification of 21 basic needs to classify suicides by which need was being frustrated, needs such as the need for achievement and the need for autonomy.

(7) Baechler (1979) suggested four types: escapist (a flight from an intolerable situation), aggressive (vengeance by eliciting remorse or social opprobrium for someone else or an appeal for help), oblative (a sacrifice to gain something or transfiguration to attain a better state),and ludic (an ordeal through risk-taking or a game played with life).

(8) Henderson and Williams (1974) proposed depression, extra-punitive, alienation, operant, modeling and avoidance as the basis for a typology.

(9) Wold (1971) developed an empirically based set of 10 categories derived from cluster analyzing variables for 500 suicides, such as "down and out" and "I can't live without you."

Using the 484 suicides from the files of medical examiners, Reynolds and Berman used 37 raters to judge the suicides, with two raters to each suicide. Eighty of these were labeled unclassifiable since they did not fit into at least two typologies. For the remaining 404 suicides, the percentage that were classifiable ranged from 61% for Leonard's system to 86% for Baechler's system. The percentage of inter-judge agreement ranged from 76% for Leonard's system to 98% for Baechler's.

Menninger's and Leonard's systems resulted in roughly similar numbers in all three categories, which was unusual for the systems. For Mintz's system, 40% were classified as desire to escape (from pain, emotional distress, etc); for Shneidman's system based on Murray's needs, 29% were classified as harmavoidance; for Shneidman's (1966) system, 47% were classified as psyde-seekers; and for Baechler's system 64% were escapist. The other systems produced at least two categories with a fair percentage of suicides.Reynolds and Berman then investigated the inter-dependence between the different typologies and identified five clusters:

> Escape (90 suicides)
> Confusion (54 suicides)
> Aggression (76 suicides)
> Alienation (23 suicides)
> Depression (112 suicides)

This typology was found to describe 86% of the suicides. Most of the typologies failed to meet meaningful criteria for typologies, including having too many unclassifiable cases, poor inter-judge agreement, and too many cases falling into one category. It is interesting that the oldest system, from Menninger in 1938 proved to be one of the best with 77% of the suicides classified, 90% inter-judge agreement, and a good proportion of suicides in each type (20% to 28%). However, the system proposed by Reynolds and Berman may be superior.

The study by Reynolds and Berman highlights one of the major issues with psychologically-based typologies. Is it better to base typologies on the speculations of scholars, or should they be empirically based. Of those examined by Reynolds and Berman, only the typology proposed by Wold was based on an empirical study of suicides.

The Bases For Typologies

There are several possible bases for typologies of suicide (or any behavior): classic theories of psychology, "arm-chair" speculation and empirical studies. Let us look at each of these possibilities.

Classic Theories

The classic theories of personality can provide a basis for typologies. For example, it would be possible to classify people on the basis of psychoanalytic theory into oral, anal, and phallic types. One of the more well-researched typologies is that based on Eysenck's (1967) theory of personality. Eysenck used two broad dimensions of personality (extraversion–introversion and neuroticism–stability) to form four types: neurotic introverts, stable introverts, neurotic extraverts and stable extraverts. (This corresponds to famous typology proposed several thousand years ago by Galen: melancholia, phlegmatic, choleric and sanguine.) It would be of interest to see whether the rates of suicide differ between these four types. Benjaminson, Krarup and Lauritsen (1990) found that attempted suicides did not differ from nonsuicidal psychiatric patients in extraversion or psychoticism, but they did have lower neuroticism scores. However, no zonal (or typological) analysis has appeared yet.

One typology based on classic theories of personality has been explored in a couple of studies. Carl Jung proposed three major dimensions of personality: extraversion–introversion, thinking–feeling and sensing–intuiting. Myers and Briggs (Myers & McCaulley, 1985) developed a psychological test to measure these dimensions and added judging–perceiving . This provides 16 types (2-by-2-by-2-by-2). Although the research has not focused on completed suicides, Lester (1989) found that suicidal ideation in college students was associated with lower sensing, thinking and judging scores (but was not associated with extraversion). Komisin (1992) found that the INFP type (introverted, intuitive, feeling and perceiving type) had the highest rate of both suicidal ideation and suicide attempts among college students, while the ESTJ type had the least. Street and Komrey (1994) found that prior non-lethal suicidality was more common in college students of type ISF, INP and ENJ for males and IP for females.

It might be thought that studies of this form might be impossible to carry out on individuals who have died by suicide because they are deceased and cannot complete psychological tests. However, reliable and valid assessments of personality have been carried out by having significant others complete the psychological tests as they think the target individuals might have done. Duberstein, Conwell and Caine (1994) had the survivors of suicides (survivors who those who have lost a significant other to suicide) complete a personality test on behalf of the deceased. The suicides were judged to have higher introversion and neuroticism scores and lower openness scores than controls, but did not differ in agreeableness or conscientious. (ratings were based on the five-factor "theory" of personality; McRae & Costa, 1987). Duberstein and his colleagues have shown, therefore, that these kinds of studies can be carried out for completed suicides, (although questions remain regarding the validly of proxy ratings). A typological analysis may, therefore, be possible in the future.

Recommendation 14.2: In order to bring suicidal behavior into mainstream psychology, it is important to develop typologies of suicidal behavior that are based on the classic theories of personality (or on theories from other fields in psychology).

Empirically-Based Typologies

Several researchers have endeavored to derive empirically based typologies (or, at least, clusters of suicidal individuals based on their characteristics). These typologies depend critically on the sample chosen, the variables used in the cluster analysis, and the interpretation given to the clusters by the investigators. It is obviously much easier to conduct empirically-based cluster analyses on living suicidal people but, unless these individuals are classified by their suicidal intent so that extrapolation to completed suicides can be made (see Chapter 2), these are not as valuable as studies on completed suicides. We should note, however, that a typology of attempted suicides and suicidal ideators might be useful for psychotherapists working with suicidal clients. It might be possible to tailor the different therapeutic tactics for specific types of suicidal clients.

Bagley, Jacobson and Rehin (1976) analyzed data from fifty completed suicides and identified three factors.[28] (i) Chronic depressed suicides had a history of suicidal behavior and psychiatric care. (ii) Sociopathic suicides were socially isolated, with a history of attempted suicide and early deprivation, and were often located in the central wards of the cities. (iii) The old and handicapped suicides were in pain, often widowed, middle class and living alone, and typically used prescribed barbiturates for the suicidal act.

Recommendation 14.3: Although it is easier to develop empirically-based typologies of living suicidal individuals (such as suicide attempters and ideators), it is important to develop empirically-based typologies of completed suicides.

"Arm-Chair" Typologies

The third basis for a typology of suicide is that from scholars using their experience of research and suicidal clients to formulate a speculative typology. Several of these were mentioned above, some of which were studied by Reynolds and Berman (1995).

An interesting typology has been proposed by Taylor (1982) based on two dimensions: (i) whether the action is inner-directed (ectopic) or other-directed (symphysic), and (ii) whether it is purposive (certainty) or merely an ordeal (uncertainty). This provides four types: thanation (ectopic/uncertain), submissive (ectopic/certain), appeal (symphysic/uncertain), and sacrifice (symphysic/certain).

Other arm-chair typologies have value if they connect to other ideas. For example, Phillips (1989) and Lester (1988) classified suicides into those that are the result of a chronic process and those what are the result of an acute crisis. Lester and Yang (1991) pointed out how this dichotomy fits well with Becker's (1962) analysis of two types of irrational behavior[29]: decisions which are a repetition of poor choices made in the past and decisions which are made from an impulsive (and perhaps random) choice from the alternatives.

Recommendation 14.4: "Arm-chair" typologies should be explored for their usefulness in generating hypotheses for research in order to identify those that are useful for increasing our understanding of suicide.

---

[28] Factor-analysis identifies dimensions of personality or characteristic rather than clustering individuals into types.
[29] Becker is an economist.

Typologies Of Attempted Suicides

There have been many attempts to use cluster analysis for samples of attempted suicides to derive typologies. Arensman and Kerkhof (1996) reviewed the results of 32 studies, some with a priori subgroups and some with no a priori subgroups. In a priori groupings, the researcher studied different groups of attempters, such as repeaters versus one-timers or high suicidal intent versus low suicidal intent. More interesting were the results of studies that carried out cluster analyses to determine the groupings.

Kiev (1976) identified seven groups: (1) suicidal gesture, (2) acute depressive reaction, (3) passive-aggressive and passive-dependent personality disorder, (4) anxiety reactions with interpersonal conflict, (5) socially isolated, (6) suicidal preoccupation, and (7) chronic dysfunctional. Paykel and Rassaby (1978) devised a typology based solely on the circumstances of the attempt: (1) non-overdoses, (2) overdosers, and (3) recurrent. Henderson and Lance (1979) identified five groups: (1) operant, non-alienated and non-avoidance, (2) repeaters, (3) depressed with high life endangerment, (4) operant, alienated and avoidance, (5) wrist-cutters, and (6) undifferentiated. Katschnig, Sint and Fuchs-Robetin (1979) identified three groups: (1) cry for help, (2) failed suicide, and (3) chronic. Kurz et al. (1987) identified three groups: (1) non-serious attempts, (2) serious attempts, and (3) repeaters. Kerkhof et al. (1988) identified five groups: (1) youngsters living with parents, (2) married/cohabiting first-evers, (3) married/cohabiting repeaters, (4) repeaters not married or cohabiting, and (5) young adults with behavioral problems. Arensman and Kerkhof concluded that the most consistent grouping was based on severity, with two groups – mild and severe.

Looking at these typologies, it appears that the majority are not based on psychological characteristics, such as personality traits or motives. A typology based on superficial characteristics such as age and marital status adds little to our understanding of attempted suicide. Similarly, typologies based on the circumstances of the suicidal action, such as severity or method, adds little information. All of these characteristics (age or method) are immediately obvious to the clinician. The typology identified by Henderson and Lance seems to be the most promising since it is based on alienation, the reward for the suicidal behavior (which they call operant), depression and avoidance, characteristics which move toward a psychological understanding of the suicidal act.

Recommendation 14.5: Typologies of non-fatal suicidal behavior (attempts and ideation) should be explored for their usefulness in generating research that increases our understanding of suicidal behavior, in predicting short-term and long-term outcomes, and in formulating psychotherapeutic plans.

Discussion

The identification of meaningful typologies of suicides, both attempted and completed, is a crucial task for suicidologists in the future. Not only are new proposals for typologies needed, those already proposed should be examined for their reliability and validity. Only one study has hitherto examined the reliability of the major typologies proposed (Reynolds & Berman, 1995), and more such studies should be carried out.

The typologies should be examined for their research and clinical usefulness. Do all or only some of the types fit into a particular theory of suicidal behavior? For example, Lester (1994b) applied fifteen theories of suicide (based on the major theories of personality) to thirty famous suicides and found that, for example, Carl Jung's theory of suicide was more appropriate to the women who committed suicide than to the men. The older suicides were more consistent with Ludwig Binswanger's theory than with other theories, while those suicides who had experienced early loss of a parent were more consistent with the theory of Gregory Zilboorg.

Perhaps even more important, do the typologies have any implications for psychotherapy? Is one system of psychotherapy better for some types of clients than others and, if so, which types? For example, there is some evidence that Linehan's (1993) dialectical behavior therapy is suitable for suicidal women and especially for those with borderline personality disorder. We need more links of this type so that we may provide better counseling for suicidal individuals.

References

Arensman, E., & Kerkhof, A. J. F. M. (1996). Classification of attempted suicide. *Suicide & Life-Threatening Behjavior*, 26, 46–67.

Baechler, J. (1979). *Suicides*. New York: Basic Books.

Bagley, C., Jacobson, S., & Rehin, A. (1976). Completed suicide. *Psychological Medicine*, 6, 429–438.

Becker, G. S. (1962). Irrational behavior and economic behavior. *Journal of Political Economy*, 70, 1–13.

Benjaminson, S., Krarup, G., & Lauritsen, R. (1990). Personality, parental rearing behavior, and parental loss in attempted suicide. *Acta Psychiatrica Scandinavica*, 82, 389–397.

Brevard, A., Lester, D., & Yang, B. (1990). A comparison of suicide notes written by suicide completers and suicide attempters. *Crisis*, 11, 7–11.

Duberstein, P. R., Conwell, Y., & Caine, E. (1994). Age differences in the personality characteristics of suicide completers. *Psychiatry*, 57, 213–224.

Durkheim, E. (1897). *Le suicide*. Paris: Felix Alcan.

Faber, M. D. (1970). *Suicide and Greek tragedy*. New York: Sphinx Press.

Henderson, S., & Lance, G. N. (1979). Types of attempted suicide (parasuicide). *Acta Psychiatrica Scandinavica*, 59, 31–39.

Henderson, S., & Williams, C. L. (1978). On the prevention of parasuicide. *Australian & New Zealand Journal of Psychiatry*, 8, 237–240.

Hitchcock, J. T. (1967). Fatalistic suicide resulting from adaptation to an asymmetrical sex ratio. *Eastern Anthropologist*, 20, 133.142.

Kaplan, K. J. (1987). Jonah and Narcissus. *Studies in Formative Spirituality*, 8(1), 33–54.

Katschnig, H., Sint, P., & Fuchs-Robetin, G. (1979). Suicide and parasuicide. In R. Farmer & S. Hirsch (Eds.), *The suicide syndrome,* pp. 154–166. London, UK: Croom Helm.

Kerkhof, A. J. F. M., Wal, van der J., & Hengeveld, M. W. (1988). Typology of persons who attempted suicide with predictive value for repetition. In H. J. Möller, A. Schmidtke & R. Welz (Eds.), *Current issues of suicidology,* pp. 193–203. Berlin–Heidelberg: Springer-Verlag.

Kiev, A. (1976). Cluster analysis profiles of suicide attempters. *American Journal of Psychiatry,* 133, 150–153.

Komisin, L. K. (1992). Personality type and suicidal behaviors in college students. *Journal of Psychological Type,* 24, 24–32.

Kurz, A., Möller, H. J., Baindl, G., Burk, F., Torhorst, A., Wachter, C., & Lauter, H. (1987). Classification of parasuicide by cluster analysis. *British Journal of Psychiatry,* 150, 520–525.

Leonard, C. V. (1967). *Understanding and preventing suicide.* Springfield, IL: Charles Thomas.

Lester, D. (1988). Suicidal individuals. *Crisis,* 9, 130–134.

Lester, D. (1989). Jungian dimensions of personality, subclinical depression and suicidal ideation. *Personality & Individual Differences,* 10, 1009.

Lester, D. (1994a). Applying Durkheim's typology to individual suicides. In D. Lester (Ed.), *Durkheim's Le Suicide 100 years later,* pp. 224–236. Philadelphia: Charles Press.

Lester, D. (1994b). A comparison of 15 theories of suicide. *Suicide & Life-Threatening Behavior,* 24, 80–88.

Lester, D. (2000). *By their own hand.* Chichester, UK: Aeneas Press.

Lester, D. (2008). *Exit weeping.* Hauppauge, NY: Nova Science.

Lester, D., Beck, A. T., & Mitchell, B. (1979). Extrapolation from attempted suicides to completed suicides: A test. *Journal of Abnormal Psychology,* 88, 78–80.

Lester, D., & Yang, B. (1991). Suicidal behavior and Becker's definition of irrationality. *Psychological Reports,* 68, 655–656.

Linehan, M. M. (1993). *Cognitive-behavioral treatment of borderline personality disorder.* New York: Guilford.

McRae, R. R., & Costa, P. T. (1987). Validation of the five-factor model of personality across instruments and observers. *Journal of Personality & Social Psychology,* 52, 81–90.

Menninger, K. (1938). *Man against himself.* New York: Harcourt, Brace & World.

Mintz, R. S. (1968). Psychotherapy of the suicidal patient. In H. L. P. Resnik (Ed.), *Suicidal behaviors,* pp. 271–296. Boston: Little Brown.

Myers, I., & McCaulley, M. (1985). *Manual: A guide to the development and use of the Myers-Briggs Type Indicator.* Palo Alto, CA: Counseling Psychologists Press.

Paykel, E. S., & Rassaby, E. (1978). Classification of suicide attempters by cluster analysis. *British Journal of Psychiatry,* 133, 45–54.

Phillips, D. P. (1989). Recent advances in suicidology. In R. F. Diekstra, R. W. Maris, S. Platt, A. Schmidtke & G. Sonneck (Eds.), *Suicide and its prevention,* pp. 299–312. Leiden: Brill.

Pompili, M., Lester, D., Innamorati, M., Tatarelli, R., & Girardi, P. (2008). Assessment and treatment of suicide risk in schizophrenia. *Expert Review in Neurotherapeutics,* 8(1), 51–74.

Reynolds, F. M. T., & Berman, A. L. (1995). An empirical typology of suicide. *Archives of Suicide Research,* 1, 97–109.

Sharma, A. (1978). Emile Durkheim on suttee as suicide. *International Journal of Contemporary Sociology,* 15, 283–291.

Shneidman, E. S. (1966). Orientation toward death. *International Journal of Psychiatry,* 2, 167–200.

Shneidman, E. S. (1968). Classifications of suicidal phenomenon. *Bulletin of Suicidology.* July, 1–9.

Shneidman, E. S. (1980). A possible classification of suicidal acts based on Murray's need system. *Suicide & Life-Threatening Behavior*, 10, 175–181.

Street, S., & Komrey, J. D. (1994). Relationships between suicidal behavior and personality type. *Suicide & Life-Threatening Behavior*, 24, 282–292.

Taylor, S. (1982). *Durkheim and the study of suicide*. London: Macmillan.

Wold, C. I. (1971). Sub-grouping of suicidal people. *Omega*, 2, 19–29.

Conclusions

15

Conclusions

It is very easy to be critical of theory and research in general and of theory and research in suicidology in particular. As anyone who has submitted a paper to a scholarly journal can attest, the reviewers find many defects in the design, statistical analysis and writing style.

It is also very difficult to get out of the ruts that previous theorists and researchers have dug for us. For example, it is easy to criticize theories of personality, whether it be Sigmund Freud's psychoanalytic theory or Hans Eysenck's biologically-based theory. It is very difficult to devise a new theory that is totally different from those already proposed. Indeed, it might be easier to do so if one had never read those other theories.

There have been many critiques of the field of suicidology in the past, with long accounts of what others have done incorrectly and incompletely. Our aim in this book has been not to simply add another critique of the field, but rather to make recommendations for the future. In this way, rather than leaving readers with a pessimistic view of the field of suicidology, we hope we have left you with optimism and ideas for your future research and theorizing.

Rather than simply re-iterate here what we have said in the previous chapters (although we have listed all of our recommendations in an Appendix), what we would like to do is present a few examples of innovative research to indicate what can be done.

A Study of Murder

First, let us mention a study that has nothing to do with the field of suicidology – one taken from the field of homicide studies. Many years ago, Stuart Palmer (1960) was interested in the violent backgrounds and abuse suffered by murderers. Palmer thought that frustration could result in murderous behavior, and his study found indeed that his sample of 51 murderers had experienced a huge amount of physical and psychological frustration as children and adolescents. For example, nine of them had injuries from the forceps during delivery (including torn mouths and lacerated ears). The murderers had 19 surgical operations and 23 serious accidents in their first twelve years of life, while eleven had serious illnesses in the first year of life. Ten had visible congenital defects, and fifteen acquired more physical deformities after birth. Their mothers had typically not wanted to be pregnant, had been rigid with their children, and more punitive.

What makes this study important? The control group (a topic and a problem that was discussed in Chapter 2 as well as referenced in other chapters)! Palmer made a fascinating choice. He chose the non-murdering brothers of the murderers as his control group, taking care to have as many younger brothers as older brothers. By making this choice, Palmer controlled for all kinds of psychological and social variables for which unrelated control groups cannot control. Palmer found that the average frustration score for the murderers was 9.2 incidents, whereas the average score for their brothers was only 4.2.

We have not yet come across a study of completed or attempted suicides which has chosen siblings as the control group. What would such a design uncover that our traditional designs have not? An interesting question indeed!

Combining Psychological and Physiological Measures

There are a couple of other studies which we think herald new and innovative approaches to the study of suicide. Typically, researchers interested in the physiology of behavior utilize only physiological measures, while those interested in psychological variables utilize only psychological variables. Sheila Crowell and her associates have combined these variables in a single study. For example, in one study (Crowell et al., 2005), 23 adolescent girls recruited from psychiatric clinics who had made multiple suicide attempts (labeled parasuicides by Crowell et al.) were compared with a control group of high school girls matched for age.

All the girls were given a battery of self-report inventories to complete, including measures of depression and positive and negative affect. In addition, the girls' parents and teachers also completed inventories about the girls, thereby supplementing the girls' self-reports and permitting investigation of the validity of both the self-reports and the parent and teacher reports. Psychophysiological measures were also made, including vagal influences on cardiac activity and skin conductance responses, in order to measure parasympathetic and sympathetic activity (in the autonomic nervous system). Blood samples were taken to measure peripheral serotonin levels. The parasuicidal girls had more psychopathology, had higher rates of drug use, and had a more attenuated parasympathetic tone than the control girls, as well as lower levels of peripheral serotonin.

To be sure, if we were reviewing this paper, we would have criticisms and we would make suggestions for improving the report. (We were not, however, asked to review the paper!) But what we would like to focus on here is the decision of the researchers to include parent and teacher reports as well as self-reports for the inventories and, perhaps even more importantly, to include physiological measures as well. In later studies, Crowell and her associates have included parent-child interactions, making her research the *most comprehensive* examination of attempted suicides we have seen.

Cusp-Catastrophe Models

In Chapter 3, we discussed how chaos and catastrophe theory may provide useful insights into the study of suicidal behavior. Armey and Crowther (2008) recently tested a cusp-catastrophe model for predicting non-suicidal self-injury. Using a sample of college students, in whom the incidence of deliberate self-injury was rare, Armey and Crowther used a variety of psychological scales to predict deliberate self-injury, including measures of response styles (such as rumination and distraction), positive and negative affect, and dissociative experiences.

Armey and Crowther found that a cusp-catastrophe model provided a better fit for the data than a logistic or linear regression model (a technique that was criticized in Chapter 2). The cusp-catastrophe model assumes that small variations in the predictor variables result in *catastrophic* changes in the target variable (Gilmore, 1981), and this proved to be the case for predicting deliberate self-injury in college students.

Final Point

Periodically throughout this book we have referenced the ideas of "protective factors" and "buffers" related to suicidal behavior. Clearly a trend over the past ten years has been to explore these constructs as differentiated from suicide "risk" factors. However, we have yet to see convincing evidence that suggests that protective factors or buffers are substantively different than the opposite of identified risk factors. In fact, it reminds us of a lyric from *Melt Your Heart* by Jenny Lewis:

"What's good for your soul is bad for your nerves if you reverse it."

Conceptually, research in the area of protective factors and buffers needs to first empirically demonstrate that these constructs are independent from factors shown to be related to increased risk for suicide as opposed to their opposites. We believe that this area of research is ripe for conceptual development and empirical investigation.

In conclusion, the point of these examples and this book is to attempt to encourage researchers to move well beyond the typical research strategies and methodologies that have become the mainstay of the field of suicidology. While the use of relying primarily on convenience samples, self-report data, and epidemiological data-bases among other strategies may be resource efficient and cost effective when conducting research in the area of suicide, we believe that these approaches have not advanced our understanding of suicide and suicidal behaviors. In fact, we argue that research in suicidology hitherto has led to more questions than it has provided answers. Consequently, we encourage researchers to think outside of the proverbial box that has characterized much of the literature in suicidology by critically evaluating their research methods and the assumptions that underlie them and by applying innovative approaches to understanding suicide.

References

Armey, M. F., & Crowther, J. H. (2008). A comparison of linear versus non-linear models of aversive self-awareness, dissociation, and non-suicidal self-injury among young adults. *Journal of Consulting & Clinical Psychology, 76,* 9–14.

Crowell, S. E., Beauchaine, T. P. McCauley, E., Smith, C. J., Stevens, A. L., & Silvers, P. (2005). Psychological, autonomic, and serotonergic correlates of parasuicide among adolescent girls. *Development & Psychopathology, 17,* 1105–1127.

Crowell, S. E., Beauchaine, T. P. McCauley, E., Smith, C. J., Vasilev, C. A., & Stevens, A. L. (2008). Parent-child interactions, peripheral serotonin, and self-inflicted injury in adolescents. *Journal of Consulting & Clinical Psychology, 76,* 15–21.

Gilmore, R. (1981). *Catastrophe theory for scientists and engineers.* New York: Wiley.

Palmer, S. (1960). *A study of murder.* New York: Crowell.

Appendix

Appendix

This appendix, beginning with Chapter 2, provides a chapter by chapter listing of the recommendations that we have made throughout the book.

Chapter 2. General Methodological Issues

Recommendation 2.1: It is important for sound epidemiological research and sociological studies of suicide that rates of completed suicide are accurate. Public health agencies should work with coroners and medical examiners to ensure that death records supplied to central government agencies are free from bias introduced by differing professional, legal, religious and economic perspectives. For example, coroners in Pennsylvania have for many years prepared two death certificates, one for the government and a special one for funeral directors to ensure that insurance companies do not withhold payment of the death benefit.

Recommendation 2.2: Since suicide in very young people is rarely, if ever, classified as such, rates should be calculated on a population base that does not include young children so as to provide a more accurate statistical picture of suicide. It would be appropriate if an organization like the World Health Organization convened a meeting to suggest an appropriate age range to use for this population base.

Recommendation 2.3: More use should be made of age-adjusted suicide rates in research, as well as suicide rates that are adjusted for other demographic variables such as sex and religious affiliation when those characteristics are relevant to the research question.

Recommendation 2.4: Rather than being tied to the typical 'rate per 100,000 per year' measure, researchers should explore the effect of using suicide rates calculated in logical, alternative ways on the results of their studies. Inclusion of alternative approaches may lead to a more fine-grained understanding of suicide and impact the refinement and development of theories of suicide.

Recommendation 2.5: Efforts must be made, perhaps by the WHO, to get more nations to report suicide rates and to encourage nations to collect data by ethnicity.

Recommendation 2.6: Although it is important to agree upon a set of terms for deliberate self-harm, it is more critical that researchers use both objective and subjective approaches to assessing the suicidal intent and medical lethality involved in the acts of their research subjects. Only if this is done can researchers evaluate the comparability of the samples used in the different published reports of research.

Recommendation 2.7: In judgments made based on an analysis of "residuals" of suicides, consideration must be given to the issue of the reliability of those data including the potential for recall and confirmatory bias in methods such as the psychological autopsy. In addition, appropriate control groups must be incorporated in these approaches, and those making judgments must be "blind" as to who is a suicide and who is a control subject.

Recommendation 2.8: Researchers studying attempted suicides with the hope of generalizing the results to those who have died by suicide must classify the attempted suicides into at least three groups based on their suicidal intent.

Recommendation 2.9: Researchers studying attempted suicides should include attempters who do not come to the attention of medical services.

Recommendation 2.10: Researchers should consider potential sources of subject bias in creating research designs, and they develop strategies to control for this critical research confound. In the absence of control, researchers should identify potential uncontrolled sources and interpret their results accordingly.

Recommendation 2.11: Studies of suicidal individuals should always control for the level of depression and the type and severity of psychiatric disturbance among other potentially confounding factors.

Recommendation 2.12: Alternative comparison groups should be utilized in studies of suicidal individuals, such as assaultive people and those with other acting-out behaviors.

Recommendation 2.13: It is important to obtain adequate sample sizes for research into suicide, especially for physiological studies.

Recommendation 2.14: Researchers must provide sample-specific evidence for the reliability and validity of the measuring instruments used in their research, especially when using measures devised in one type of setting or population but applied by the researchers in a new type of setting or population.

Recommendation 2.15: Researchers should make an effort to determine whether their results apply to variations in suicide rates over time, over place or both.

Recommendation 2.16: Researchers should investigate the impact of their choice of their sample of regions on the results of their ecological studies.

Recommendation 2.17: Researchers must continue to move beyond a sole reliance on statistical significance in interpreting quantitative research in suicidology to address issues of the clinical and practical usefulness of their results.

Recommendation 2.18: Researchers should remain cognizant of the limitations of online and CD-ROM access to the literature and take care to acquaint themselves with research on and theory about suicide prior to the last few years.

Chapter 3. Psychology Research into Suicide

Recommendation 3.1: The major classical theories of personality and human behavior, plus more recent proposals, should be explored further for their implications for explaining suicidal behavior. Testable hypotheses should be proposed, and research to test these predictions carried out.

Recommendation 3.2: Research should be based on hypotheses derived from psychological theory rather than conducted at a purely empirical level and then related back to any theory that seems relevant.

Recommendation 3.3: Efforts should be made to summarize the findings from the existing atheoretical research, using meta-analyses where appropriate to identify reliable findings and their range of applicability.

Recommendation 3.4: Previously proposed micro-level and post hoc theories should be identified and reviewed, and testable (and competing) hypotheses derived and tested.

Recommendation 3.5: More theories derived from the study of other behaviors should be explored for their applicability as explanations for suicidal behavior.

Recommendation 3.6: Alternatives to the deficit-oriented models of suicidal behavior should be proposed (for example, models based on "positive psychology" and resilience), and theories proposed to explain suicidal behavior carried out for growth-oriented (as conceived by humanistic psychologists) motives.

Recommendation 3.7: Efforts should be made to develop new macro-theories of suicidal behavior based on previously applied micro-theories of suicidal behavior or by drawing upon theoretical developments in other fields and disciplines.

Recommendation 3.8: Testable hypotheses should be derived from these macro-theories of suicidal behavior so that the relevance and applicability of the theories can be tested.

Chapter 4. Psychiatric Research

Recommendation 4.1: Psychiatric research into suicide requires the development of a better diagnostic system, one that takes into account causes rather than relying on the phenomenology of symptoms.

Recommendation 4.2: Psychiatric research into suicidal behavior must take into account the treatment history (especially medications), current medications and adherence to treatment regimen of the subjects.

Recommendation 4.3: Research into suicide should experiment with the use of other control groups beyond depressed non-suicidal patients. Aggressive and impulsive subjects might provide interesting and useful insights.

Recommendation 4.4: Research on suicidal behavior in twins must employ more rigorous methodologies to address these and other potentially confounding issues.

Recommendation 4.5: MZ twins reared apart MUST be studied if interpretations are going to be drawn regarding genetic versus environmental influences.

Recommendation 4.6: Twin studies of suicide must control for depression in order to decide whether it is suicidal behavior *per se* that is inherited or merely depression.

Recommendation 4.7: Research into suicidal behavior in twins should focus on non-fatal suicidal behavior.

Recommendation 4.8: Studies of the brain of suicides must utilize large sample sizes.

Recommendation 4.9: Suicides and controls must be matched, not only for sex, age, ethnicity and post-mortem delay, but also confounding factors such as depression.

Recommendation 4.10: Researchers should study more than one brain area. Indeed, it might be useful for researchers into brains to come to some consensus about which brain areas should be sampled in research so that research from different research teams can be more easily compared.

Recommendation 4.11: Research on the brains of suicides would be improved if the research was designed to study suicidal behavior and not merely a peripheral analysis of data collected for a project on some other behavior (such as schizophrenia or depressive disorders).

Recommendation 4.12: Psychiatric research should be carried on a variety of clinical and non-clinical subjects in order that the generality of the associations between PTSD and suicidal behavior can be ascertained.

Recommendation 4.13: Since there typically exists a variety of operational measures for each target behavior, researchers should consider using two or more operational measures and comparing the results obtained with each measure.

Recommendation 4.14: The strengths and limitations of these three different methodologies should be identified, and the associations examined for each methodology separately. Attempts to synthesize the results from these approaches should be grounded in a theoretical framework that can advance understanding of the relations.

Recommendation 4.15: Psychiatric research must take into account the timing and sequencing of experiential events, the appearance of symptoms and behaviors, and the development of the target behavior.

Chapter 5. The Sociological Study of Suicide

Recommendation 5.1: Tests of Durkheim's theory of suicide must consider all combinations of levels of social integration and social regulation and test for curvilinear relationships rather than assuming linearity.

Recommendation 5.2: Tests of Durkheim's theory of suicide must classify suicides by type and calculate four rates of suicide – egoistic, anomic, fatalistic and altruistic.

Recommendation 5.3: Researchers must seek to validate their presumed measures of social integration and social regulation.

Recommendation 5.4: Sociologists must move on from an excessive reliance on Durkheim's theory of suicide.

Recommendation 5.5: Henry and Short's theory is worthy of examination and needs modification to overcome its inherent inconsistencies.

Recommendation 5.6: The study of homicide together with suicide can provide important comparisons and contrasts leading to a better understanding of both behaviors.

Recommendation 5.7: Alternative measures of status integration need to be devised for adequate tests of Gibbs and Martin's status integration theory.

Recommendation 5.8: Alternative sociological theories of suicide need to be explored, and those proposed need to be explored for competing predictions which can then be tested empirically.

Recommendation 5.9: Sociological theories of suicidal behavior and research must include both fatal and nonfatal suicidal behavior.

Chapter 6. Anthropological and Suicide

Recommendation 6.1: Anthropologists should devote more thought and research to the topic of suicidal behavior than they do at the present time.

Recommendation 6.2: Anthropologists should identify and document the definitions of suicide in different cultures.

Recommendation 6.3: Anthropologists should document the *meanings* and psychodynamics of suicidal behavior in different cultures.

Recommendation 6.4: Anthropologists should document the phenomenon of suicidal behavior in cultures to identify which aspects of the phenomenon are culture specific and which are found across all cultures.

Recommendation 6.5: Anthropological research should focus on the role of cultural conflict in suicidal behavior and the effect of different styles of coping with the conflict on suicidal behavior.

Recommendation 6.6: Anthropologists should endeavor to devise theories of suicide based on their studies of cultures rather than attempt to fit anthropological data within psychological and sociological theories.

Recommendation 6.7: Anthropologists should study suicidal behavior in the different ethnic groups within developed nations, groups which have been ignored by suicidologists hitherto.

Recommendation 6.8: Anthropologists should endeavor in their research to identify which aspects of suicidal behavior are (relatively) culturally invariant and which vary with culture.

Recommendation 6.9: The entries for suicide for all cultures in the Human Relations Area Files need to be gathered together, rated by independent judges so that inter-judge reliability can be assessed, specified by era, and explored for cross-cultural correlates.

Recommendation 6.10: Anthropologists should explore indigenous cultures for their theories of suicide and endeavor to test these theories empirically.

Chapter 7. Studies of Attitudes Toward Suicide

Recommendation 7.1: Researchers investigating attitudes toward suicide and other suicidal behaviors should identify their underlying conceptualization of "attitudes" and consider the implications of that conceptualization since it impacts the methodology and the interpretation of the results of the study.

Recommendation 7.2: Attitude researchers should move beyond a simple assessment of the valence of attitudes and include measurement techniques related to commitment and conviction that can help differentiate between attitudes and non-attitudes.

Recommendation 7.3: In addition to measures of conviction, suicide attitude researchers should include an assessment of relevant individual characteristics in order to interpretation attitude strength.

Recommendation 7.4: Researchers interested in studying attitudes toward suicide using established measures should consider the possibility that items developed in the past may not reflect current understandings of suicide and suicidal individuals.
Thus, it is important to reestablish support for the validity of interpretations intended to be drawn from the scores on the attitude measure.

Recommendation 7.5: In developing new measures to identify attitudes toward suicide, researchers must provide empirical evidence supporting the assumption that items are interpreted by respondents as anticipated and provide sample-specific evidence for the reliability of scores and the validity of interpretations based on those scores.

Chapter 8. Studies of Sexual Abuse and Suicidality

Recommendation 8.1: Researchers must not only be clear about the definitions of the terms that they use, but efforts must also be made to reach consensus of how variables should be measured in a reliable and valid manner.

Recommendation 8.2: The measurement of variables should not be overly simplified. The complex aspects of the variables should be taken into account.

Recommendation 8.3: Because of the reconstructive nature of memory, researchers should attempt to gather corroborating reports of sexual abuse (or other antecedent behavior) and other relevant moderating factors whenever possible in order to overcome possible biases in self-report. While not intending to discount the accuracy and value of self-report information, there are abundant data suggesting the need for independent verification of recalled information (e.g., Pope, 1996). Concern over the reconstructive nature of memory may be especially heightened in clinical samples where co-occurring psychological and psychiatric conditions may substantially impact the memory retrieval process.

Recommendation 8.4: When assessing CSA, researchers should attend to the relevant moderators of the impact of CSA discussed in the literature rather than only asking for the presence of past sexual abuse. The literature is relatively clear that the perception of impact, type, frequency, and duration of the abusive behaviors are important components for assessment as are co-occurring histories of emotional abuse, physical abuse, and neglect. Additionally, attention to significant positive and negative events that may have occurred subsequent to the sexual abuse and prior to the suicidal behaviors would be important. This recommendation applies to the study of other antecedent behaviors.

Recommendation 8.5: Research on antecedent behaviors and suicidality should be conducted in both clinical and non-clinical samples so that the generality of the research findings can be assessed.

Recommendation 8.6: Since correlational cross-sectional research does not permit cause-and-effect conclusions to be drawn, more long-term, longitudinal studies should be undertaken so that the causal chains that may be identified are more plausible.

Recommendation 8.7: Research should be conceptualized in an a priori fashion from a theoretical perspective and developed to test theoretically derived hypotheses. Knowing only that there is a relationship between CSA and suicidality is not particularly useful without an explicit consideration of the related mechanism of operation. Prior to the question of whether or not there is a relationship between CSA and suicide, the question of why such a relationship is expected should be asked. This recommendation applies to the study of other antecedent behaviors.

Chapter 9. Assessing Suicidal Risk

Recommendation 9.1: We think that it is premature to abandon the goal of predicting suicide. In addition to the many advances in our understanding of suicidal behavior in the thirty years since the first efforts to predict suicide, there have been concomitant advances in statistical and mathematical modeling procedures. A move away from simple linear modeling to the application of more complex approached such as models based on chaos and catastrophe theories and self-organized criticality may lead to more successful efforts to predict suicide.

Recommendation 9.2: Examination of the reliability, validity, specificity and sensitivity of suicide assessment scales is paramount and ongoing as these characteristics tend to vary over time and across groups and settings. Therefore, suicide assessment scales, whether used for prediction or assessment, should be examined for their applicability to men and women, people of different ages and cultures/ethnicities and in different settings. For example, it is foolish to expect the same scales to be useful in all settings whether a telephone crisis counseling service or a prison.

Recommendation 9.3: In developing suicide risk assessment measures and protocols, research should be undertaken to examine the impact of the clinician, the client, and their interaction.

Recommendation 9.4: Additional models and approaches, which may hold potential for improving the quality of the assessment relationship and the resulting judgment of risk, should be explored. Beyond the therapeutic assessment and feminist models explored here, alternative methods based on age, gender, and culture/ethnic perspectives should be considered.

Recommendation 9.5: While collaborative and other empowerment models may make intuitive sense with regard to their potential to increase the validity and reliability of risk assessment data, appropriate effectiveness and efficacy research needs to be conducted to support their usefulness.

Chapter 10. Fads in Research: Sex Differences in Suicidal Behavior

Recommendation 10.1: Identifying the existence of sex ratios in death by suicide and non-lethal suicidal behavior should be viewed as only the preliminary step for research in this area. Beyond identifying broad social/economic differences, research should focus on identifying underlying reasons for both the general consistency in sex differences in suicidal behavior as well as exploring the factors that contribute to differences.

Recommendation 10.2: Observed aggregate differences in suicidal behaviors related to professional and marital status provide little information with regard to understanding suicidal behavior. As we discuss again in Chapter 11, most married men and women do not engage in suicidal behaviors nor do most professional women. What is needed is for research in this area to move forward by beginning to identify specific characteristics of marriages and professions that may interact with individual characteristics to lead to suicidal behavior.

Recommendation 10.3: Many hypotheses have been offered in an attempt to understand differences in choice of method for suicide. Testing these different hypotheses have the potential to increase our understanding of this important aspect of suicidal behavior and are long overdue.

Recommendation 10.4: Despite claims in the field of suicidology that suicidal behavior is multidetermined, research continues to be primarily discipline myopic. The limited data on physiological aspects of suicidal behavior suggests that a fuller understanding of suicide should result from research that includes attention to social, psychological, psychiatric and physiological factors related to suicidal behavior.

Recommendation 10.5: Suicidologists should not abandon research issues until a thorough examination of the phenomena has been undertaken and before hypotheses proposed for explaining the phenomena have been tested.

Recommendation 10.6: Suicidologists should cooperate with researchers grounded in other academic disciplines to form collaborative relationships to explore suicidal phenomena.

Chapter 11. Studies of Social Relationships

Recommendation 11.1: Research investigating the relations between marital status and suicide needs to move beyond the broad epidemiological approach to begin to identify more specific qualitative differences within those statuses that can advance the understanding and prevention of suicide.

Recommendation 11.2: Investigations of the relations between suicide attitudes and other social demographic characteristics through the use of epidemiological survey research must move away from the tendency to rely on simplistic approaches to assessing attitudes if meaningful interpretations are to be drawn.

Recommendation 11.3: Researchers need to carefully consider their selection of control group participants and the potential biasing impact of the experience of the suicidal crisis when studying the relation between social support and suicidal behavior to avoid potentially miss-interpreting state influenced ratings of social support as more trait-like evaluations.

Recommendation 11.4: Although investigating the role of relationship stress as a contributing factor in suicidal behavior by studying gay, lesbian, and bisexual samples may be appropriate give the theoretical expectations that relationship stress may be more significant for these individuals, caution must be used in attempting to generalize study results from samples to populations. Consideration should be given to newer technologically-based sources of relationship support and arguments for the validity of interpretations of measures of social support should be empirically defensible.

Recommendation 11.5: Tests of the modeling effect related to suicide and suicidal behaviors must move away from simple broad epidemiological analyses to include tests of more specific theoretical relations.

Recommendation 11.6: Investigations of the modeling effect on suicidal behavior must be based on comprehensive model development including attention to both model and observer characteristics and a consideration of the "reward" characteristics for behavioral engagement. Specifically in this regard, social response or "reward" for engaging in suicidal can be positive (resulting in increased social support and resources) or negative (i.e., social marginalization, anger, frustration). Clearly, a consideration of the reward or consequences resulting from engaging in suicidal behavior will be related to the probability of that behavior being modeled.

Recommendation 11.7: Research should move from the study of distal and superficially-measured variables to the study of actual interactive patterns between suicidal individuals and their significant others, observed and coded by the researchers.

Chapter 12. Suicide Notes and Other Personal Narratives

Recommendation 12.1: Investigating differences between suicide note writers and non-writers must move beyond a comparison of simple demographic and status variables to include a consideration of the more relevant psychological and psychodynamic similarities and differences.

Recommendation 12.2: In order to make appropriate comparisons and interpretations, genuine suicides notes must be compared with notes written by the same individuals at an earlier point in time.

Recommendation 12.3: Coding categories for suicide notes and other materials (diaries, poems, etc.) should be devised, preferably based on theories of suicide and theories of personality.

Recommendation 12.4: Typologies of suicide notes need to be developed and studied for their inter-judge reliability and comprehensiveness.

Recommendation 12.5: Personal documents and narratives of individuals who kill themselves, other than suicide notes, should also be studied in order to further our understanding of the psychodynamics of suicidal behavior.

Chapter 13. Studies of the Suicidal Personality

Recommendation 13.1: It is important for researchers in the area of personality characteristics and suicide to explicitly identify their underlying theoretical position with regard to the state versus trait or stable versus malleable issue in personality research.

Recommendation 13.2: Beyond the state versus trait distinction, researchers should take into consideration potential developmental influences, especially in studies with adolescents and youths, as they interpret the relationships between personality and suicidal behavior.

Recommendation 13.3: Researchers investigating personality characteristic should develop data collection strategies that do not rely solely on single methods such as self-report (both for the personality variables and for suicidal behavior) and to include an assessment of impression management as part of their research design.

Recommendation 13.4: Authors should identify a theoretically linked and psychometrically sound operational definition for personality constructs to ensure clarity of results and allow for replication.

Recommendation 13.5: Researchers should clarify the theoretical underpinning for focusing their research on risk factors versus protective factors. In particular, the polarities of the personality traits and states investigated should be made explicit.

Chapter 14. Typologies

Recommendation 14.1: It is important to developed meaningful psychology-based typologies of suicidal individuals.

Recommendation 14.2: In order to bring suicidal behavior into mainstream psychology, it is important to develop typologies of suicidal behavior that are based on the classic theories of personality (or on theories from other fields in psychology).

Recommendation 14.3: Although it is easier to develop empirically-based typologies of living suicidal individuals (such as suicide attempters and ideators), it is important to develop empirically-based typologies of completed suicides.

Recommendation 14.4: "Arm-chair" typologies should be explored for their usefulness in generating hypotheses for research in order to identify those that are useful for increasing our understanding of suicide.

Recommendation 14.5: Typologies of non-fatal suicidal behavior (attempts and ideation) should be explored for their usefulness in generating research that increases our understanding of suicidal behavior, in predicting short-term and long-term outcomes, and in formulating psychotherapeutic plans.